Given all of this, one might suppose that we would write off children altogether and leave them to their own devices until they reach the "age of reason." But of course we do not do that, for we must willy-nilly see them as tomorrow's citizens, albeit often with dismay, and we are deeply committed to them, but our commitment all too often has a strange flavor consisting of part scorn because they must be classed with the Great Excluded, and envy because they can violate the joyless principles of the Puritan Ethic and get away with it, a crime we would all dearly love to commit.

Natalie Babbitt

Publishers' Weekly, July 19, 1971
Copyright, Xerox Corporation

# Children's Literature

## Volume 1

Including Essays Emanating from
The Modern Language Association Seminar on
Children's Literature

Established by the
University of Connecticut, 1969

Temple University Press
Philadelphia

Editor-in-Chief: Francelia Butler

Associate Editors: William Moynihan, Matthew N. Proser, Barbara Rosen, David
   Sonstroem, Marcella Spann

Editorial Assistants: Jan Bakker, Lee Burns, Bernard Horn, Michael Michanczyk,
   Robert G. Miner, Jr.

Consultant for the School of Education: Julie Carlson McAlpine

Consultant for the Library: William E. Peters


Editorial correspondence should be addressed to:
   Editors, *Children's Literature*
   English Department, U–25
   University of Connecticut
   Storrs, Connecticut 06268

Manuscripts submitted should conform to the second edition of the Modern Language Association *Style Sheet*. An original and one copy are requested. Manuscripts should be accompanied by a stamped, self-addressed envelope.


Temple University Press, Philadelphia 19122

Published 1972
Previously published in Storrs, Connecticut as *The Great Excluded: Critical Essays
   on Children's Literature*
Printed in the United States of America


International Standard Book Number: 0-87722-082-4 cloth; 0-87722-081-6 paper
Library of Congress Catalog Card Number: ~~75-21550~~ *mc78-2585*


Fourth printing, 1975


Cover design: "Hookah Smoking a Caterpillar" by Charles F. Bendzans

# CONTENTS

# THE EDITOR'S HIGH CHAIR

Up to now, children's literature has been ignored by many humanists and by most critics. There are a number of possible reasons for this situation.

First, simplicity is too readily equated with triteness. Many forget that the greatest literature—like the Psalms of David, Christ's Parables, Blake's Songs—possesses the same simplicity as children's stories. Nor are these critics aware of the attitude of such writers as C. S. Lewis, who said, "A children's story is the best art form for something you have to say."

Second, children's literature usually lacks the verbal sophistication and complexity with which people in higher education have been traditionally trained to deal. As a result of this, children's literature is difficult to teach and, as the head of the English Department of one of the leading Ivy League Universities wrote me, the teaching of it is "deplorable."

Third, children's literature, good and bad, tends to be lumped together with no clear critical standards. Moreover, the generally unrecognized but pernicious influence of commercial interests and children's "experts" upon both the writers and reviewers tends to discourage criticism of a quality comparable to that available for adult literature. (Of course, commercialism affects the criticism of adult literature, too, but not to such an extent.)

Naturally, scholars have avoided a field where art is smothered by political and economic interests.

It is my feeling that the trouble started four hundred years ago when children's literature became a separate field. In Shakespeare's day, for example, there was not one literature for children and another for adults. Everyone together enjoyed the oral literature, including Aesop's Fables, the chapbooks, and so on. Even after the separation of the literature, the great books for children have been those which adults and children shared. Alice in Wonderland, Huckleberry Finn, Winnie-the-Pooh are for the man as well as the child.

Preliminary research has led me to believe that children's literature as a separate field came about as a result of certain economic interests. Indications are that the separation might have begun with the "Warnings to Apprentices," published by commercial interests in the seventeenth century. These bear a striking resemblance to the warnings to little children, the "deathbed confessions" of children who disobeyed moral "laws" and reformed too late. Numerous books of these confessions were published in England and America by the Puritan merchant class in the late seventeenth and eighteenth centuries. These "deathbed confessions" and other dire warnings to children were continued in the hundreds of Sunday School tracts which grew out of the Sunday School movement begun by Robert Raikes. Raikes, a wealthy shipowner, acknowledged that he began the Sunday Schools to keep working children from depredations on Sundays. I should like to delve into the significance, if any, of Raikes' ties with John Newbery, regarded by educators as the "father" of children's literature, who bolstered the waning market for adult chapbooks by writing some books for children. I believe children's literature began as an exploitation of children—threatening them with death if they did not behave. I should like to see whether there is an historic link between the economic undercurrents in early children's literature and much of the current writing for children—promising them success if they follow a certain social pattern. Perhaps the scorn of the literature on the part of the humanists is due to a confusion in terminology. Perhaps many current books should not be considered "literature" but rather, cleverly disguised propaganda for moral or economic purposes.

Children's literature is almost entirely in the hands of those in education or library science, who emphasize the uses of literature in the classroom, methodology, biographies of current writers, graded reading lists, book reports—good things but not the concern of those in the Humanities.

What, then, should be the concern of humanists? Perhaps more than with other literature, they should be concerned with the quality of the literature available to our children and youth, especially since they have neglected it for so long. The obvious influence of available literature on the young of each generation makes the careful study of this literature—whether in written or in oral or visual form—increasingly more urgent. If literature and life are indeed closely related, as those in Departments of Literature maintain, then one cannot scorn the literature of children and youth without scorning those for whom the literature is designed. This scorn, neglect, oversight, (blind spot) may be one key to our present problem with youth. It points to the psychological attitude upon the part of the adult (even the "thinking" adult) which aggravates the problem.

The purpose of this collection of essays is to stimulate the writing, teaching, and study of children's literature by humanists—to encourage humanists with the best (and open) minds to enter the field. The intention would be to begin the process of resolving each of the above reasons for its neglect.

We want to acknowledge our indebtedness to Professor David Sonstroem, who three years ago pointed out the need for a critical journal of children's literature. We want to thank Rowena James, editor of the Iowa State University Press, for suggesting the title of this issue. We also wish to express our gratitude to the Research Foundation of the University of Connecticut for encouraging progress in a new field in the Humanities.

# AESOP AS LITMUS: THE ACID TEST OF CHILDREN'S LITERATURE[*]

Robert G. Miner, Jr.

> "Ask now the beasts, and they shall teach thee;
> and the fowls of the air, and they shall tell thee."
>
> Job, xii. 7

The basic English children's edition of <u>Aesop's Fables</u> is by Sir Roger L'Estrange and came out in two volumes, 1692 and 1699. After establishing in his introduction that his book is "for the Use and Edification of Children," L'Estrange goes on to insist that

> Nothing spoils Young People, like Ill Example; and that
> the very Sufferance of it, within the Reach of Their Ken,
> or Imitation, is but a more Artificial way of Teaching them
> to do Amiss . . . Now this Medly, (such as it is) of
> Salutary Hints, and Councels, being Dedicated to the Use,
> and Benefit of Children, the Innocence of it must be pre-
> served Sacred too, without the least Mixture of any Thing
> that's Prophane, Loose, or Scurrilous, or but so much as
> Bordering That way.

A normal enough sentiment, of course, but interesting in the light of some of the fables that follow it. On page 7, for example:

### Socrates and Calisto

> There happen'd a Dispute betwixt Socrates and Calisto; the
> One, a Famous Philosopher, and the Other, as Famous a
> Prostitute. The Question was only This; which of the Two
> professions had the greater Influence upon Mankind.
> Calisto appeals to Matter of Fact, and Experiment: for
> Socrates, says she, I have Proselyted Ten times as many
> of Your People, as ever you did of Mine. Right, says
> Socrates, for Your Proselytes, as you call them follow
> their Inclinations, whereas Mine are forc'd to work
> against the Grain. Well well! says Lais (Another of
> the same Trade,) the Doctors may talk their Pleasure, of

---

[*] Notes preliminary to a doctoral dissertation on <u>Aesop's Fables</u>, given at the Modern Language Association Seminar on Children's Literature, Chicago, Illinois, December 27, 1971

> the force of Virtue and Wisdom, but I never found any
> Difference yet, in all my practice, betwixt the Flesh
> and Bloud of a Fornicator, and that of a Philosopher; and
> the One Knocks at my Door every jot as often as the Other.

No philosophers and fewer fornicators knock on children's doors these days. The difference in attitudes that this suggests may be significant.

The L'Estrange edition of Aesop set me thinking about other editions of Aesop, before and after 1699. Were there any? What were they like? Where did they come from? What or who was Aesop, for that matter? And did all this bear looking into, anyway? Perhaps, there was more to Aesop and his fables than that certain dusty ennui that I remembered from my childhood—after all, that courtesan had a point, didn't she? And if only I had heard of it when young, things might have turned out differently. As it was, I had had to wait for High School and Freud to discover what any well-bred eighteenth century tot would have known from his nursery days.

Even the briefest of histories of Aesop's Fables is complicated. It turns out that there were, for instance, several hundred editions and variations of Aesop before L'Estrange. Beginning, it seems, sometime in the sixth century, B. C. And in at least a score of basic languages. None of these editions were for children (children, of course, were not invented until the seventeeth century); but much of the content of these editions came to be considered particularly suitable for children (which is an interesting fact in itself: must certain kinds of great basic literature eventually end up the exclusive property of children— folk tales, ballads, fables, myth, the Bible?).

It seems likely that a man named Aesop did exist in Greece in the sixth century, B. C. He was a slave, seems to have lived in Samos, and most probably died a violent death at the hands of the Delphinians. Joseph Jacobs, the eminent Aesop scholar, argues that Aesop did not invent the "beast-tale with a moral" (as he calls it) but rather invented a new use for it. Before Aesop it was used to amuse children; Aesop used it to convince men, to make political points in the age of the tyrants when direct speech could be unhealthy. Even indirect, metaphorical stories seem to have been unhealthy for Aesop, however, and for one reason or another he was killed in 671 B. C. by outraged citizens of Delphi— perhaps for making a point too well.

After his death fables continued to be attributed to him and his influence can be traced through references in Plato, Aristotle, Xenophon, Herodotous, Aristophanes. Socrates is even said to have turned some Aesop into verse while awaiting death. After the founding of the democracies in Greece, fables became part of the rhetorical tradition and continued to grow as a form: they were considered the exclusive property of the well-educated and a sophisticated way to make a point. In 300 B. C. Demetrius Phalereus, who founded the Alexandria Library, collected all the available fables in his Assemblies of Aesopic Tales. Then a first century A. D. Latin version in verse appeared. This was by Phaedrus, like Aesop a slave from Greece, who seems to have added some fables of his own and whose Aesop is the first we know of intended to be read as literature rather than a mere collection of folk wisdom. The earliest extant Greek collection is in prose and was written about the second century A. D. It is known in the trade as the <u>Augustana</u>. Also in the second century Babrius produced a Greek <u>Aesop</u> in verse upon which many of the later versions came to be based. The Latin verse <u>Aesop</u> of Avianus in the late fourth century, A. D. continued the tradition of <u>Aesop</u> as literature that culminates in the seventeenth century with the work of Jean de la Fontaine.

The Middle Ages drew their versions of <u>Aesop</u> chiefly from prose paraphrases of Phaedrus and Avianus that appeared from the fifth century onward. In the ninth century a prose collection of fables appeared under the name of "Romulus." Sometime before 1030 Ademar of Chabannes produced a prose collection, too. Collections appeared in France from then on, the most important before La Fontaine being one by Marie of France which she claimed was translated from the English--of King Alfred.

The history of English editions of <u>Aesop's Fables</u> begins with Marie of France's assertion about [King] Alfred's version. Whether or not he actually produced one is questionable (there is an <u>Aesop</u> by <u>an</u> Alfred in the 1170's--some years after King Alfred's death), but the story ought to be true. It would be appropriate that Alfred, attempting to revitalize his ravaged society, should have chosen to translate <u>Aesop</u> into the vernacular as a basic text for popular education. Nothing is really known about "King Alfred's" <u>Aesop</u>, but the idea of there having been one then, and for that reason, helps emphasize the very real connection between <u>Aesop</u> and education (and, therefore, children) that developed in England several centuries later.

England was the home of <u>Aesop</u> in the centuries following King Alfred, and the popularity of the fables with the Normans led to numerous French versions (done in England) and to the inclusion of several fables in the Bayeux Tapestry of the twelfth century. The fables then show up in the popular literature of anecdote-- and in sermons--of the thirteenth and fourteenth centuries. Collections of fables appropriate for use in sermons (one wonders what <u>they</u> include) were made by Holkot, Bromyard and others. And of course Chaucer, Lydgate and Gower all used some fables in their works.

It was not until the fifteeth century that another complete English collection of <u>Aesop</u> appears. That was Caxton's edition of 1484 and one of the very first books printed in English. Interesting enough in itself, this fact takes on added significance when you realize that Caxton took the time to translate, as well as print, it: all this for <u>Aesop</u> while Caxton was engaged in his frenetic attempt to print everything of importance to his time. <u>Aesop</u>, then, was important (and popular: Caxton was sensitive to popular needs) in the fifteenth century. With Caxton's help it became more so. Because from his time onward a surprising number of important men begin to mention Aesop in their writing, usually with the same particular focus: learning and children.

In <u>The Book Named the Governor</u>, printed in 1531, Sir Thomas Elyot was quick to grasp the potential of <u>Aesop</u> for the education of children. Elyot develops a theme that is echoed again and again in the years leading up to L'Estrange's <u>Aesop</u> of 1692:

After a fewe and quicke rules of grammer, immediately, or
interlasyge it therwith, wolde he redde to the childe Esopes
fables in greke: in which argument children moche do delite.
And surely it is a moche pleasant lesson and also profitable,
as well for that it is elegant and brefe, (and not withstanding
it hath moche varietie in wordes, and ther wis moche helpeth
to the understandinge of greke) as also in those fables is
included moche morall and politike wysedome.

In Elyot's view, _Aesop_ should be the very first book a child reads. His argument
for _Aesop_ is little changed by the time it is used by L'Estrange:

For as the Foundations of a Virtuous and a Happy Life,
are all laid in the very Arms of our Nurses, so 'tis but
Natural, and Reasonable, that our Cares, and Applications
toward the Forming, and Cultivating of our Manners, should
Begin There too. And in Order to Those Ends, I thought I
could not do better, than to Advance That Service under the
Veyle of Emblem, and Figure, after the Practice, and the
Methods of the Antients. . .For Children must be Ply'd with
Idle Tales, and Twittle-Twattles; and betwixt Jeast and
Earnestness, Flatter'd, and Cajol'd, into a Sense, and
Love of their Duty. A Childs lesson, must be fitted to a
Childs Talent and Humour . . .

Between Elyot and L'Estrange several prominent men talk about _Aesop_, among
them Sir Philip Sidney, Francis Bacon, and John Locke. Before them, however,
and just after Elyot, comes an illuminating event in the history of _Aesop_ and
its connection with learning. _Aesop_ was such a popular and influential book,
apparently, that William Bullockar used it as the best way to make his point.
In 1585 he brought out his _Aesopz Fablez in tru Ortography_, spelled new, to con-
vince his fellow countrymen of the excellence of his method of spelling.

Both Sidney and Bacon make essentially the same comment about _Aesop_. They
are primarily interested in how _Aesop_ works, both emphasize its power to instruct
and delight at the same time: through indirection and entertainment the fables
elevate the human mind. Locke's emphasis is different. He is interested in the
proper reading for children and what influence it can have. He suggests that
what is needed in England is an edition of the fables specifically for children.
Which is where L'Estrange got the idea.

By the time L'Estrange's version begins to come out in 1692, _Aesop_ is not only
one of the basic books in Western (and an even more basic book in English) culture, but also a vitally important book for children (according to the adults, anyway). Children's books are beginning to exist in response to the discovery that
children exist and what they first read could be a matter of first importance.

The eighteenth century experienced a great expansion of books for children
under the energetic John Newberry and others of his business-like mien. Not

unexpectedly, Aesop figured prominently in this development. It is not that there were so many different versions, but rather that unrecorded numbers of bits and pieces of Aesop appeared as chapbooks and pamphlets. These appeared continually—and promptly disappeared. From overwork (this, too, is in the proper Aesopic tradition: scholars note for example that only three copies of Caxton's Aesop survive today and only one of them in decent shape. The rest have been thumbed out of existence. How many other popular, much printed books can that be said for?). Two major new versions of Aesop did appear during the eighteenth century, one by the Reverend Samuel Croxall in 1722 and another by (of all people) Samual Richardson. Croxall's Aesop was a translation, not merely a revision of L'Estrange or Caxton, and it is less extravagant—and less earthy—than L'Estrange's. At the same time it is livlier than Caxton's. Croxall, too, had children in mind when he did his edition. Each fable was supplied with a drawn conclusion, and the book ends:

> It is not expected that they who are versed and hackneyed
> in the paths of life should trouble themselves to pursue
> these little loose sketches of morality; such may do well
> enough without them. They are written for the benefit of
> the young and inexperienced; if they do but relish the
> contents of this book, so as to think it worth reading over
> two or three times, it will have attained its end; and
> should it meet with such a reception, the several authors
> originally concerned in these fables, and the present com-
> piler of the whole, may be allowed not altogether to have
> misapplied their time, in preparing such a collation for
> their entertainment.

In his introduction to the 1889 edition of Caxton's Aesop, Joseph Jacobs has something to say about both L'Estrange and Croxall:

> He (L'Estrange) inflicted on Aesop the indignity of "applica-
> tions" in addition to "morals"; these were intended to pro-
> mote the Jacobite cause . . . L'Estrange was succeeded on
> the Aesopic throne of England by the Rev. S. Croxall, whose
> reign lasted throughout the eighteenth century, and whose
> dynasty still flourishes among us in the Chandos Classics.
> It says much for the vitality of Aesop that he has survived
> so long under the ponderous morals and "applications"—
> Whig aginst L'Estrange's Jacobitism—with which the reverend
> gentleman loaded his author.

With characeristic earnestness, Richardson attempted to correct these "excesses" by neutralizing Aesop. His version is entitled Aesop's Fables. With Instructive Morals and Reflections, Abstracted From All Party Considerations, Adapted to all Capacities. It does not seem to have been popular and may serve as a lesson

13

to those who try to purge literature for children of all living and breathing blemishes.

The point about these eighteeth century editions is that they reflect the attitudes and prejudices of their times towards children and literature for children. As did the L'Estrange edition for its time. Which brings us to a further point: Since Aesop is such a basic book in England through the ages, and since as a basic book it came naturally to be thought of as a basic book for children, then perhaps we could tell something about that intangible and elusive something in the air that characterizes different ages by looking carefully at what each did to its Aesops. More specifically for our purposes, it would seem to me, at least, that Aesop might prove a quick and convenient indicator of the basic attitudes of an age toward its children and what they read. The idea deserves a thorough look. It also suggests related questions that may have some light shed on them in the process.

What, for example, gives Aesop its longevity? its almost universal appeal (among the better known languages Aesop has appeared in are the following: Chinese, Basque, Bengali, Breton, Catalan, Esperanto, Estonian, Gascon, Hindustani, Icelandic, Marathi, Hyanja, Pushto, Sanskrit, Serbo-croat, Swahili, Tonga, Turkish, Welsh)? Is it that animal stories appeal somehow to that ancient human wish to belong? Maybe to hear of animals making our mistakes, proving our points is somehow comforting in an anthropomorphically primitive way. Or maybe the necessary impersonality of an animal fable tickles the fancy: objective and simple that way, life seems subject to solid, comfortable, consistent laws. No ifs and buts about what an animal does.

Another question that arises is related to changes in moral values. Which of the fables is consistently repeated in every age? Which for children? Which not? And why? Is it still fashionable, for instance, to be happy with one's lot? or emulate the tortoise in a nuclear age? And how did the eighteenth century react to a fable chastising the monkey for wanting to cover and decorate his private parts?

And what of American Aesops? It would not be surprising to see them take on different shape from English ones—or would it? Is there anything of the pioneer in, say, the boy who cried wolf, or the wolf in sheep's clothing? the dog in the manger? Is Sour grapes a tale to suit post-colonial tastes?

Of course the psychological, scientific, and sociological claims on Aesop cannot be neglected. Anne Caldwell, author of Origins of Psychopharmacology from CPZ to LSD, has suggested that the connection between fables and hallucinogens needs exploring (any child prone to nightmares can verify that, I bet). And what about some sort of statistical-sociological study of the relationship between the number of editions of Aesop in any age and its intensity of feeling for its children? The possibilities, like the versions of Aesop, seem endless.

Perhaps after all this we shall discover that Aesop is one of those books that future millennia (if there are any) will say were vital to our civilization (look, after all, at the sheer numbers) but which we never noticed because it was so thoroughly basic. I cannot remember when I first heard of the hare and the tortoise, but I can distinctly remember yawning ostentatiously when it was used by my second grade teacher to make a point about (my lack of) diligence. I wonder which version I had read?

Alexander Calder's drawing for Sir Roger L'Estrange's children's version of Aesop, published by Harrison of Paris in 1931 and republished by Dover Publications, 1967

# CHILDREN'S LITERATURE IN OLD ENGLISH*

Hugh T. Keenan

The Old English riddles, lyrics, and tales are not primarily literature for children. In tone, subjects, and techniques, the Old English examples of these genres seem designed instead for an adult audience.[1] Possibly children shared in their enjoyment with adults, but the world reflected by them is not a child's world. The complexity, allusiveness, and serious moral tone of major poems such as Beowulf, The Seafarer, Brunnanbrugh, Maldon, Exodus, and Elene exclude them from consideration too. In all probability, the children's literature that remains to us is to be found in a few didactic works, pagan and Christian. These prepared the child for his adult roles in that serious and heroic Anglo-Saxon society, so similar in its attitudes and goals to the nineteenth century.

Such Old English works as the collections of gnomes, the alphabetic Rune Poem, and Ælfric's Colloquy suggest why their number is so few and how the necessary and vital distinction between literature for children and children's literature arose. It is not inconceivable that Christianity provided the sympathy which underlies that distinction and which leads to the later development of a literature more on the level of children.

This is not to imply that the Anglo-Saxons did not care deeply for their children. Various references in the poetry indicate parental concern for their well being.[2] From Beowulf, it is evident that they were sent to board at foreign courts to learn necessary skills and graces if they were nobles.[3] Besides feats of arms, they learned pithy words of wisdom. Thus the youthful Beowulf has ready words to answer Hrothgar's numbing grief at the death of Æschere, his friend:

> 'Ne sorga, snotor guma! Selre bið æghwæm,
> þæt he his freond wrece, þonne he fela murne.[4]

> Do not grieve, wise warrior! It is better for each one
> that he avenge his friend than that he mourn greatly.

Characters and narrators resort to such gnomic expressions throughout Old English verse. Perhaps they were instructed in such formal sentiments as children.

Besides being embedded in other works of Old English literature, such gnomes are found in two separate collections, the Exeter Gnomes and the Cotton Gnomes. Such repositories may have been designed for the instruction of youngsters who were taught for example:[5]

* Given at the Seminar on Children's Literature, Modern Language Association, Chicago, Illinois, December 27, 1971.

As the sea is serene when the wind wakes it not,
so peoples are peaceful when they have settled a
dispute; they sit in happy circumstances and then
hold with comrades. Bold men are mighty by their
nature. A king is eager for power. Hateful is he
who lays claim to land, loved is he who gives more.
. . . . . . . . . . . . . . . . . . . . . . . . .
The shield shall be for the warrior, the shaft
for the spoiler, the Eucharist for holy men, sins
for the heathen.
. . . . . . . . . . . . . . . . .. .. .. . .
No man acquires too much. Well shall one keep a
friend in all ways; often a man passes by the village
afar off where he knows he has no certain friend.
. . . . . . . . . . . . . . . . . . . . . . . . .
Weary shall he be who rows against the wind; full often
one blames the timid with reproaches, so that he loses
courage, draws his oar on board. Guile shall go with
evil, skill with things fitting; thus is the die stolen.[6]

As these lines speak of diplomacy, generosity, and the fitness of things, they answer the practical aim of fitting the child into that amalgamation of the heroic and the Christian that was Anglo-Saxon society.

In such an elementary education, gnomic words of wisdom were supplemented by a poem on the letters of the ancient Germanic runic alphabet. The matter of the poem is somewhat more elaborate than modern ABC's such as "A is for Apple." Each of the 29 letters receives a descriptive stanza, incorporating the name of the rune.[7] For example, the rune þ which is our <u>th</u> sound has the name <u>thorn;</u> its verse reads:

> þ (thorn) is very sharp; for each of the thanes, the
> grasp is evil, cruel without measure for each of men
> who may rest among them.

The similarly-shaped rune ᚹ or <u>wynn</u> means "joy" and represents a <u>w</u> sound:

> He possesses ᚹ (joy) who knows little of misfortunes,
> of affliction and of trouble, and who has for himself
> glory and bliss and the abundance of cities too.

For the rune ᚢ or <u>ur</u> "wild ox" and which represents a <u>u</u> sound, we read

> ᚢ (The wild ox) is grim and great horned, a very fierce
> animal, the famous traverser of the moors; it fights with
> its horns; that is a brave creature.

Such verses would help students to remember the letters and to keep similar runes from being confused.

But it is in another didactic work, Ælfric's <u>Colloquy,</u> which is designed to teach students Latin by means of an Anglo-Saxon interlinear gloss and by dialogues between students and teacher (a forerunner of the modern oral approach to teaching foreign languages) that we first find evidence of an imaginative sympathy for the world of children and an allowance for the exercise of fantasy through role-playing. Ælfric conducts the lessons with playful sternness and teasing, to which the students respond in kind. He asks how the student has spent his day and arrives at more personal matters in the following exchange:

| | |
|---|---|
| Teacher. | When will you sing evensong and compline? |
| Pupil. | When it is time. |
| Teacher. | Were you flogged to-day? |
| Pupil. | I was not, for I carefully restrained myself. |
| Teacher. | And how about your companions? |
| Pupil. | Why do you ask me that? I dare not reveal our secrets to you. Every one knows whether he was flogged or not. |
| Teacher. | What do you eat during the day? |
| Pupil. | As yet I feed on meat, for I am a child living under the rod. |
| Teacher. | What else do you eat? |
| Pupil. | Herbs, eggs, fish, cheese, butter, and beans, and all clean things, I eat with great thankfulness. |
| Teacher. | You are extremely voracious, since you eat everything that is set before you. |
| Pupil. | I am not so voracious that I can eat all kinds of food at one meal. [8] |

Such sassy interchanges show Ælfric knew children well. He used these realistic exchanges of dialogue to keep their interest keen in the learning process and to make the accompanying moralizing more palatable too. He let his students take such roles as Plowman, Shepherd, Hunter, Fisherman, Fowler, Merchant, Shoemaker, and Counselor, so that as they were caught up in playing a part they learned the language more readily. The following dialogue between Teacher and Fowler brings in a third participant, the Hunter:

| | |
|---|---|
| Fowler. | In many ways I entice birds—with nets, with nooses, with lime, with whistling, with a hawk, or with traps. |
| Teacher. | Have you a hawk? |
| Fowler. | I have. |
| Teacher. | Can you tame them? |
| Fowler. | Yes, I can. What good would they do me if I did not know how to tame them? |

18

| Hunter. | Give me a hawk. |
| Fowler. | So I will gladly, if you will give me a swift hound. Which hawk will you have, the bigger one or the smaller? |
| Hunter. | Give me the bigger one.[9] |

Such a lively, human exchange is rare even in today's oral lessons. Ælfric has caught the frank, bold, even greedy spirit of children.

Our brief survey of these evidences of children's literature suggests that the native Anglo-Saxon society was adult oriented, conscious of fully grown heroes.[10] It needed the influence of Christianity with its Child in the Manger, its Holy Innocents, and its promise that of such is the Kingdom of Heaven to produce what may be truly called the first children's literature in English. Ironically, as has been the case so often since, a childless adult like the tenth-century monk Ælfric writes the most memorable work in that genre.

---

[1] Most of the riddles are learned; a few are obscene; a number are simply strained or dull. See the discussion of this genre and of the lyrics by Stanley B. Greenfield, A Critical History of Old English Literature (New York, 1965), pp. 204-208, 213-228. F. H. Whitman, "Medieval Riddling: Factors Underlying Its Development," NM, LXXI (1970), 177-185, appeared too late for consideration in my essay. Whitman's stimulating article suggests that the Latin riddles especially were devices for teaching grammar and elementary facts of natural history, as well as providing practice in elementary allegorical exegesis. This article may possibly lead to a reexamination of the OE riddles.

[2] Cf. Wealhtheow's concern for the safety and the inheritance of her sons in Beowulf.

[3] Frederick Klaeber, ed. Beowulf and The Fight at Finnsburg, 3rd ed. (Boston, 1950), ll. 1836-1839, 2426-2434; Beowulf was only seven then.

[4] Old English quotation taken from Klaeber's ed. of Beowulf, ll. 1384-1385.

[5] Blanche Colton Williams, Gnomic Poetry in Anglo-Saxon (New York, 1914; rptd. 1966), p. 113, says of the Cotton Gnomes that later this poem "may have been used as a school exercise; perhaps for copy-books, perhaps for memorization, possibly as a model for alliterative compositions." The Exeter Gnomes are of the 8th or 9th c.; the Cotton is somewhat later. Miss Williams gives the Old English texts of both and discusses both the nature of gnomes and their use in Old English literature.

[6] Translations by R. K. Gordon, Anglo-Saxon Poetry, 2nd ed. (New York, 1954), pp. 310, 312, 313. This volume in the Everyman series gives accurate, readable prose translation of most Old English poetry.

[7] Similar runic poems are found in Old Norwegian and Old Icelandic. The Old English example dates from the 8th or 9th c. For text and discussion, see Elliott Van Kirk Dobbie, ed. The Anglo-Saxon Minor Poems, Vol. VI, of ASPR (New York, 1942). Nearly all of the extant Old English poetry can be found in the six volumes of The Anglo-Saxon Poetic Records.

[8] Trans. by Mary W. Smyth in Albert S. Cook and Chauncey B. Tinker, eds., Select Translations From Old English Prose (Cambridge, Mass., 1935), p. 135. According to the Benedictine Rule, which this student is following, meat is allowed to the very young, the very old, and the infirm. The rest had to do with vegetables.

[9] Cook, Select Translations, pp. 181-182.

[10] Cf. the gnome in Gordon, Anglo-Saxon Poetry, p. 310:
> One shall teach the young man, strengthen and urge
> him to know well, until one has subdued him. Let
> him be given food and clothing till he be brought
> to understanding. He shall not be rebuked as a
> child before he can declare himself. Thus shall
> he prosper among the people, so that he shall be
> firm of purpose.

# CHILDREN'S LITERATURE IN THE MIDDLE AGES [1]

Meradith Tilbury McMunn and William Robert McMunn

Because western notions about children have changed radically since the Middle Ages, modern conceptions of "children's literature" are anachronistic as applied to that earlier period. Children in medieval society were thought to be essentially the same as adults, except that they were smaller and less experienced. A child's world was that of the adult in miniature. His clothing imitated adult clothing in every detail, as can be seen, for example, in the diminutive suits of armor in museums. Portraiture presenting children as wizened adults, mature in feature if not in size, persisted into the nineteenth century. Our modern society's preoccupation with the physical, moral, and sexual problems of childhood was unknown in medieval civilization. Indeed, there was no separation of generations in the Middle Ages as there is today. Soon after he had been weaned (much later than is common now), the child became the natural companion of the adult, sharing his interests and recreation.[2]

· The description of children in early medieval literature indicates very little about their daily lives or literary interests. In the epic literature children, like women, are mentioned infrequently, and then often only as heritors, as in the passage in the Old French epic Le Charroi de Nimes where Guillaume d'Orange tells King Louis that he will not take the lands of an infant whose father has died valiantly in the King's service.[3] The lives of heroes are narrated with few details about childhood except those that reveal precocious prowess, and the exploits themselves are archetypal adult feats—exceptional skill in arms and athletics, the killing of a monster, and the like. Similar idealizations occur in medieval saints' lives, which generally describe the saints as having been supernaturally good children.

Later in the Middle Ages the representation of children was sometimes more realistic.[4] The advent of courtly literature with its emphasis on the domestic as well as the militaristic aspects of society brought the appearance of "family scenes," at least as vignettes, in the romances of Marie de France, Chretién de Troyes, and others. Childhood episodes in the lives of heroes such as Arthur, Tristan, Perceval, Havelok, and Guy of Warwick became more important. Occasionally inferences concerning the behavior of children and parents can be drawn from the actions in beast fables. For example, the outraged accusations of the mother hawk against her brood on seeing the nest befouled, the baby hawks' "it was him" responses, and the mother's harsh punishment of the young culprit, are told in the fable of "The Hawk and the Owl," which was widely repeated in English, French, and Latin in the twelfth and thirteenth centuries.[5] It is easy to infer that such slapstick episodes must have amused old and young alike, but neither the medieval beast fables nor the tales with human characters give any information about the literary interests of children.

Because we lack direct and explicit evidence of "children's literature" in the Middle Ages, that is, literature written specifically for the entertainment of children as opposed to adults, it seems logical to investigate the related field of educational literature for clues about what medieval children may have read and enjoyed. Of course, not all education is conducted with written literature. Often the media of education have been games, songs, legends, and personal demonstration. Nor is there always a clear line of demarcation between the purely instructive and the entertaining. The modern child who "plays house" or "doctor" or the medieval youth who "jousted" with blunt sticks or hunted birds with bow and arrow or javelin are ready examples of play that combines instruction with amusement. Surely the heroic legends of Beowulf and Roland must have been told with an awareness of their potential for instruction as well as entertainment. Conversely, the legends of the saints were entertaining as well as morally edifying, and they often reflected as many of the ideals and details of the secular society as of the clerical—for example, the lives of St. Edmund, St. Goderic, and St. Nicholas.

Were medieval children literate? There certainly existed in the Middle Ages a body of literature meant for instruction, and there is evidence that instruction in literacy began then, as now, when children were about six or seven years old.[6] The first song schools and Latin grammar schools in England after the withdrawal of the Roman army were probably established in the late sixth or early seventh century.[7] We do not know whether these earliest schools admitted students other than those destined for occupations in the Church, but it is possible that they did and it is likely that schools of a somewhat later period educated a wide cross-section of medieval society. In the ninth century King Alfred proposed that the sons of English freemen be taught to read English, and those that wanted to learn further, Latin as well.[8] Lynn Thorndike argues that "in the period of developed medieval culture elementary and even secondary education was fairly widespread and general."[9] Arthur F. Leach, M. L. Laistner, Charles Jourdain, James W. Thompson, and others have adduced evidence of elementary schools in England and on the continent that date from before the twelfth century.[10] Later medieval schools do not seem to have been exclusively for the education of the clergy and nobility. There were decrees such as that of the third Lateran Council of 1179 which advocated the establishment of church-sponsored schools for the education of clerks of the Church and poor students whose parents could not afford to pay their way.[11] And Thorndike cites, among others, the example of some fourteenth-century English villeins who were "apparently willing to pay further (in addition to the cost of the education itself) a  fine at the manorial court for having sent their sons to school without their lords' permission."[12]

It would seem then that a significant number of citizens in the Middle Ages could read and had available to them for instruction a body of literature that included classical authors, medieval poets (Latin and vernacular), saints' lives, histories, and the psalter, much of which had considerable value as entertainment.[13] That entertaining stories were used in programs of instruction is attested by Pierre Dubois' recommendation (1309) that histories, rather than "the usual superfluous tales," ought to be used as the subjects of student compositions.[14] Most medieval students were probably delighted to have the opportunity to read entertaining schoolbooks. The life of Saint John (Joannis Laudensis, Italian, A.D. 1026-1106) tells how young John refused to take any pleasure from the salacious stories of profane authors that were so interesting to his schoolmates.[15] In addition to entertaining works of instruction intended for readers of all ages, there were a few instructional works specifically designed for children. Aelfric's _Grammar_ was prepared for "little boys who know nothing," but its format and style do not distinguish it much from works written for a general audience of children and adults.[16] Children's primers, such as the one that Chaucer mentions in his "Prioress's Tale," contained the alphabet, prayers, excerpts from scripture, and edifying catalogues of deadly sins, principal virtues, etc., but they seem to have included very little that might be called entertaining.[17] Aelfric's _Colloquy_ seems definitely to have been designed for children, rather than adults, and it has considerable value as entertainment. Written in the form of a dialogue between a Latin master and his pupils, most of the _Colloquy_ consists of a series of speeches in which characters belonging to the various occupations (a monk, a ploughman, a shepherd, a hunter, a fisherman, etc.) describe their daily work.[18] By taking advantage in this way of the delight that most children take in role-playing, Aelfric made his Latin textbook entertaining as well as instructive. Nevertheless, Aelfric's _Colloquy_ and other similar didactic dialogues of the Middle Ages are primarily works of instruction, rather than entertainment, and so differ essentially from modern children's literature in which the entertainment is not merely a sugar-coating.[19]

Despite the spread of grammar schools, not all of the literate could read Latin. To accommodate those who could read only in their native languages, there was a growing enthusiasm, from the ninth century onward, for translating works into the vernacular languages. King Alfred (d. 899) was so concerned about the need for works in English that he inaugurated a program of translation and even did some of the work himself.[20] The author of _Grant mal fist Adam_ (middle twelfth century) translated his work for the "simple people" because there was enough literature for those who read Latin and because readers would more readily understand the language that they had spoken since childhood.[21] By the later twelfth century the practice had become so widespread that Marie de France decided to versify some Breton lais that she had heard, rather than translating "aukune bone estoire" from Latin into French, since so many others had already done so.[22]

Besides the primers, the only vernacular works specifically designed for medieval children seem to have been the didactic courtesy books that gained enormous popularity in the fourteenth and fifteenth centuries.[23] Such works generally consist of dull lists of maxims concerning the rules of etiquette, frequently in uninspired verse. In them one may learn much about the role of young men serving as "squires" in the homes of their patrons. In return for acting as waiters and valets, these adolescents hoped to be given wives with large dowries and influential relatives. Young women's courtesy books were similarly didactic, exhorting their readers to avoid sexual advances and encouraging them to obey their parents and patrons. The most famous such book for young women, _The Book of the Knight of La Tour-Landry_ (French, fourteenth century; English translations, fifteenth century), contains an encyclopedic catalogue of anecdotes, each with a very explicit moral.[24]

The existence of these courtesy books supports the claim that vernacular literacy was widespread among the upper and middle classes in the late Middle Ages. It might be expected that the courtesy books would prescribe reading matter proper for children, but most of them are silent on this topic. One exception is Caxton's Book of Curtesye (c. 1477-8) which urges "lytyl Iohn" to read all the best poets— Gower, Chaucer, Hoccleve, and especially Lydgate.[25] No mention is made of any literature written explicitly for children, nor do we know of children's versions of "adult literature" in the Middle Ages. Caxton, then, advocated that "lytyl Iohn" read the same literature that literate adults were reading.

Because there was no secular literature written or redacted primarily for the entertainment of children, it seems almost a certainty that the "children's literature" of the Middle Ages was simply the literature of the entire culture.[26] For illiterate children and adults, as well as for literate ones, this included a vast body of legends and tales which were transmitted orally, often by professional reciters and bards. Perhaps it would be an anachronistic modern inference to suppose that medieval children would have preferred the beast fables to the courtly romances. But whatever the children of the Middle Ages preferred, they had a wide variety of literature from which to choose. One of the earliest explicit allusions to a child's interest in the oral literature of the Middle Ages occurs in an eleventh-century biography of Alfred the Great. Although Alfred was allegedly illiterate through the age of twelve, his biographer tells how the boy listened "day and night" to the recitation of Anglo-Saxon poems and memorized them. On one occasion, when his mother offered to give a book of poetry to whichever of her sons could learn it first, young Alfred won the prize by immediately taking the book to a master who read it to him and then returning to recite the poetry to his mother.[27] Whether or not this anecdote is literally true of the ninth-century King Alfred, it proves that Alfred's eleventh-century biographer considered young Alfred's delight in heroic poetry plausible, and hence that at that time the heroic Germanic poems were not exclusively for adults but were enjoyed by children, too.

In the twelfth century Wace wrote that he had heard minstrels in his childhood who sang "how William long ago blinded Osmunt and dug out the eyes of Count Riulf and how he caused Ansketil to be slain by trickery, and Balzo of Spain to be guarded with a shield."[28] Children then apparently enjoyed violent action as much as they do today. In the same century Chrétien de Troyes narrated a charming scene in Yvain in which the hero enters a garden where he sees a young girl "not sixteen" who is reading to her father and mother from a romance.[29]

Further evidence, though of a much later date, of the reading habits of children in their leisure time is given indirectly by Montaigne, who in his essay "On the Education of Children" (c. 1580) comments on his own reading habits at the age of eight. He writes that he preferred the fables of the Metamorphoses of Ovid to "the Lancelots of the Lake, the Amadises, the Huons of Bordeaux, and such books of rubbish on which children waste their time."[30] Similarly, Hugh of Rhodes in his Book of Nurture (1554) urged that children be kept from the "reading of feigned fables, vain fantasies, and wanton stories and songs of love, which bring much mischief to youth."[31] It is obvious from these that unexpurgated romances or chansons de geste were available to sixteenth-century children as well as to adults. Such poems of adventure and love must have been appealing in their time much as stories of exploration, battles, and romantic intrigue are to boys and girls today.

These scattered examples, which could be multiplied, serve to confirm what we would reasonably have expected, given the role of children in medieval society. The absence of specifically "children's literature" should by no means be interpreted as signifying that children were without literary experience. Even those children who, like the young Alfred, could neither read nor write were not cut off from the mainstream of the secular literature of their day. Indeed, if any children are culturally deprived by being isolated from the literature of their culture, they are the modern children who are encouraged to read only "children's literature."

------

[1] We would like to thank Professors Margaret Schlauch and Rossell Hope Robbins for valuable bibliographical suggestions.

[2] J. H. Plumb, "The Great Change in Children," Horizon, 13 (Winter 1971), 5-13; Philippe Ariès, Centuries of Childhood, tr. Robert Baldock (New York: Knopf, 1962), p. 411; Bilderatlas zur Schul- und Erziehungsgeschichte, ed. Robert Alt (Berlin: Volk und Wissen Volkseigener Verlag, 1960), vol. I, passim. See also Isabelle Jan, Essai sur la littérature enfantine (Paris: Les Éditions ouvrières, 1969), pp. 18-19, for the claim that Jean-Jacques Rousseau invented the modern concept of "childhood."

[3] Le Charroi de Nimes, ed. J. L. Perrier (Paris: Champion, 1963), p. 12, lines 365-70.

[4] A rare exception to the pervasive literary treatment of children as miniature adults occurs in the thirteenth-century prose romance Lestoire del Saint Graal, in which Queen Sarracinte recalls her inability as a child to imagine the invisible God of the Christians. A saintly, bearded hermit had invoked God's cure of her mother's chronic illness, and her mother asked the little girl to believe in the God who had cured her. "But I was a child and simple, and I thought that she spoke of the good man; and I told my mother that I dared not. And she asked me why, and I said it was because he had too great a beard. And the good man commenced to smile at what I said of him," Medieval Narrative: A Book of Translations, tr. Margaret Schlauch (New York: Prentice-Hall, 1928), p. 199; the text of the original is in The Vulgate Version of the Arthurian Romances, ed. Heinrich Oskar Sommer, vol. I: Lestoire del Saint Graal (Washington: The Carnegie Institution, 1909), p. 68.

Helen M. Mustard and Charles E. Passage have suggested that "Wolfram (von Eschenbach)'s portraits of children strike one as particularly modern. No other medieval author, indeed, perhaps no author before the nineteenth century, has shown such keen and sympathetic insight into the mind of a child," "Introduction,"

_Parzival_, tr. Mustard and Passage (New York: Vintage, 1961), p. ix. For instance, when young Parzival wept at the sweetness of birdsong, he was unable to tell his mother why he was weeping, "as is still the way with children":

> ern kunde es ir gesagen niht,
> als kinden lîhte noch geschicht.

Mustard and Passage, p. 67; _Wolfram von Eschenbach,_ ed. Karl Lachmann, 6th ed., rev. Eduard Hartl (Berlin and Leipzig: Walter de Gruyter, 1926), Book 3, §118, lines 21–22, p. 66.

The best instance in support of Mustard and Passage's claim occurs in Book 7 where Wolfram tells how the little girl Obilot persuaded Gawan to remain and fight for her and her family. Her playmate Clauditte points out that Obilot owns nothing that she might give Gawan as a token of her favor except dolls, and she offers Obilot one of her dolls to use if they are any nicer than Obilot's (§372, lines 16–21).

This reference to dolls and Gawan's earlier remark that Obilot would have to be five years older before she could give a man her love (§370, lines 15–16) both emphasize the fact that Obilot is a child. Nevertheless, she comports herself throughout like an adult, and much of the interest of the episode for a modern reader results from her authentic portrayal of an adult role, that of the courtly lady. Indeed, she is much more mature than her overweening older sister Obie. See David Blamires' excellent analysis of Obilot's behavior, _Characterization and Individuality in Wolfram's 'Parzival'_ (Cambridge: Cambridge University Press, 1966), pp. 387–92; see also Xenja von Ertzdorff, "Fräulein Obilot: Zum siebten Buch von Wolframs Parzival," _Wirkendes Wort_, 12 (May-June 1962), 129–40.

Obilot's precocious maturity is not treated as a prodigy but as a good and natural way for a child to behave. We would not want to maintain here that Wolfram considered all children to be as mature and civilized as little Obilot, but we think it is clear that he saw her as an ideal child, one to be emulated by children and admired by adults. Wolfram's presentation of Obilot is the contrary of a modern portrait of a child. Obilot is not distinctly a child at all, but rather a miniature adult.

[5] _The Owl and the Nightingale_, ed. Eric G. Stanley (Edinburgh: Nelson, 1960), pp. 52–53, lines 101–26; see also p. 107, note 99f, and the Appendix, pp. 159–64.

[6] Bede wrote that his own education began when he was seven, _A History of the English Church and People_, tr. Leo Sherley-Price (Harmondsworth and Baltimore: Penguin, 1955), p. 329 (Bk. V, Ch. 24). At the age of seven Beowulf was sent to the home of relatives for his education, though we have no indication of what studies he pursued, _Beowulf and the Fight at Finnsburgh_, ed. Frederick Klaeber, 3rd ed. (Boston: Heath, 1950), pp. 91 and 212–13, line 2428 and note. The author of a _Tractatus_ on the Waltham Holy Cross College School (1060–1177) recalls that he was sent to the school at the age of five, _Educational Charters and Documents 598-1909_, ed. Arthur F. Leach (Cambridge: Cambridge University Press, 1911), pp. 56–57. The seven-year-old song school pupil in Geoffrey Chaucer's "Prioress's Tale" had to learn _Alma redemptoris_ by rote because he could not yet read, though he was learning to read with a primer, _Works_, ed. F. N. Robinson, 2nd ed.

26

(Boston: Houghton Mifflin, 1957), pp. 161-62, lines 495-529. Gilles de Muisis says that he was sent to school at the age of eight, Poesies, I, 8, quoted in the Histoire litteraire de la France, XXXVII, 254, cited by Lynn Thorndike, "Elementary and Secondary Education in the Middle Ages," Speculum, 15 (1940), 405. Young Floris and Blancheflour, in the thirteenth-century French and fourteenth-century English romances named for them, began their education at the age of five (French version) or seven (English version) and, after five years of school, knew Latin and how to write on parchment; particularly interesting is the English poet's implication that such an education was usual among "both high and low"—Floire et Blancheflor, ed. Margaret Pelan, Publications de la Faculté des lettres de l'Université de Strasbourg, Textes d'étude 7, 2nd ed. (Paris: Les Belles Lettres, 1956), pp. 8-10, lines 191-268; King Horn, Floriz and Blancheflur, The Assumption of Our Lady, ed. J. Rawson Lumby, rev. George H. McKnight, Early English Text Society, original ser. 14 (London: Kegan Paul, 1901; 1st ed. 1866), p. 71, lines 7-34.

According to Thorndike, p. 404, Pierre Dubois proposed that the ideal educational plan should begin with children of four, five, or six years old. Thorndike, p. 405, also cites an anonymous Latin treatise on education in a manuscript at the Vatican (Vatic. Palat. lat. 1252, fols. 99v-109r, "De commendatione cleri") that proposed a plan of education beginning with seven-year-old boys. The pseudo-Boethean De disciplina scholarium (Patrologia Latina, ed. J. P. Migne, LXIV, 1223-38), probably composed at Paris in the first half of the thirteenth century, proposed a curriculum starting with grammar at the age of seven; it is discussed by Charles Homer Haskins, "Manuals for Students," Studies in Mediaeval Culture (Oxford: Clarendon, 1929), pp. 73-74.

[7] Arthur F. Leach, The Schools of Mediaeval England (London: Methuen, 1915), pp. 1-5.

[8] Alfred's preface to the West Saxon version of Gregory's Pastoral Care, ed. Henry Sweet, Anglo-Saxon Reader, 14th ed., rev. C. T. Onions, (Oxford: Oxford University Press, 1959), pp. 4-6; also in Educational Charters, ed. Leach, pp. 22-25.

[9] Thorndike, "Elementary and Secondary Education," p. 401.

[10] Leach, Schools; Max L. Laistner, Thought and Letters in Western Europe, A.D. 900-1500, rev. ed. (Ithaca: Cornell University Press, 1957); Charles Jourdain, "Mémoire sur l'éducation des femmes au moyen âge," Excursions historiques et philosophiques à travers le moyen âge (Paris, 1888), pp. 463-509; James Westfall Thompson, The Literacy of the Laity in the Middle Ages, University of California Publications in Education, 9 (1939; rpt. New York: Burt Franklin, 1963).

[11] Educational Charters, ed. Leach, contains similar excerpts from King Edgar's Canons (c. 960), pp. 34-35, the Council of 994 (?), pp. 36-37, "Asser's" account (c. 1001) of King Alfred's educational reforms (c. 887), pp. 30-35, King Canute's

policies (c. 1020), pp. 52-53, and others, including the Lateran decree, pp. 122-23. Leach casts doubt on whether the reforms promulgated in these documents were widely implemented, The Schools of Mediaeval England, pp. 67-85. However, despite the lack of reliable contemporary documentation, Leach implies that the circumstantial evidence favors the thesis that literacy was common outside the Church, pp. 47, 74, and passim. James Westfall Thompson, Literacy of the Laity, weighs the evidence for and against widespread knowledge of Latin among the secular European nobility in the Middle Ages, and concludes that literacy was more common than has been supposed, but by no means uniform from region to region or generation to generation.

[12] Thorndike, "Elementary and Secondary Education," p. 403.

[13] R. Davis, "Bede's Early Reading," Speculum, 8 (1933), 179-95.

[14] De recuperatione terrae Sanctae, ed. C. V. Langlois (Paris, 1891), pp. 58 ff., cited by Thorndike, p. 404, note 1.

[15] Thompson, Literacy of the Laity, p. 64.

[16] Educational Charters, ed. Leach, pp. 48-51.

[17] Chaucer, Works, p. 162, lines 516-22. A facsimile of a fourteenth-century English primer is printed in George A. Plimpton, The Education of Chaucer (London and New York: Oxford University Press, 1935), pp. 18-34.

[18] Educational Charters, ed. Leach, pp. 36-48; Aelfric's Colloquy, ed. George N. Garmonsway, 2nd ed. (London: Methuen, 1947).

[19] For a brief discussion of the dialogue genre in ancient and medieval instructional literature, see Haskins, Studies in Mediaeval Culture, pp. 82-84.

[20] See note 8 above.

[21] Reimpredigt, ed. H. Sachier (Halle, 1879), stanza 127.

[22] Marie de France, "Prologue," Lais, ed. A. Ewert (Oxford: Blackwell, 1944), pp. 1-2.

[23] Several such books are conveniently collected in Early English Meals and Manners, ed. Frederick J. Furnivall, Early English Text Society, original ser. 32 (1868; rpt. London: Oxford University Press, 1931). See also Caxton's Book of Curtesye, ed. Frederick J. Furnivall, Early English Text Society, extra ser. 3, (1868; rpt. London: Oxford University Press, 1932), and A Fifteenth-Century Cour-

tesy Book, ed. R. W. Chambers, Early English Text Society, original ser. 148, (1914; rpt. London: Oxford University Press, 1937). Clara P. McMahon gives an excellent survey of all phases of education in the late Middle Ages, together with a useful annotated bibliography, in Education in Fifteenth-Century England, Johns Hopkins University Studies in Education, 35 (Baltimore: Johns Hopkins Press, 1947).

[24] The Book of the Knight of La Tour-Landry: Compiled for the Instruction of His Daughters, ed. Thomas Wright, Early English Text Society, original ser. 33, (1968; rpt. London: Kegan Paul, 1906).

[25] Caxton's Book of Curtesye, pp. 32-43

[26] Similar conclusions, without much discussion, have been stated by Cornelia Meigs, A Critical History of Children's Literature, 2nd ed. (New York: Macmillan, 1969), p. 3; Percy Muir, English Children's Books 1600-1900 (London: Batsford, 1954), p. 23; and John Rowe Townshend, Written for Children (London: Garnett Miller, 1965), pp. 11-12. Muir's account, though brief, is the clearest and most scholarly. He cites the Tatler, no. 95 (1709), in which Steele's "Mr. Bickerstaffe" recounts that his godson's favorite reading includes Aesop's Fables, Don Bellianis of Greece, Guy of Warwick, and the Seven Champions, while the boy's sister prefers fairy tales. From this Muir plausibly infers that up to and including the early eighteenth century "there were few books written expressly for the entertainment of children, who were thus compelled to select from the reading of their elders anything that especially appealed to them, supposing that they could obtain or evade approval of their choice" (p. 23). Townshend, p. 12, quotes Sir Philip Sidney's allusion to "a tale which holdeth children from play, and old men from the chimney corner," An Apology for Poetry or The Defense of Poesy, ed. Geoffrey Shepherd (London: Nelson, 1965), p. 113.

[27] Educational Charters, ed. Leach, pp. 24-27.

[28] Wace, Roman de Rou, ed. H. Andresen, 2 vols. (Heilbronn, 1878-79), I, lines 1361-67, quoted by Urban Tigner Holmes, Jr., "Norman Literature and Wace," Medieval Secular Literature, ed. William Matthews (Berkeley and Los Angeles: University of California Press, 1965), p. 63.

[29] Yvain (Le Chevalier au Lion), ed. T. B. W. Reid (Manchester: Manchester University Press, 1942), p. 146, lines 5360-70.

[30] The Complete Essays of Montaigne, tr. Donald M. Frame (Stanford: Stanford University Press, 1957), p. 130 (Bk. I, Ch. 26); Oeuvres complètes, ed. Albert Thibaudet and Maurice Rat (Paris: Gallimard, 1962), p. 175.

[31] Quoted by Townshend, Written for Children, p. 12.

# RED RIDING HOOD*

Lee Burns

Behind the darkest folk tales lie attempts to interpret fear. Although the tales take place in domestic settings, the events in the stories dramatize fears which are universal. One folk tale which has endured is <u>Red Riding Hood</u>. The fears projected into the tale are: fear of the invasion (natural or supernatural) of the home, fear of becoming subject to the destructive will or power of another, and the fear of deception. That this tale should be an echo of older fears involving natural forces (which have been incorporated into myths) should not be surprising. Fear of the changeability and violence in human nature that appears in folk tales has its counterpart in myth in the fear of natural forces and their changeability and violence. In <u>Red Riding Hood</u>, the evil, mesmerizing darkness of the Wolf echoes the image of the darkness of night and death. The character of Red Riding Hood is the counterpart of day, light, and innocent gaiety. Some folklorists claim that the tale echoes a myth of sunrise and sunset. Henry Bett cites the red cloak as evidence:

> The Letts have a story which tells how the daughter of
> the sun hung her red cloak on an oak tree. At the other
> end of the world, the Australians of Encounter Bay say
> that the sun is a woman and has a lover among the dead
> who has given her a red kangaroo skin in which she appears
> at her rising.

Bett then explains the wolf as "personification of night." He cites the recurrence of the wolf in Norse mythology as a destroyer of light.[1] In the <u>Index of Fairy Tales Myths, and Legends</u>, there is a similar claim for the myth of Helge, who, to escape his enemies, disguised himself as a wolf and who turned out to be a God of night and darkness.[2]

Although it seems farfetched to think that so simple a tale as <u>Red Riding Hood</u> should have come from such dynamic legends, the particular vividness and enduring qualities of the red hood and the figure of the wolf do have their roots in traditional symbols which strengthen this supposition. The color red, and its association with blood and passion, would prefigure the violence to come. It is interesting that the substitution of color (for instance, gold) should make a difference. In <u>Little Golden Hood</u>, there are none of the ominous overtones of <u>Red Riding Hood</u>. The golden hood is not only divine, linked to golden flowers and the sun, but it

---

* Given at the Modern Language Association Seminar on Children's Literature, Chicago, Illinois, December 27, 1971.

serves as protection for the little girl. Faith in human good sense is exhibited: Grandmother kills the wolf, there is a lesson learned, and a happy ending.[3] The red hood incorporates qualities of life, light, and sexual energy.[4] The use of the hood and its association with death adds to the ominous quality of the tale.[5]

The figure of the wolf arouses terror, not only because of his savage wildness, but because of traditional connotations of darkness and evil. In the Dictionary of Symbols, he is cited as being the "symbol of evil," the "monster" who lived in the depths of the earth and who would "break out of this prison . . . devour the son."[6] Medieval Christian thinking marks him as a symbol of the devil, the whore, a beast who massacres "anybody who passes by with a fury of greediness." He also has the eyes of the Devil and is capable of mesmerizing his victims, if he chooses.[7] The combination of evil, sexual aggression, and gluttonous violence, then, is historically connected with the wolf. It is surely his nature in Red Riding Hood. His association with darkness and destruction links him, and by extension the tale, to the ancient myths.

The fear of sexual power characterizes all versions of the tale. It represents an irresistable force, a force in the service of greed and death. In the French tales this sexuality is more explicit: the little girl is lured into the bed. The rhythmic, intimate repetition of questions leading to the moment of climax (or anti-climax) is extremely sexual. The mesmerizing qualities of the wolf as male power add to the eroticism. But sexual eroticism is obvious only to the adult. The terror the tale holds for the child occurs because the eroticism exploited is one of far deeper significance—that of the intimacy with another's body, be it mother, father, or grandmother—a tactile desire which is far deeper than the desire for heterosexual intercourse. This deepest desire and trust betrayed is what makes the wolf's violence so much more horrifying.

In male chauvinistic terms, this tale is an act of sex in itself. Perrault's version is explicitly an act of aggression against the female because of its faintly disguised prurience and enthusiasm for the final "kill," with its expression of male exaltation and triumph. The penetration of the house (with its fragile latch, bobbin, or string guarding the door) as a feminine stronghold, the enactment of destruction and violence by a male, is obvious. It is interesting that when the tale comes from the male-female storytelling tradition of folklore, the female figures emerge with more luck. The wolf is cut up and his "head" is chopped off (a bit of feminine fantasy creeping in). In Grimm, fantasy is even greater in the dumping of rocks into his stomach, revenge for the "infliction" of pregnancy.

The versions of the tale vary in the exploitation of fear of violence, and the use of erotic stimulation, and work to achieve different ends. Some are amoral, some contain moral values. Some are highly erotic, some much less so, to the point where sexual eroticism is almost suppressed. All assume certain social attitudes toward children as a result, and deserve looking at for this reason.

Two versions of the tale still published relatively intact are the French tale of Perrault and the German folk version collected by the Grimm brothers. The plot of both tales is derived from an old French tale called the Story of Grandmother.

31

There is no special moral in this tale; the cannabalistic, sexual, and scatological events are matter-of-factly stated. No maternal warning foreshadows the grisly future. The end is farcical and anticlimactic in comparison with the Perrault and Grimm versions.

Suspense caused by sexual tension and fear of violence builds up as the bzou (werewolf) directs her to undress:

> "Undress, my child," said the bzou, "and come and sleep
>      beside me."
> "Where should I put my apron?"
> "Throw it in the fire, my child; you don't need it any more."
> And she asked where to put all the other garments, the
>      bodice, the dress, the skirt, and the hose, and the
>      wolf replied:
> "Throw them in the fire, my child; you will need them no more."

The vision of the wolf as a diabolic being comes through here. His mesmerizing qualities hold the little girl hypnotized as she does her medieval strip tease. The provocative qualities of the passage are inflamed by the acquiescence of the little girl; here our enjoyment of the game almost makes us forget that the game is almost up. When the child says, "Oh, Grandmother, that big mouth you have!" and the wolf replies, "All the better to eat you with, my child!", she decides she has to relieve herself. In spite of the bzou's insistence that she do it in bed, she has her way and goes outside, tieing the leash he has attached to her to a tree. The bzou, growing impatient, snaps, "Are you making cables?" and jumps out of bed to fetch her, only to find she has escaped. [8]

Because of its scatological wit and nonviolence, the ending undercuts the violence of the plot. It domesticates the supernatural werewolf and assumes that children are capable of the cunning of adults. There is a down-to-earth order in the tale that is much different from the moral tales or the tales idealizing children.

Another quality of the tale which adds to this order is the rapidity, the matter-of-fact nature of the act of violence. Within one short paragraph, the wolf has killed Grandmother, put her flesh in the pantry, and a bottle of her blood on the shelf. The chilling vision of evil occurs with the deliberate, casual invitation to the little girl to eat the "meat" and "wine", the blood and body of her own Grand-mother. The mixture of sacrilege with barbarity adds to the shock value of the act.

Perrault fills the old amoral horror story with an erotic tale of warning in his Red Riding Hood. Although it is told with amusement and relish, it is a moral tale: pretty little girls should not talk to wolves (males) on the path. Jacques Barchilon in his article "L'ironie et l'humour dans les 'Contes' de Perrault," explores this erotic warning in detail. He speaks of Perrault's penchant for amusing himself as well as the children by entering into their game. [9] He is amusing himself vicariously with the thought of seduction while warning little girls who are innocent and pretty to be careful. The moral is implicit in the plot, and early in the story there are presentiments of the end: " . . . the poor child, who did not know how dan-

gerous it is to stop and speak to wolves . . ." [10] In spite of her innocence, there
is evidence that she (like her predecessor in the Story of Grandmother), has more
than a bit of erotic curiosity. The violence is darker, not in spite of the eroticism,
but because of the nature of this eroticism; it exhibits the tragedy of innocence
betrayed. The innocent eroticism in the child is bound up in the tender intimacy
of close contact with a beloved adult. This innocent trust followed by a brutal
death is what shocks and frightens children. It is the adult who sees himself as
a wolf, who seems to pick out sexual seduction in the tale, not the child. The
tale is also more frightening because of its finality. There is no recourse, no
comforting denouement. It summons up the ancient mythical vision of the end of
the world, an eternity of night.

The Grimm tale of Red Riding Hood, which appeared in the early 1800's, evokes
a more exact memory of the daylight myth because the rescue is analogous to the
return of day.[11] But the tale does not contain the comforting qualities of the myth.
The sly eroticism in Perrault is missing; there is repressed sexuality in the German
tale. The explicit request to come to bed is gone. However, the scene on the
path, the incantation, the erotic mesmerizing of the little girl before the wolf
springs, is still there. This repressed sexuality (also symbolized by the guilt involved with picking flowers, the forgetting herself in sensual delight) is accompanied by increasing violence and a barbaric, sadistic sense of justice. What
could be more sexually perverse than the wolf's strange "pregnancy" with the two
females inside? What could be more brutal than the following "pregnancy" of
rocks ? It is also significant that it is sweet, innocent Red Riding Hood who
fetches the rocks and helps to fill his belly. He dies, ripped by the weight of the
rocks when he tries to escape.

The novelty and ingenuity of this revenge lends sadistic appeal to this tale. It
acts against a humanistic involvement a child might have toward pain and suffering. Unlike Perrault, who has written a moral story about innocence and its frailty
in the face of raw violence, the Grimms' tale has its roots in the necessity for
obedience. "I will never again wander off into the forest as long as I live, when
my mother forbids it," intones Red Riding Hood.[12] Stressing justice and obedience,
the tale shows torture committed with ingenious flippancy; the tale reveals a dark
humor as potent as any of the moderns. The frightening thing is that the torture
is meant to serve the idea of the story—that of the necessity of obedience to authority and the administration of justice. Compared to Perrault's vision of the
child as erotic innocent, Grimms' tales reveal the child to be erotically cruel, as
cruel as the old werewolf in the Story of Grandmother.

While both versions of the tale continue to be published, proving their irresistable strength, there have been rewrites of Red Riding Hood which exhibit divergent and interesting views toward the character of Red Riding Hood and, by extension, children.

Some late nineteenth and earlier twentieth-century versions tamed both the violent and erotic incidents, watering down the purity of emotion of the older tales.
There are long, sissyfied descriptions of Red Riding Hood and drawn out sections
of plot which tend to turn a lesson about deception and violence into an unreal

vision of the child as an innocent, beautiful fool, protected in life. The interpreter of the tale has deceived his child reader about the true meaning of danger. In the selection from a set of books entitled The Young Folks Treasury, for instance, there are three pages of long vague, rambling and sentimental prose, compared to half a page of action. Red Riding Hood doesn't even meet the wolf until the third page of the four-page story. There is the assumption that to be sweet and innocent is enough in life. Someone will always rescue the weak and good from the mean and cruel. Virtue is its own reward (plus the added bonus of God's grace, presumably).

Walter de la Mare wrote a witty version of Red Riding Hood which compares interestingly with the sentimental Red. His Red Riding Hood is vain, and this vanity sets the stage for her deception. The eroticism is back in this tale—stylish, deliberate and subtle in the suggestive behavior of the wolf. His voice is "queer and husky," "his jaws opened and grinned; and then in tones as wheedling and buttery-smooth as his tongue could manage, he said, 'Good afternoon, my **dear.** I hope you are refreshed after your little nap. But what, may I ask, are you doing here, all alone in the woods and in that beautiful bright red hood, too?' As he uttered these words, he went on grinning at her in so friendly a fashion that Little Red Riding Hood could not but smile at him in return." De la Mare's point seems to be this: seduction is an exploitation of vanity. The wolf then, is not wholly the villain. In fact, he is quite the stereotype of the dandy. When Red Riding Hood describes her method of signalling Grannie, he says, "But how clever, and where does your poor dear Grannie live and which way are you going?" [13] By making the wolf's dialogue chatty and urbane, and adding the dimensions of vanity and the parody of slick, seductive behavior, de la Mare has humanized the Wolf to a greater degree. Mixed feelings for the reader accompany the justice of the wolf's end. He is so comical in Grannie's nightie, and so vulnerable:

> "At this faraway strange sound in his dreams, the Wolf
> opened—though by scarcely more than a hair's breath—
> his dull, drowsy eyes. But at glimpsing the woodman,
> his wits came instantly back to him and he knew his dan
> ger. Too late! Before even, clogged up in Grannie's
> nightgown, he could gather his legs together to spring
> out of bed, the woodman, with one mighty stroke of the
> axe, had finished him off." [14]

Far from being harmed, the two females appear happy and gay; in fact, Grannie's rheumatism is cured from all the "warmth and squeezing" in the wolf's belly.

Walter de la Mare has written a version superior to all of the modern versions I found. His wit, his amused tone reminiscent of Perrault, is true to the erotic humor of the old French tale. His sense of justice is complicated and much more sensitive than the cruel justice of the German folk tales. His refining of the moral warning of Perrault to include vanity makes the story richer for children, without being preachy.

One of the interesting topics in twentieth-century literature is the relationship between victim and victimizer. Genet, Reage, and others have written complicated and perplexing novels and plays about this subject. Ionesco, in The Lesson, uses the Red Riding Hood tale as the spirit of his play (whether or not it is intentional), for example. Ann Sexton, in her new book of poetry, Transformations, attempts to get at the deepest level of Grimms' fairy tales. In her poem "Red Riding Hood," she examines the vague, dual nature of actions involving deception and cruelty.

Like de la Mare, she makes the wolf strangely vulnerable. In her first few lines she writes:

> Long ago
> There was a strange deception:
> a wolf dressed in frills.
> A kind of transvestite.[15]

The wolf is described as quite an impulsive fellow, not cruel but very hungry: ". . . he planned to eat them both,/the grandmother an old carrot/and the child a shy budkin/in a red, red hood." He does his job in a hurry, eating Grandmother "as quick as a slap./Then he put on her nightdress and cap and snuggled down in-to the bed/A deceptive fellow." He "gobbled Red Riding Hood down like a gum-drop. Now he was fat." This is almost a complete reversal of roles. He is child-like in his disguise and in his eagerness. He does not act like the humans, who cut him open while he is still alive and fill his belly with rocks and sew him up. He is sad, grotesquely funny, without the ability of humans to abstract ideas to justify their own brutality:

> "The wolf, they decided, was too mean to be simply shot
> so they filled his belly with large stones and sewed him up.
> He was as heavy as a cemetery and when he woke up and
> tried to run off he fell over dead. Killed by his own weight.

Sexton suggests that his "crime" did not approach theirs:

> Those two remembering
> nothing naked and brutal
> from that little death,
> that little birth,
> from their going down
> and their lifting up.

It is interesting that this adaptation of the Grimm tale (the most direct echo of the old myth of sunset and sunrise) should be also the occasion for such words as these, which suggest both the fetus in the womb, birth, and sunrise and sunset imagery.

Darkness and light, good and evil, male and female, the home and the wilder-ness are the forces of opposition in the tale of Red Riding Hood. From the matter-of-fact erotic horror of the old French tale to the relativistic humanism of Ann Sexton with her ironic, gentle treatment of aggression, the story casts an enchantment which is ageless in its dark appeal.

[1] Henry Bett, M. A., Nursery Rhymes and Tales (Detroit, Mich., 1924), pp. 20-22.

[2] Index of Fairy Tales, Myths, and Legends, 2nd ed. rev. and enl., (Boston, 1926), p. 746.

[3] Andrew Lang, Red Fairy Book (London, 1959), pp. 225-229.

[4] J. E. Cirlot, A Dictionary of Symbols, (New York, 1962), p. 52.

[5] Ibid., p. 143.

[6] Ibid., p. 355.

[7] T. H. White, ed., The Book of Beasts; being a Translation from a Latin Bestiary of the Twelfth Century (London, 1955), pp. 56-61.

[8] Paul Delarue, ed., The Borzoi Book of French Folk Tales (New York, 1956), pp. 230-232.

[9] Jacques Barchilon, "L'ironie et l'humour dans les 'Contes' de Perrault," Studi Francesi, II (1967), p. 260.

[10] Perrault, "Little Red Riding Hood", Favorite Fairy Tales (New York, 1907), pp. 87-91.

[11] Bett, Nursery Rhymes and Tales, p. 21. Bett says, ". . . the German version of the story, Rothkappchen, ends with the arrival of the hunter, who rips up the sleeping wolf, when the little damsel in her red cap comes out again safe and sound. It is the picturesque story of the adventure of the red sun devoured by the monstrous darkness at sunset, and then disgorged again at sunrise."

[12] Jacob and Wilhelm Grimm, Fairy Tales (Cleveland, 1947), p. 63.

[13] Walter de la Mare, Told Again; traditional tales told by Walter de la Mare (Oxford, 1927), pp. 110-111.

[14] Ibid., p. 117.

[15] Ann Sexton, Transformations(Boston, 1971), pp. 77-79.

# THE SAGE OF LA FONTAINE OR A CERTAIN ART OF LIVING

Dominique Tailleux

Few readers are aware of the philosophic depth of fables and their role in establishing a way of life. In the epistle to Madame de Montespan, at the beginning of the second volume of his Fables, La Fontaine proposes to ". . . ériger en divinité /Le sage par qui fut ce bel art inventé." The sage, the sage par excellence, is Aesop, who knew how to transfigure the world through his symbols and accord to the imagination its right. Wisdom, for La Fontaine, is therefore an art of seeing the world, of transforming it into a parallel universe with a poetic essence that would elevate the fable to the ranks of the fine arts. Such a reflection in the "Pouvoir des Fables" (VIII, 4) would seem to invite us to believe this. But the wise man for La Fontaine is also the one who can resign himself like the sheep (VIII, 14) who lets himself be led without complaint to the slaughter. "La mort ne surprend point le sage" (VIII, 1). This type of wise man is closely related to the traditional one who, before the eighteenth century, was also called the "philosophe."

Even in the middle of the second volume, in 1678, there still remains a traditional element in La Fontaine's conception of the sage, but if the word "sage" appears frequently under the pen of the poet in this second volume, it does not always appear with the same meaning. New and modern elements make La Fontaine's wise man a precursor to the philosophers of the eighteenth century. Personal elements, inseparable from the temperament of the fabulist, bring in turn their own particular coloration. Finally, as in Montaigne's Essais, the conception of the sage in La Fontaine's Fables evolves progressively with age. La Fontaine is forty-seven years old when, in 1668, in the first volume of Fables, he presents, with a certain conventional indifference, the ordinary sage, prudent and judicious, clothed in attitudes woven with epicurean threads and a stoic border. The philosophy of Gassendi opens new horizons to the fabulist who, at age fifty-seven, in the second volume, becomes deeply involved with questions concerning wisdom, the pursuit of which becomes his principal reason for living. Then comes the winter: at age seventy-three, in the last book of Fables, in 1694, the sage is another man, more sedate and austere.

Leaving aside the conventional volume of 1668, let us try to describe the evolution of the image of the sage which La Fontaine creates, and determine what it represents for him.

The Fables of 1678 do not abruptly annihilate the practical empiricism taught by Aesop and all the fabulists who preceded La Fontaine. They remain faithful to a morality of experience which is translated into advice addressed to others: one should know how to reply "en normand," like the fox at the lion's court (VII, 7); to extricate oneself skillfully from a difficult situation as does the deer after the death of the lioness queen (VIII, 14). One also has to be able to adapt without troubling himself with mere scruples: the dog who fiercely defends his master's dinner comprehends very quickly that he is mistaken and that he must be first in line if he wants to have "part au gâteaux" (VIII, 7).

The foundation of this empirical morality is enlightenment. How many times does La Fontaine remind us of this! The sage must, before all else, be conscious of his own fate. This consciousness leads to an active prudence which may help to avert a menacing danger, as in the case of the capon who sees the cook's knife (VIII, 21); or may lead to a passive resignation, like that of the pig (VIII, 12). Self-pre-servation always presents itself as a first and absolute necessity. The wise man is the one who sees clearly: in the fable just evoked, "Le cochon, la chèvre et le mouton," the resignation of the goat and that of the sheep who "ne voyaient nul mal à craindre," is sheer foolishness and ignorance. The cries of the pig prove his alertness. "Mais que lui servait-il? Quand le mal est certain, / La plainte ni la peur ne changent le destin." Resignation is therefore necessary but only after having acquired a lucid insight into one's destiny. The ideal attitude of the sage would combine those of the goat and the sheep. It is to this theme of enlightened resignation that La Fontaine most often returns. This is the richest heritage that tradition bequeathed him.

From tradition the fabulist also borrows some general precepts, particularly ap-plicable to politics: the mediating pigeons in the vulture's war are victims of their good office (VII, 8); it is preferable to leave "divisés les méchants." The leopard sultan does not distrust the young lion from the neighboring forest; he has only scorn and pity for him, mistakenly, however, since the lion soon becomes the mas-ter (XI, 1): one should always be friendly toward those who might become powerful. The shepherd (X, 9) learns at his own expense that one should beware of kings and courts. These are the traditional precepts which La Fontaine embellishes in his Fables, and which may be epitomized in "l'art d'esquiver" dangers, wicked men and imbeciles.

La Fontaine remains equally faithful to the epicurean morality: the sage must en-joy everything without becoming attached to anything. Life is a banquet from which one must depart sufficiently satiated so as to feel no unbecoming regrets at the leave-taking. One must know how to avoid the pitfalls of ambition and cupidity. The happy medium, the "médiocrité" taught so well by Horace, lives on as the ideal; the cobbler (VIII, 2), and the couple in the "Souhaits" (VII, 7) adequately bear witness to this ideal, and the title of one fable, "Rien de trop" (IX, 11), con-firms it. From the epicurean philosophy La Fontaine especially retains, as an en-dorsement of the wise man, the virtue of rest: it is futile to run after Fortune; it is preferable to wait for her in one's bed. The concept of passivity for La Fon-taine's sage is again that of Epicure's gods who from their height of serenity glance at the human comedy in the same tranquil and amused way that Diderot will evoke later in a letter to Sophie Volland. Finally, for La Fontaine, rest is sleep, a sleep which could have delighted Ronsard beneath the shadows of Vendômois. The invocation of Diderot and Ronsard with regard to La Fontaine leads us to the realization that for him, as for them, happiness is a preoccupation.

In effect, while adopting elements from a traditional way of life, La Fontaine places them in a perspective which intermingles wisdom with happiness to the point of confusion. More than the establishment of a morality, La Fontaine is concerned with the search for finding a basis for an optimism which occasionally echoes that of the Renaissance and is a prelude to the philosophies of happiness of the eighteenth century. Then again his idealistic optimism surpasses traditional epicureanism and comes closer to Gassendi.

In his Syntagma, written between 1656 and 1658, Gassendi, rediscovering the epicureanism of the Renaissance, rehabilitates the body in general, its instincts and its nature. In 1674 Bernier had just published an abridged edition of Syntagma; another edition appeared in 1678, the same year as the second collection of Fables. La Fontaine, meeting Bernier at Madame de la Sablière's salon, had only to be lured by his temperament. Between the Christian epicureanism of the Renaissance and the materialistic optimism of the eighteenth century, Gassendian philosophy forms a stage which is literarily most faithfully represented by La Fontaine. Certain verses from the fable "Un animal dans la lune" (VII, 18) prove that reason only works on sense data and illustrate one of the fundamental principles of Gassendi, who says in fact that "rien n'est dans l'entendement, qui n'ait d'abord été les sens." Gassendi thus paves the way for the sensualism of Locke, Condillac and Diderot. La Fontaine's sage will therefore follow Gassendi's philosophy because of this priority accorded to the senses.

In addition, he will follow this philosophy because it is oriented in the direction of a pagan wisdom without breaking with religion and because it resolves the contradiction that La Fontaine feels in himself between the call of the senses and the fear of God. Bernier's abridgement furnished La Fontaine with the idea of a transcendent, sovereign and protecting God, "qui peut être appelé cause Première et premier Moteur, la Source de tout être, l'Origine de toute perfection, le Maître de l'Univers." This God, whose perfect work can be seen in "Le Gland et la citrouille" (IX, 4), is not far removed from the Providence of Zadig. According to La Fontaine, the sage is already a man of the eighteenth century, who declares his hostility toward foolishness and superstition in fables such as "l'Horoscope" (VIII, 16) or "Les Devineresses" (VII, 15).

The fabulist and the sage have scientific minds. Still faithful to the ideas of Gassendi, La Fonaine believes in a universal soul in which every being participates:

> . . . la nature
> A mis dans chaque creature
> Quelque grain d'une masse où puisent les esprits.
> (X, 14, Discours a M. le duc de La Rochefoucauld)

He believes in a hierarchy of souls from the superior soul to that of the animals, for each living being has his own individuality, which he wants to safeguard at any price, as we see in the last part of "La souris métamorphosée en fille" (IX, 7). Here again it is possible to evoke a man of the eighteenth century, the Ddierot of the Rêve de d'Alembert.

A philosophy that reconciled pleasure and virtue in a sort of modern hedonism, sheltered from the stoic and Christian, which left a predominant place for God in

a universe where the importance of matter and the senses were, however, unequiv-
ocally affirmed, which permitted the free exercise of intelligence in all scientific
questions, could only have been attractive to a curious and restless intellect.

Thus, there appeared beyond the moral tradition, without, however, disregard-
ing it, a new type of sage who allows a glimpse of the man of the eighteenth century. This sage is all the more evidently a precursor of the eighteenth century for
his thinking in terms of happiness. More precisely, his wisdom is founded on the
right to happiness, on the search for what Gassendi calls natural felicity, a state
"dans lequel il se trouve autant de bien et aussi peu de mal qu'il est possible,
et dans lequel l'on puisse par conséquent passer la vie doucement, tranquillement,
constamment."

Such a quest for tranquility obliges the wise man to accept the established
order, whether in politics or in individual destiny: the serpent's tail should not
want to take the place of the head (VII, 17); the fox can not make himself a wolf
(XII, 9). The destiny of all living creatures being death, one should become accustomed to death; detach himself as much as possible in order to suffer as little
as possible. In this matter La Fontaine is very close to Montaigne, uneasy as is
he at the prospect of death. Each of them seeks to convince and reassure himself.

Applying to the letter the lessons of Gassendi's philosophy, the sage, according
to La Fontaine, succeeds in reconciling the matter of individual fate, predestina-
tion, chance, and liberty. Fate, commanded by a kindly Providence, corrects the
absurdities of blind Fortune; as for our liberty, it consists especially in the possibility of becoming aware of our nature and condition, thus, assuring ourselves
sedate happiness.

To Gassendi's new type of sage La Fontaine, who would not be content simply
being a disciple of a philosophy, adds some personal elements. The image of the
ideal  sage acquires more suppleness and human truth. These elements become
especially pronounced in books VIII through X of the Fables, book VII being more
clearly influenced by the enthusiastic discovery of Gassendian philosophy. With
all of his persuasive power, La Fontaine insists on the necessity of refining our
own nature: "Faute de cultiver la nature et ses dons, / Oh! combien de Césars
deviendront Laridons" (VII, 24, "l'Education"). He instills in the sage an inquiring
mind: "le savoir a son prix," even though it does not permit brilliant material
successes.

Aside from these intellectual qualities, indulgence is also needed by the sage:
irritated by the human race, Jupiter  only hurls his lightning in a desert: "Tout
père frappe à côté" (VIII, 20). The lesson is worthy of meditation. Too, fantasy
and imagination have their rights; the sage likes fables for he cannot live without
illusions and dreams: "Si Peau d'Ane m'était conté . . ." (VIII, 4).

These diverse directions, these variations on a basic philosophy and on tradition
indicate a reflected search. The sage must do more than merely understand; it is
necessary for him to make others understand. He has a responsibility to others:
he has to teach that happiness is not only a right of every man but also a duty.

The approach of death and nothingness sometimes changes intellectual perspectives and Gassendi's philosophy becomes progressively dominated by an austere
Christianity influenced by the frequenting of Protestant milieux in Madame de la

Sablière's salon and by Jansenist friendships, in particular that with La Roche-roucauld.  The enjoyment of rest gives way to the delight of retreat; already there appears the theme of the man of quality retired from the world, who will be best illustrated by l'Abbé Prévost.  The need for friendship is dominated by the need for solitude.

From book XI, and especially from "le Songe d'un habitant du Mogol," this evo-lution of the sage, as La Fontaine conceives of him, is perceivable, but it affirms itself especially in the last fable of the last book (XII, 25), a true spiritual testa-ment of the poet.  The recognition of our nature and its growth is now incompatible with the turmoil of the world, for those who coped so well with the effervescence of the salon conversation in the preceding books.  They demand "des lieux pleins de tranquillité": "Pour vous mieux contempler demeurez au désert. / Ainsi parla le solitaire."  Parabolic tone and Jansenist vocabulary; we are far from epicur-eanism, midway between the Renaissance and the eighteenth century.  Reflection is no longer oriented toward the search for happiness, but rather toward the search for salvation.  The advice given by the recluse, in this last fable, is a "conseil salutaire," and it appears that the word "salutaire" is not simply there for the rhyme.  The sage now withdraws from the world.  Where does he retire?  To Port-Royal, the syntax would lead us to believe, but the engraving accompanying the fable depicts a Trappist.  To the very end, the sage refuses to belong to one sect rather than another, as in the time of Gassendi enthusiasm, La Fontaine had re-fused to be solely and strictly a follower of Gassendi.  The principle of solitude is now all that counts for him and for his salvation.  On the practical level, what is the last word of the solitary wise man?:  A little money, not to be wasted, not to be thrown out the window, as the monkey does with the miser's ducats (XII,3), and much tranquility in order to have the pleasure of exercising, to the fullest extent, one's reason and intellect.

In only one domain, the sage experiences difficulty finding a fixed point, in the domain of passions.  If one believes the reproaches addressed to Ulysses' com-panions (XII, 1), the sage must not be a slave of his passions; however if one believes the lesson of the "Philosophe Scythe" (XII, 20), neither must he curtail them entirely.  Even though salvation may be of prime importance, in this last phase of wisdom, the heart equally exerts its rights.  The true final attitude of the sage, and of La Fontaine himself, is given to us in a letter written by the fabulist to Bonrepaux: "Je concilierai tout cela le moins mal et le plus longtemps qu"il me sera possible."  Once again, we think of Diderot and of his unsolvable contradictions.

La Fontaine belongs, in effect, to the same intellectual family as Diderot—to those minds nourished at the same time by classical thought and by modern philos-ophy, who loyally seek a solution to the problem of living and of "Connais-toi, toi-même."  Although he evolves from Aesop to Port-Royal, by way of Gassendi, La Fontaine's sage still offers, in his variations, the same fundamental dosage of enlightenment and sensibility, still influences the attitudes toward life of gener-ations of children.

(Translated from the French by Ronald Margolin)

# PILGRIM'S PROGRESS AS A FAIRY-TALE

Alison White

The vogue for J. R. R. Tolkien's Lord of the Rings trilogy may have something in common with the three hundred years' "vogue" for John Bunyan's Pilgrim's Progress. The thirst of readers for Bunyan has abated somewhat during the past generation or two, but the fervor with which the young today contemplate Tolkien's elfin heroes in their crusades against the Dark Riders in Mirkwood suggests that themes of spiritual earnestness clothed in an entertainment of marvels and perils, maintain their hold. To play with the idea that Pilgrim's Progress and Lord of the Rings have links is tempting. Tolkien's Frodo is a battling pilgrim of Christian's stamp. Gandalf, the benign wizard, is Frodo's Evangelist. In Bunyan's Dark Land, Valiant-for-Truth prefigures Tolkien's heroic Strider. In accounting for his romances, Tol-kien has analyzed what he directly calls fairy-tale. The term is uneasy; it should perhaps be confined to tales in which there are fairies. Faerie as a name, however, was imaginatively extended in such ballads as "Thomas Rhymer" and also in Spenser and Keats. The dim, marvel-steeped terrain of Pilgrim's Progress in no way resembles Bunyan's England, or any earthly kingdom. It is Faerie—if we can extend that realm to include the landscapes of Revelation. By importing a dragon and a woman, among other Apocalyptic apparitions, Spenser brought Revelation into Faerie. Bunyan did the same. And the term fairy-tale has been loosened by others of Bunyan's literary descendants besides Tolkien. Pilgrim's Progress fathered a succession of literary fantasies by such clergymen as Charles Lutwidge Dodgson (Lewis Carroll), George Macdonald, and Charles Kingsley. Though fairies were absent from it, Lewis Carroll called Alice in Wonderland this "love-gift of a fairy-tale." A literary follower of Bunyan, George Macdonald, wrote romances, he said, to help people who sought truth in a nutshell because they could not "see the fairy-tale in the mustard-seed." Bunyan saw the fairy-tale in the mustard-seed, in the burning bush, in Aaron's rod, and the fiery chariot. I plead that fairy-tale has been so dignified by its practitioners—lovers and imitators of Bunyan—that, in its more fanciful aspects, Pilgrim's Progress may be dubbed an evangelical fairy-tale.

To return to the Tolkien-like Valiant-for-Truth, a Strider in his murky Dark-Land, let us hear from his lips what his parents had told him about Christian and his Progress. All that Valiant relates is folklorish. He has missed all the allegory, even as did countless thousands of child readers of Bunyan. Valiant says: "They (his parents) told me of the Slough of Despond, where Christian was well-nigh smothered. They told me that there were archers standing ready in Beelzebub's Castle, to shoot them that should knock at the wicket-gate for entrance. They told me also of the wood, and dark mountains, of the Hill Difficulty, of the lions, and also of the three giants, Bloodyman, Maul, and Slay-Good. They said, more-over that there was a foul fiend haunted the valley of Humiliation and the Christ-ian was by him almost bereft of life. Besides, said they, you must go over the

42

Valley of the Shadow of Death, where the hobgoblins are, where the light is darkness, where the way is full of snares, pits, traps, and gins. They told me also of Giant Despair, of Doubting Castle, and of the ruins that the pilgrims met with there. Further, they said I must go over the Enchanted Ground, which was dangerous. And that after all this I should find a river, over which I should find no bridge, and that that river did lie betwixt me and the Celestial Country." Then Valiant sings the fine Pilgrim song which was so moving a part of the funeral of Sir Winston Churchill: "Who would true valour see,/ Let him come hither;/ One here will constant be/ Come wind, come weather./ There's no discouragement/ Shall make him once relent/ His first avowed intent/ To be a pilgrim./ Hobgoblin nor foul fiend/ Can daunt his spirit,"

I see Pilgrim's Progress as a fairy tale in that it is possibly the world's greatest Cinderella story. A man in rags and with a "magic" burden is clothed (as by a fairy godmother) in a "broidered coat," is made "as fair as the moon" by a seal on his forehead, and wins a crown in a city of gold where he feasts with the greatest of princes. The singular thing about this Cinderella story is that it was read as absolute, totally personal, actuality and truth by millions of the devout. Pilgrim's Progress is a passionately earnest book. It concerns the fate of the soul. But it is as far from being abstract as theology can get. As a literary work its greatness lies in its equipoise of realism and fantasy. The realism—especially where it timelessly reveals human nature—is what commends it most to modern taste. Still, if we remember all those Tolkien addicts, we must admit that the appetite for Bunyan-esque marvels and perils is perhaps as strong today as it ever was.

It is odd to note how often Pilgrim's Progress recalls the Odyssey in the latter's aspect as a collection of Greek fairy tales. Bunyan gives no sign of having known Homer, except that he mentions Hercules, also satyrs and a goddess. But the Odyssey tales have many popular forms, and the daydreams and threats they express are inherent in the human condition. As Bunyan tells us, he was in youth addicted to chapbook romances about giant-slayers, dragons, and magic. Anyhow, there are oddities among resemblances to Homeric episodes in Pilgrim's Progress. Mount Sinai, the hanging hill, threatened to fall on Christian, and "There came words and fire out of the mountain." Evangelist explained that the hanging hill is "in a mystery" a bondwoman in bondage with her children. It is rather like the Greek Scylla, and it is also rather like that other Homeric topographical menace, Charybdis. In Bunyan, too, there are Sirens. (They go after Faithful, not Christian.) These are called Wanton and Lust of the Flesh, Lust of the Eyes, and Pride of Life. Christian faces Lotus-Eater perils, the Enchanted Ground and Forgetful Green. There is a Circe: Madame Bubble, the witch who tempts Stand-Fast. Honest says to Stand-Fast: "Madame Bubble! Is she a tall comely dame?.... Doth she not speak very smoothly, and give you a smile at the end of a sentence? This woman is a witch, and it is by virtue of her sorceries that this ground is enchanted. Whoever doth lay their head down in her lap had as good lay it down upon that block above which the axe doth hang. She has given it out in some places that she is a goddess, and therefore some do worship her."

The folk-lore motifs that abound in Pilgrim's Progress are given enormous sub-stance and evocative power by their being attached to a religious structure which was, at the time of the book's composition, massive indeed. In applied power, only the folk-lore of the Bible excels that of Pilgrim's Progress, and Bible folk-lore suffuses Bunyan's book. Interpreter starts the great dream in its career of meta-physical marvels. He shows a fire that burns hotter when the Devil casts water on it, for the oil of Christ's grace keeps it burning. The unremovable burden on Christian's back is loosed by the sacred magic of Christ's cross. Pilgrims are given "furniture," gospel armor, a weapon called "all-prayer," shoes that will not wear out. Christian is shown Bible "engines": Samson's jawbone of an ass, David's sling, Jael's nail and hammer, Gideon's pitchers, trumpets, lamps. He confronts Apollyon, the angel of the bottomless pit, from Revelation. Apollyon "was clothed with scales like a fish (and they are his pride) he had wings like a dragon, feet like a bear, and out of his belly came fire and smoke, and his mouth was as the mouth of a lion." Christian faces Apollyon as St. George had faced his dragon and, as, later in Pilgrim's Progress, Greatheart defeated Giants Grim Bloody-Man, Maul, Slay-Good and Despair. The wounded Christian was ministered to by a hand with leaves from the tree of life which... "Christian applied to the wounds... and was healed immediately." In the Valley of the Shadow of Death he meets hobgoblins, satyrs, and dragons of the pit. Fiends whisper things he thought came from his own mind. In his deliverance the pilgrim sings "O world of wonders." On the "realistic" side of his adventures, Christian encounters figures who seem to have emerged from fable—such as Talkative, son of Saywell, in Prating Row. Like an Alice in Wonderland grotesque (or a Shakespearean grotesque named Polonius) Talk-ative prates: I will talk of things heavenly, of things earthly; things moral, or things evangelical; things sacred, or things profane; things past or things to come, things foreign, things at home; things more essential or things circumstantial." When Christian, like any chapbook giant-killer, is imprisoned, starved, and flog-ged in Doubting Castle, he remembers his magic key of Promise in his bosom. At its approach the jail door flies open. Next, Christian looks through the Shepherds' magical perspective glass which shows him his own face, or, when tilted, the face of the Savior.

In Part II, the rather relaxed and indulgent tale of Christiana's progress with Mercy and the four boys, there is even more holy magic, more wishfulfillment. Young Mercy's dream of entering heaven is a Cinderella vision—one of the most naive touches in the book. One with wings, she says, wiped her eyes, clad her in silver and gold, put a chain about her neck and earrings in her ears, and a beautiful crown on her head. When the boy Matthew eats green plums from Beelzebub's orchard, he is dosed with a witch's brew: blood of a goat, ashes of a heifer, juice of hyssop. But he requires the stronger medicine of the body and blood of Christ. On Forgetful Green the pilgrims forget the favours they have received. Birds then sing to them in words, praising God's goodness. At Enchanted Ground "a great mist and a darkness fell upon them all." In its ominousness, this sentence evokes the mood of romance from Malory through Tolkien. The book ends with one of the most irrational and strange of its conceits. Despondency and his daughter, Much-Afraid, declare that their fears are ghosts, "the which we entertained.. and could never shake them off, and they will walk about and seek entertainment of the pilgrims... but shut ye the doors upon them."

It is little wonder that Huckleberry Finn should have passed his ineffable judgment upon Pilgrim's Progress in saying "The statements was interesting but tough."

Where else in literature can one find such a blend of spiritual force, of humane good sense, and of fairy-tale in the mustard-seed? All in all, it's one heaven of a book.

OUT OF THE ORDINARY ROAD: JOHN LOCKE AND ENGLISH
JUVENILE FICTION IN THE EIGHTEENTH CENTURY

Robert Bator

John Locke in 1693 could list few books for children's reading. "Some pleasant Book suited to his [the child's] Capacity" (Aesop and Reynard the Fox) were
all he could find: "What other Books there are in English of the kind of those
above-mentioned, fit to engage the liking of Children, and tempt them to read, I
do not know . . . And nothing that I know has been consider'd of this kind out of
the ordinary Road of the Horn-Book, Primer, Psalter, Testament, and Bible."[1] To
Locke's list might be added the devotional tracts of James Janeway and his suc-
cessors plus John Bunyan's The Book for Boys and Girls or Country Rhimes for
Children (1686).[2]
The Puritan works included, there is still little for the child reader by the end
of the seventeenth century. Largely because of Locke, the child in the eighteenth
century was prodigally supplied with books designed for him. Besides providing a
touchstone into what was available for children's leisure reading at the end of one
century, Locke shaped the educational work of the following century. "Undoubtedly the greatest factor in moulding the general theory of the age was the work of
Locke, and his disciplinary conception of education is perhaps the underlying basis of most of the successful educational work in the century."[3] Locke's teaching on the absence of innate ideas in the child is pervasive in educational reform.
Once granted the child's mind is a tabula rasa, the responsibility is squarely on
education, since ideas enter only through experience, that is, by learning. Locke
improved the status of the child so often seen in the early eighteenth century as a
miniature adult. "He brings the child—seen but not heard, at best— out of his ob-
scurity, his invisibility, into the light, even the glare, of philosophical examination; the child becomes a philosophical subject."[4]
Locke's well-documented popularity with parents and writers in the eighteenth
century[5] is witnessed in Pamela in which Some Thoughts Concerning Education is
reviewed favorably. As late as 1769, Goldsmith hailed "the great Mr. John Locke
who may be justly said to have reformed all our modes of thinking in metaphysical
inquiry," and found him "still useful at present."[6] Locke's views reigned through
the eighteenth century right on up to the heyday of Rousseau.[7]
Not so well documented is Locke's influence on the production of a new literature for children. Not only spotlighting a definite need for books for children,
Locke urged that children be given a "Liking and Inclination" to what it is proposed
they learn, (STCE, pp. 74-75). "And if Things were order'd right, Learning any
thing, they should be taught, might be made as much a Recreation to their play, as
their Play is to their Learning," (STCE, p. 77). Locke's innovation, that learning
be made play, bore fruit in the quality and quantity of juvenile books produced in
the eighteenth century.
In 1740-1742, when Locke's influence on English parents and teachers was

still pervasive, Thomas Boreman's ten-volume <u>Gigantick Histories</u> appeared. None too imaginative, they do differ from anything available before that date. The first secular works for children in England outside of school texts, Boreman's books have the acknowledged aim of amusing: "During the Infant-age ever busy and always inquiring, there is no fixing the attention of the mind, but by amusing it."[8] Like Locke, Boreman criticizes the bulk of the books for children before his time: "Most of the Books which have been made use of to introduce children to a Habit of Reading . . . tend rather to cloy than entertain them."[9] Boreman's works are important for what they represent. Secular books meant for children exclusively, they were the sort of books Locke looked for which were to become commercially successful once Newbery capitalized upon them.

Another pre-Newbery writer for children whom Locke influenced is Mary Cooper who succeeded to her husband's printing business and published until 1761.[10] In 1743 she put out <u>The Child's New Play-Thing</u> and <u>Tommy Thumb's Pretty Song Book</u>.[11] An advertisement in the latter for the former heralds "The Child's Plaything / I recommend for Cheating / Children into Learning / Without any Beating."[12] This seems to follow Locke's recommendation for teaching the eight-year old son of Edward Clarke to read, "Cheat him into it if you can but make it not a Business for him," (STCE, p. 182). Other sections in STCE also parallel the Cooper method: "Thus Children may be cozen'd into a Knowlege of the Letters; be <u>taught to read</u>, without perceiving it to be any thing but a Sport, and play themselves into that others are whipp'd for," (STCE, p. 178).

Locke also recommended the use of alphabets in play, not as mere drill: "There may be Dice and Playthings, with the Letters on them, to teach Children the Alphabet by playing; and twenty other ways may be found, suitable to their particular Tempers, to make this kind of Learning a Sport to them," (STCE, pp. 177-178). Apparently influenced by Locke's suggestions, Cooper included in her book not only an alphabet but a "Preface Shewing the Use of the Alphabets" which paraphrases Locke:

> With this ALPHABET a Child may easily be taught its Letters by playing with them. For instance, let an Alphabet be put into a Hat or Box, and let the Child draw the Letters out one by one, and be told at first what they are, as he draws them out. By degrees he may be set to guess what they are, and be rewarded or encouraged when he finds them out. . . . Several other diverting Methods may be found out with this loose Alphabet, by which Children in a very little time may be taught their Letters, which I leave to the Ingenuity of their several Parents or Tutors.[13]

One of the first books for children is thus linked to Locke: ". . . It is impossible to compare one of the first attempts to produce a play-book, 'The Child's New Play-Thing,' with the advice written to his friend, Edward Clarke, without feeling that the progress from the religious books to primers and readers . . . and then onward to story-books was largely the result of the publication of his letters under the title of 'Thoughts on Education.' "[14]

Locke influenced not only fledgling efforts towards a true children's literature but also the work of the most important figure in the production of children's books in the century, John Newbery. Newbery was the first to weave the various threads of interest in children's books voiced by Locke, Richard Steele [15] and others into sustained, consistent work directed at children's interests. A Little Pretty Pocket-Book (1744), Newbery's first juvenile book, lists itself as "intended for the Instruction and Amusement of little Master Tommy and pretty Miss Polly." The open avowal of amusement as a direct intention of a book for youth runs counter to the John Bunyan and Isaac Watts tradition which may have provided amusement but reluctantly admitted it. At this stage the Newbery book, if not greatly different in kind, is at least different in degree from earlier juvenile books. The preface shows an indebtedness to John Locke's Some Thoughts Concerning Education. Reading like a synopsis of Locke, the Newbery book credits and paraphrases him: "Would you have a Hardy Child, give him common Diet only, cloath him thin, let him have good Exercise, and be as much exposed to Hardships as his natural constitution will admit. The face of a Child, when it comes into the world (says the great Mr. Locke) is as tender and susceptible of Injuries as any other part of the Body; yet by being always exposed, it becomes Proof against the severest Seson and the most inclement Weather."[16] Compare: "The Face, when we are Born, is no less tender than any other part of the Body: 'Tis use alone hardens it, and makes it more able to endure the Cold," (STCE, p. 4). Newbery's debt to Locke is obvious from his first published work for children on.

Besides A Little Pretty Pocket-Book (ten editions by 1769), Newbery produced until his death in 1767 at least fifty original books for children. The Newbery family firm to 1802 produced for youth nearly four hundred works. [17] In The Circle of the Sciences (1745-1746), seven volumes for youth on grammar, rhetoric, arithmetic, etc., Newbery is less obviously following Locke. The volumes on logic and rhetoric would have met the disapproval of Locke who saw little advantage in teaching such subjects to children since it might make them contentious, [18] (STCE, pp. 223-4). The books were also more primers to aid parents than the reading books Locke asked for.

Newbery's most famous work for children, The History of Little Goody Two-Shoes, was the most significant of the stories for children written in the eighteenth century. Originally printed in 1765, it went through innumerable editions. One writer located 174 English and American editions of the work by the nineteenth century. [19] It is still in print. The first sustained narrative written expressly for children, it epitomizes the innovations which Newbery brought to a primitive field. To look at the book is to see at once how Newbery and children's literature improved in the twenty years since his first book for children. The book fits the typical Newbery pattern. The story of Margery Meanwell (alias little Goody Two-Shoes) is narrated for those "Who from a State of Rags and Care / And Having Shoes but half a Pair, / Their Fortune and their Fame would fix, / And Gallop in a Coach and Six."[20] In part two, "The Renowned History of Mrs. Margery Two-Shoes, President of ABC College," poor peasant rises by book learning to become principal of a rather progressive neo-Lockean school in which Ralph the Raven arranges upper-case letters while Tom the Pigeon tends the lower-case ones. Goody, as did Locke, disavows rote learning; instead she scatters the alphabet around the classroom, making learning a game. If Goody did not read Locke, it is evident that her author did.[21] The letter games Goody invents are among the twenty other ways Locke hinted at to cozen children to read.[22] As evident from some of the works cited, Locke figures as an important influence on Newbery. Those who imitated Newbery's success stories helped disseminate Locke's ideas. By deciding the form and substance of children's literature for three or four generations, Newbery spread the Lockean ideas he favored.

A Description of Millenium Hall (1762), which is usually seen as the work of Sarah Robinson Scott, illustrates the debt of others to Newbery and therefore to Locke. The book is dedicated to Newbery in a Lockean preface that compares the minds of children to sheets of white paper.[23] Compare with: "Children are but Blank Paper, ready Indifferently for any impression, Good or Bad" (STCE, Preface, 1694, n.p.) and ". . . A Gentleman's Son who being then very little, I considered only as white paper or wax, to be moulded and fashioned as one pleases," (STCE, p. 261). Since only a few books in England for children to 1765 did not come from Newbery's press, literature for children in the first two-thirds of the century largely shows the influence of John Locke. While Locke's influence can be charted until the end of the century, his vogue is mainly from 1725 to 1765.[24] In the last part of the eighteenth century in England, after the English translation of Emile (1762), Jean-Jacques Rousseau becomes more influential on English juvenile writers but not instantaneously. In 1772 for example, Francis Newbery (John Newbery's nephew) produced The Prettiest Book for Children. A character, Don Stephano Bunyano, argues against nursery rhymes and fairy tales, countering that if children are to learn to read they might as well get reason and understanding at the same time.[25] Bunyano is still pretty much in the employ of Locke, not Rousseau who permitted Émile a single book, Robinson Crusoe.

Not until the 1780's is Rousseau mentioned in a juvenile book, Lady Eleanor Fenn's Fables in Monosyllables by Mrs. Teachwell (ca. 1783). While Locke's influence declines somewhat when Rousseau's rises, both philosophers agree in many areas. Both show a respect for children and a belief in their capacities, markedly absent in the Puritan writers of the seventeenth century. Both writers reject abstractions, stress the useful and distrust the fanciful. In adult and in children's literature, this is seen in an emphasis on reason as a guide, the exaltation of the useful and the recognition of the humble and the primitive.[26] It was hard to know where Locke ended and Rousseau began:

> People had taken a few ideas from Locke and Rousseau, mixed
> them up with more or less of puritan sentiment, a little ration-
> alism, and from this strange leaven sprouted a quantity of works.
> . . . They were inspired first of all, by the idea that there was
> not a single hour in the child's life but must be consecrated to
> usefulness. Like Madame de Genlis, but with this difference,
> that the English are more tenacious, more obstinate and more
> formidable. The French often stop along the way, but nothing

stops the English once they have started; they are slow but intrepid. [27]

Lady Eleanor Fenn, one of the first juvenile writers to take note of Rousseau, shows in <u>Cobwebs to Catch Flies</u> (<u>ca</u>. 1783) that her eagerness to impose object lessons does not have its origin solely in Rousseau. Her dedication to this book claims that if the child's mind is as Locke saw it, then "Who would leave their common-place book among fools, to be scrawled upon? Yet how often are <u>nurses</u> and <u>common servants</u> allowed to give the first intimation to children, respecting the objects with which they are surrounded." [28] Compare this with Locke's warning about "those foolish flatterers," servants "The first impressions which infants receive, and the first habits which they learn from their nurses, influence the temper and disposition long after the slight causes which produced them are forgotten." (STCE, pp. 58, 9).

The work of Madame de Genlis (1746-1830) for children popularized the principles of Rousseau's <u>Emile</u>. Yet her <u>Adele and Theodore</u> (in English, 1783) was cited by Sarah Trimmer as containing not only Rousseau but also Locke in a more pleasing form than the original. [29] As late as 1794 or 1795 a writer (Priscilla Wakefield in <u>Mental Improvement</u>) still claims the kind of amusement and instruction that Locke had recommended. She used dialogue since it blended amusement and instruction and because she wanted her books read from choice not compulsion. She promised entertainment, not "dry preceptive lessons." [30] A few years later, in <u>Domestic Information</u> (1798) Wakefield displays her corruption of what Locke recommended. In this book two girls beg to go to a Punch and Judy show. Replying that they are too old for such nonsense, their mother whips out a solar microscope and projects a mass of reticulated rootlets. When the children ask for novelty, the mother says, "Behold the wing of an earwig!" [31]

Maria Edgeworth uses Locke with a twist in <u>The Parent's Assistant</u> (1795). "The Purple Jar" tells of seven-year-old Rosamond, whose mother lets her spend her money on a purple jar. The jar, she later discovers, is not purple but holds dyed water. Because of her imprudent choice, Rosamond has to wear her non-watertight shoes for a month. The work concludes with Rosamond's promise, ". . . I hope I shall be wiser another time." [32] Locke would have cheered the leaking shoes ploy, but not as punishment. To condition the child, Locke wrote, "I would advise . . . to have his <u>Shoes</u> so thin, that they might leak and <u>let in Water</u>, when ever he comes near it," [33] (STCE, p.5). Locke's influence on Maria Edgeworth, the most important writer for children in the 1790's, is seen in at least five areas: (1) the push for private as opposed to public education (2) the stress on the importance of good company (3) making learning attractive (4) the condemnation of memory work (5) the belief in the unlimited power of education and the small place for natural endowment. [34]

Unlike Locke, Rousseau proscribed books for children since they might teach bad habits to the natural child who is to be uninhibited by civilization. Ironically, his imitators produced hundreds of books for youth. Locke was better served. He asked for books out of the ordinary road for children, and informed an educational theory that resulted in a whole new industry—books specially designed for child-

ren. Where there were no books of amusement at all, suddenly there were the
children's novel, closet drama, familiar essays, miscellanies, books of letters
and even the first magazine for children. Thanks largely to John Locke the child
in the eighteenth century had every type of literature known to the modern child.
Granted the range of quantity of books available to him, the eighteenth-century
child need not be pitied [35] as Locke had pitied his seventeenth-century counterpart.

---

[1] Some Thoughts Concerning Education (London, 1693), pp. 185-186. All references to this edition will be indicated by page numbers in parentheses in the
text.

[2] See William Sloane, Children's Books in England and America in the 17th
Century: A History and Checklist. . . (New York, 1955) on the books available
to the Puritan child.

[3] Alfred H. Body, John Wesley and Education (London, 1936), pp. 33-34.

[4] Rosalie L. Colie, "John Locke and the Publication of the Private," PQ,
XLV (January, 1966), p. 33.

[5] See Kenneth MacLean, John Locke and English Literature of the Eighteenth
Century (New Haven and London, 1936) for further documentation of the influence
of Locke on adult literature.

[6] Oliver Goldsmith, An History of England in a Series of Letters from a Noble-
man to His Son. A New ed., corrected. (London, 1769), II, p. 137.

[7] A[lice] Paterson, The Edgeworths: A Study of Later Eighteenth Century Education (London, 1914), p. 63.

[8] Wilbur Macey Stone, The Gigantick Histories of Thomas Boreman (Portland,
Maine, 1933), p. 9.

[9] Cited by Christina Duff Stewart, Preface to Facsimile Reprint of A Description of Three Hundred Animals (1786). (New York and London, 1968), n.p.

[10] H. R. Plomer, and others, A Dictionary of the Printers and Booksellers who
were at Work in England, Scotland and Ireland from 1726 to 1775 (London, 1932),
pp. 60-61.

[11] The latter work is extant only in a second volume without date in the British
Museum. Most writers place both works at 1744 but M. F. Thwaite, A Little
Pretty Pocket-Book: A Facsimile (London, 1966), p. 15 opts for 1743 for the 2nd
ed. of The Child's New Plaything. The year 1744 becomes important in the history

of children's literature. Judith St. John, private interview, Aug. 24, 1967, sees Newbery as taking over Mary Cooper's publications while Plomer, pp. 60-61 says John Hinxman of York succeeded her.

[12] B. M. copy II, 64, cited by F. J. Harvey Darton, Children's Books in England: Five Centuries of Social Life (Cambridge, Mass., 1932), p. 102.

[13] The Child's New Play-Thing (London, 1775), pp. 4-5.

[14] Rosalie V. Halsey, Forgotten Books of the American Nursery: A History of the Development of the American Storybook (Boston, 1911), p. 41.

[15] See Tatler #95, Sept. 17, 1709.

[16] Thwaite, p. 56.

[17] Sydney Roscoe, Newbery-Carnan-Power; a Provisional Check-List. . . (London, 1966).

[18] That Newbery had not forsaken Locke is seen in vol. 5 of the series: Logic Made familiar and easy . . . (London, 1748), p. iv, in which Newbery cites a modern logician "to whose excellent writings we own ourselves indebted."

[19] Wilbur Macey Stone, "The History of Little Goody Two Shoes," Amer. Antiquarian Soc. Proceedings, XLIX (Oct., 1939), p. 367.

[20] Foreword, The History of Little Goody Two-Shoes (Westport, Conn., 1947), p. ix.

[21] Credit for authorship is split among John Newbery and three men who were all writing for him in 1765: Giles Jones, Griffith Jones and Oliver Goldsmith. See Florence V. Barry, A Century of Children's Books (London, [1922]), p. 235; N & Q, 4th ser. VIII (1870), 570-572 and Sister M. Charles Veronica, C. S. J., "'Goody' by Goldy?" Elementary English, XLIII (October, 1965), 574-575.

[22] Barry, p. 69. See STCE, p. 182.

[23] (London, 1762), pp. 1-2. On authorship, see Walter Marion Crittenden, "The Life and Writings of Mrs. Sarah Scott—Novelist, 1723-1795," Ph. D. diss. Philadelphia, University of Pannsylvaia, 1932.

[24] MacLean, p. 2.

[25] (London, n.d.), p. 7.

[26] Annie E. Moore, <u>Literature Old and New for Children:  Materials for a College Course</u> (Boston, 1934), p. 184.

[27] Paul Hazard, <u>Books, Children and Men</u>, trans. Marguerite Mitchell (5th ed.; Boston, 1963), p. 34.

[28] <u>Cobwebs to Catch Flies</u> (London, n.d. [<u>ca</u>. 1783]), p. viii.

[29] Gesiena Andreae, <u>The Dawn of Juvenile Literature in England</u> (Amsterdam, 1925), p. 100.

[30] (1st Amer from 3rd London ed.; New Bedford, 1799), p. iv.

[31] Geoffrey Riddehough, "Priscilla Wakefield," <u>Dalhousie Review</u>, XXXVII (1955), 346.

[32] <u>The Parent's Assistant</u> (London, 1798), I, 1-16.

[33] See also Locke's letter (3 May 1685) in B. Rand, ed. <u>Correspondence of J. Locke and E. Clarke</u> (London, 1927), p. 135.

[34] Paterson, p. 25.

[35] L[izzie] Allen Harker, "Some 18th century Children's Books," <u>Longman's Magazine</u>, XXVII (Oct., 1901), 556.

# PARALLELS BETWEEN OUR MUTUAL FRIEND AND THE ALICE BOOKS

Richard Arnoldi

> "Then pray," said Bella, sternly putting the question
> to herself in the looking-glass as usual, "what do you mean
> by this, you inconsistent little Beast?"
> The looking-glass preserving a discreet ministerial
> silence when thus called upon for explanation, Bella went
> to bed. . . .
> Charles Dickens, Our Mutual Friend (London, 1957), p. 442.

> "And here Alice's adventures are told as though they
> came from the inside of a dream." (Horace Gregory, "Foreword"
> to Lewis Carroll, Alice's Adventures in Wonderland and
> Through the Looking-Glass (New York, 1964), p. vi.)

Dicken's Our Mutual Friend was published in monthly numbers running from May, 1864 to November, 1865. The first edition of Alice's Adventures in Wonderland was published on July 4, 1865. Through the Looking-Glass was published in 1871.

On January 16, 1868, Lewis Carroll wrote an entry in his journal, from which these lines are excerpted: "I have also added a few pages to the second volume of Alice. . . . One novel has been all my reading, Our Mutual Friend, one of the cleverest that Dickens has written." Roger Lancelyn Green notes parenthetically that "the second volume of Alice" actually refers to Through the Looking-Glass."[1] It is clear that Carroll read and enjoyed Our Mutual Friend, but the time sequence suggests several additional things.

Although he could not have read all of Our Mutual Friend before he wrote Alice's Adventures in Wonderland, Carroll did read the Dickens novel at precisely the same time he was working on Through the Looking-Glass. In fact, Carroll may have read excerpts from the novel before its publication in book form and neglected to mention them. Any enthusiastic follower of Dickens would at least have known the existence of a given work at the time of its first publication—and Carroll makes it clear elsewhere that he admired some of Dickens' other novels (i.e., David Copperfield and Martin Chuzzlewit).

It is apparent that Dickens and Carroll shared certain interests and images. The looking-glass section of Dickens' description of the Veneering dinner party shows Dickens' awareness of the dramatic and symbolic possibilities inherent in mirror-images. It remained for Carroll to actualize in Through the Looking-Glass the conception of the world behind the mirror.

In Our Mutual Friend, when Wegg finally decides to drop down upon Boffin, he recites this bit of poetry:

If you'll come to the Bower I've shaded for you,
Your bed shan't be roses all spangled with doo:
Will you, will you, will you, will you come to the Bower? 2

"The Lobster-Quadrille" in <u>Alice in Wonderland</u> contains the following lines:

Then turn not pale, beloved snail, but come and join
   the dance.
Will you, won't you, will you, won't you, will you
   join the dance?
Will you, won't you, will you, won't you, will you
   join the dance? 3

It is possible that both poems are parodies of Mary Howitt's "The Spider and the Fly." However, the refrains of "will you, will you" (in the case of Dickens) and "will you, won't you" (in the case of Carroll) have no counterpart in Howitt's poem. That the two writers should each independently create such a distinctive refrain seems more than a coincidence in taste and inventiveness, particularly since Carroll's poem was added after he wrote the first version of <u>Alice</u> 4 and presumably after the publication of <u>Our Mutual Friend</u>.

<u>Our Mutual Friend</u> offers a great store of characters, situations, and observations that would have been especially appealing to Carroll. Jenny Wren is first described as "a child—a dwarf—girl—a something." She explains that she cannot get up "because my back's bad, and my legs are queer" (p. 208). She asks Bradley Headstone to guess her profession, and when he cannot guess, she says: ". . . I'll give you a clue to my trade, in a game of forfeits. I love my love with a B because she's Beautiful; I hate my love with a B because she is Brazen; I took her to the sign of the Blue Boar, and I treated her with Bonnets; her name's Bouncer, and she lives in Bedlam.—Now what do I make with my straw?" (p. 210). Compare this to the following passage from <u>Through the Looking-Glass</u>: "'I love my love with an H,' Alice couldn't help beginning, 'because he is Happy. I hate him with an H because he is Hideous. I fed him with—with—Ham-sandwiches and Hay. His name is Haigha, and he lives—'" (p. 279). Martin Gardner points out that this passage employs a popular Victorian parlor game favored by children. Obviously both Dickens and Carroll were familiar with it.

Jenny Wren continues her conversation with Headstone amiably enough until he mentions children, at which point,

"Ah, lud!" cried the person of the house with a little
scream, as if the word had pricked her. "Don't talk of
children. I can't bear children. I know their tricks and
their manners. . . .
   ". . . ever so often calling names in through a person's
keyhole, and imitating a person's back and legs. Oh! <u>I</u>
know their tricks and their manners. And I'll tell you what

I'd do to punish 'em. There's doors under the church in the Square—black doors, leading into black vaults. Well! I'd open one of those doors, and I'd cram 'em all in, and then I'd lock the door and through the keyhole I'd blow in pepper."

"What would be the good of blowing in pepper?" asked Charlie Hexam.

"To set 'em sneezing," said the person of the house, "and make their eyes water. And when they were all sneezing and inflamed, I'd mock 'em through the keyhole. Just as they, with their tricks and their manners, mock a person through a person's keyhole!"    (pp. 210-211)

Perhaps the idea of punishing obnoxious children with pepper interested Carroll, for he added the famous "Pig and Pepper" chapter to Alice's Adventures in Wonderland at some point between his presentation of the earliest extant manuscript of the Alice story (see note 4) to Alice Liddell on November 26, 1864, and the publication of Alice's Adventures in Wonderland on July 4, 1865.

In "Pig and Pepper," Alice ventures into a smoke-filled kitchen, where she finds the Duchess and the cook. The Duchess is holding a child; the air is full of pepper. The baby is "sneezing and howling alternately." Eventually the Duchess begins to sing him a lullaby, which can be seen as a caricature of Jenny Wren's philosophy on children:

> Speak roughly to your little boy,
> And beat him when he sneezes:
> He only does it to annoy,
> Because he knows it teases. . . .
>
> I speak severely to my boy,
> And beat him when he sneezes:
> For he can thoroughly enjoy
> The pepper when he pleases!    (p. 85)

Gardner comments that "The original of this burlesque is 'Speak Gently,' a happily unremembered poem" whose nine soporific verses, as recorded by Gardner, contain no mention of pepper.

Alice is given the child to nurse; but he turns into a pig, and she drops him, remarking that other children she knows would make better pigs than children. Here Gardner notes that "it was surely not without malice that Carroll turned a male baby into a pig, for he had a low opinion of little boys." Gardner goes on to quote a postscript from a letter Carroll wrote to one of his little-girl friends:

> My best love to yourself,—to your Mother
> My kindest regards—to your small,
> Fat, impertinent, ignorant brother
> My hatred—I think that is all.    (p. 87)

Gardner, in his "Introduction" to The Annotated Alice, quotes Carroll as having written, "I am fond of children (except boys)" and continues, "He professed a horror of little boys, and in later life avoided them as much as possible" (p. 11).

Carroll's antipathy to little boys is analogous to Jenny Wren's expressed hatred of all children. Jenny's physical problems may also have seemed familiar to Carroll. He was afflicted with a painful ailment popularly known as "Housemaid's Knee."5 Martin Gardner comments that Carroll was "asymmetric: One shoulder was higher than the other, his smile was slightly askew, and the level of his blue eyes not quite the same. He . . . walked with a peculiar jerky gait" (p. 10).

For us, these correspondences are merely intriguing. For Carroll, they must have been overwhelming. It is no wonder that Carroll saw this novel as Dickens' cleverest, and it is not surprising that the affinity which he felt for Our Mutual Friend led Carroll to echo some of its passages in his own classic fantasy of childhood.

---

1 The Diaries of Lewis Carroll, ed. Roger Lancelyn Green (New York, 1954), II, 265.

2 Charles Dickens, Our Mutual Friend, ed. G. K. Chesterton, reprinted by Dutton (London, 1957), p. 617. Subsequent references to this edition will be noted parenthetically.

3 Lewis Carroll, The Annotated Alice, Intro. and Notes by Martin Gardner (New York, 1960), pp. 133–134. Subsequent references to Alice's Adventures in Wonderland, to Through the Looking-Glass, or to Martin Gardner's introduction and notes will be to this title, and will be noted parenthetically in the text.

4 Alice's Adventures Under Ground, a MS written in 1864, a facsimile of which was printed in 1886, and reissued by Dover in 1965, with an introduction by Martin Gardner.

5 Isa Bowman, The Story of Lewis Carroll (New York, 1900), p. 10.

# TERMS FOR ORDER IN SOME LATE 19th CENTURY FICTION FOR CHILDREN[*]

R. Gordon Kelly

For the last century and a half, Americans appear to have been peculiarly concerned with matters of childhood and youth. European visitors to the United
States in the nineteenth century frequently commented on the American child,
whose independent behavior, in comparison to his English or French counterparts,
was at once refreshing and disconcerting.[1] Moreover, youth and innocence have
seemed, to American historians and novelists alike, to symbolize essential qualities distinguishing the cultural experience of the New World from that of the Old.
The apotheosis of the American Adam is Huck Finn. However unpersuasive these
engaging metaphors may be, it is clear that the successful transmission of a
group's culture to its young is a sine qua non of social continuity, whether the
group be a whole society or only a part. The link between the generations is at
once supremely important and peculiarly vulnerable.

During the latter part of the nineteenth century, one social group in America
left an especially rich tradition of children's literature in which the problem
of cultural transmission may be examined. This group, termed by Professor Stow
Persons the "gentry," roughly equivalent to the well-known "genteel tradition,"
has received considerable attention from historians, though seldom on its own
terms.[2] The moral idealism of the genteel tradition has been widely noted, but
its preoccupation with a particular social type—the gentleman—and its function
as a culture bearing class or elite are less widely understood.

The following brief essay is abstracted from my longer study, "Mother Was a
Lady, Strategy and Order in Selected American Children's Periodicals, 1865 -
1890."[3] Using theoretical concepts drawn from cognitive anthropology and the
sociology of knowledge, this study examines the most characteristic form of
children's literature in the period (the children's magazine) to illuminate the problems faced by the "gentry elite" in transmitting their culture. Narrative fiction is
analyzed for the terms of the gentry's world view and for the logic or "strategy"
of persuasion which they adopted in their efforts to transmit intact their vision of
social order and democratic possibilities during a period of dramatic and turbulent
change in American life.

Initially, a child is introduced to one world of meanings, presented as if it had
the authority of nature; but in a pluralistic society, alternative modes of behavior
and cognitive orientation are available which may eventually compete for his
allegiance. In practice, a variety of influences contribute to the socialization of
children. For centuries stories expressly created for tender minds and budding
consciences have been an accepted means of winning (or trying to win) the young

[*] This paper was prepared for presentation at the first annual meeting of the
Popular Culture Association, April 8-10, 1971, at Michigan State University.

to essential truths. Moreover, books aimed at the edification of Young America, unlike the actual behavioral patterns associated with child-rearing in the past, are conveniently accessible for research. Fiction created for children thus exists at one of the most potentially illuminating intersections in American culture, for it is here that the remembered past, the apparent present, and the desired future meet and interpenetrate. Functioning as both persuasion and confirmation, such literature may be studied both as an effort to attract converts to a particular point of view by means of a carefully controlled experience and as a structure of meanings capable of sustaining the allegiance of those already persuaded of the truths intended by the fiction. Given this nation's religious and cultural diversity, American children's literature may be expected to reveal variations in value and expectation as well as divergent definitions of success, of character, and of the promise of democracy.

Historians of American thought have been particularly drawn to the works of Horatio Alger, and their explanations and interpretations of his popularity are well known.[4] Alger enjoyed no hegemony over widely held values, however; the group of authors who wrote regularly for St. Nicholas and the Youth's Companion, for example, offered alternative versions of the American dream which insisted on different priorities and rested on different assumptions.

In the formula stories characteristic of these periodicals, the traditional social type of the gentleman provides the central model for youthful emulation as well as the means by which a cluster of related values and approved traits might be ordered and structured for dramatic effect. Presented as having broad social utility, the ideal is at once a concept of personality integration, a discipline for self-culture, a standard of public service, and a principle for social order in a competitive society.

The ideal gentleman of tradition was characterized by courage, self-control, refined sensibilities, graceful, dignified manners, a readiness to serve society, and by a love of honor, truth, and justice. Not all of these were equally relevant to children, of course, and the traditional attributes received selective emphasis in the fiction under discussion here. Courage, honesty, self-reliance, and service are continually stressed; manners and aesthetic response receive far less attention. Correlatively, children are warned against the dangers of carelessness, lack of personal discipline, or the various forms of tempting, but ungentlemanly (and socially disruptive), self-assertiveness. Courageous but not reckless, self-reliant but not arrogant, the gentleman is characterized in these stories as an individual whose outward manner is the perfect, harmonious expression of disciplined inner impulse and as one who remains serenely capable and cheerful despite hardship, danger, deprivation—or even death. Children who read these stories were not encouraged to regard the passage to gentility as an easy one, however. Although anyone, regardless of family or regional background, could aspire to gentility, the way was arduous and demanding as befit the acme of human perfectability.

The code of the gentleman also offered an ideal of public service, one that points up rather sharply an important contrast between the social implications of this literature and the implications of some Alger novels. Simply getting ahead, even through the agency of providential good fortune, is rarely dramatized. Rather characters in these stories are likely to discover their economic salvation (and at the same time their social role) by becoming producers, by recognizing and satisfying a need for goods or services. The stories are not dominated by the ladder image of vertical mobility, nor is one's rise pegged to the specific dollar amounts so prominently featured in the progress of Alger's heroes.

But more than a personal ideal of courage, integrity, and service, the code of the gentleman is presented as a basis for moral and social order in an aggressively competitive society. Courage and self-reliance, traditional elements of the ideal, are kept within proper limits by the insistence on prudence, courtesy, and disciplined self-control as well as by the obligation of service. The threat to social order inherent in the unbounded development of the former qualities is balanced by the latter imperatives. Given a preponderance of this social type, freedom and initiative might be preserved; the process of competition is restrained and softened; and its rewards are a function of character rather than of luck, ruthlessness, or chicanery. As it appeared in these periodicals, then, the ideal of the gentleman was a model of restraint and moderation, a strategy to preserve simultaneously the democratic concept of the free individual and the existence of an orderly society based on competing individuals. These writers sought to acknowledge the just demands of both. They recognized that social order is a precarious achievement, threatened especially, they thought, by persons who neither recognized appropriate limits to ambition nor exercised self-restraint.

The ideal presented in these stories is in many respects a generous one. It also happened to be particularly vulnerable to that shift in the social sources of moral authority which occurred during the last decades of the nineteenth century. An old world of fixed principles, a stable cosmic order thought to lie outside of time, was being undermined; a new world characterized by flux was being discovered. The assumptions basic to much of the fiction published in St. Nicholas and the Youth's Companion might be summarized by the following paradigm. The natural world is characterized by inner, essential stability—however mutable it may appear when clothed in the familiar cycles of growth and decay. Men too may not be what they seem; each experiences an inner life partially separable from the behavior through which he presents himself to others. In theory the ideal of the gentleman mediated between appearance and reality in one's relationships with others and with nature. The gentleman, as presented in etiquette book and children's fiction, not only was what he appeared to be, but he sensed immediately if another dissembled. Moreover, the gentleman or lady was uniquely prepared to perceive the laws and spirit of that stable order of which the visible, mutable elements of the natural world were but the husk.

Such a paradigm could remain plausible only so long as its constituent elements and their relationships remained plausible. With the development of evolutionary naturalism, the informing idea of natural correspondences was called into question. Random mutation appeared to deny stability or design in the natural world. To penetrate below the flux of appearances was to find only chance, not those laws needed to support the nurture, role, and social value of the democratic gentleman. As the social authority of the new scientific knowledge grew, these particular children's writers attempted the difficult task of shoring up a view that appeared increasingly implausible to many people. In their stories, we may see the strategies which they adopted in the effort to transmit persuasively their vision of social order.

---

[1] Richard Rapson, "The American Child as Seen by British Travelers, 1845-1935," American Quarterly, XVII (Fall 1965), 520-535.

[2] Stow Persons, "The Origins of the Gentry," in Robert Bremmer, ed., Essays on History and Literature (Columbus, Ohio, 1966), 83-119.

[3] Unpublished dissertation (University of Iowa, 1970).

[4] The best of these are R. Richard Wohl, "Alger: An Episode in Secular Idealism," in Reinhold Bendix and Seymour M. Lipset, eds., Class, Status and Power (Glencoe, Illinois, 1953), 388-395, and the chapter on Alger in John Cawelti, Apostles of the Self-Made Man (Chicago, 1965).

# FROM FANTASY TO REALITY: RUSKIN'S <u>KING OF THE GOLDEN RIVER</u>, ST. GEORGE'S GUILD, AND RUSKIN, TENNESSEE *

Francelia Butler

Biographers have noted that Ruskin's childhood copying of Cruikshank's illustrations to Grimms' fairy tales stimulated Ruskin's later interest in art and that Ruskin's childhood reading of Grimm influenced the form and content of Ruskin's own fantasy, <u>The King of the Golden River</u>.[1] But could it not be that this early familiarity with Grimm extends even further into Ruskin's career? One can see Ruskin's early fascination with the poor and simple folk of Grimms' tales reflected not only in the economic allegory of <u>The King of the Golden River</u>, but also in his real-life experiments with St. George's Guild and even in the writings late in his life. These writings, such as <u>Fors Clavigera</u>, have poor folk as their theme, wholly or in part, and stylistically very often border on fantasy. Further, Ruskin's imaginative projections of an ideal society for the poor became reality, at least temporarily, in tiny "Ruskin" settlements established in the United States. When these failed, the ideas which emanated from Ruskin's creative imagination can be traced into later economic movements. Just as the puppet show of Faust may have influenced Goethe's long literary life, so Grimm may have partially influenced Ruskin's long literary life, and through Ruskin, other people.

<u>The King of the Golden River</u> was written in 1841 as a gift for Euphemia Chalmers Gray, then twelve, whom Ruskin was to marry seven years later. Published in 1851, the story "attained an immediate popularity which it has ever since retained, both in England and in America."[2] Perhaps as a result of this popularity, copies are scarce, as children soon wear books out. By 1937, Charles Goodspeed, in <u>Yankee Bookseller</u>, reported copies of <u>King</u> as difficult to find.[3] Ruskin's manuscript, from which the following quotations are taken, is in Yale University Library. It seems to vary in no significant respect from published versions of the story.[4]

Briefly, it will be recalled, the story has to do with three brothers who lived in a fertile valley watered by a pure stream. Unfortunately Hans and Schwartz, the two older brothers, were selfish:

> They killed everything which did not pay for its eating. They
> shot the blackbirds because they pecked the fruit, and killed
> the hedgehogs lest they should suck the cows—they poisoned
> the crickets for eating the crumbs in the kitchen, and smothered
> the cicadas which used to sing all summer in the limetrees.

---

* An address given at the Joint Annual Meeting of the Kentucky-Tennessee American Studies Association and the East Tennessee Folklore Society, Johnson City, Tennessee, March, 1965.

They worked their servants without any wages till they would
not work any more and then quarreled with them and turned
them out of doors without paying them. It would have been
very odd if with such a farm and such a system of farming they
hadn't got very rich and very rich they did get. They generally
contrived to keep their corn by them till it was very dear and
sell it for twice its value—they had heaps of gold lying about
on their floors, yet it was never known that they had given as
much as a penny or a crust to charity. [5]

In contrast to these two exploiters of the land and labor, there was little Gluck,
only twelve (Euphemia's age). Gluck was their tool and was forced to do their
dirty work, such as cleaning their shoes, floors, and plates. Things went along
like this until there was a bad depression—"a very wet summer and everything
went wrong in the country round." Needless to say, Hans and Schwartz took full
advantage of the situation:

They asked what they liked and got it except from the poor
people, who could only beg, several of whom were starved
at their very doors, without the slightest regard or notice. [6]

At this point, while the older brothers were out, an "extraordinary looking little gentleman" appeared, with curling moustaches, and asked Gluck for shelter
and food. Gluck was reluctant to help because, as he told the little man, he
knew he would be beaten for it. (Even the good could not operate in such a situation.) And indeed, just as he was about to slice some mutton for the dwarf, his
brothers returned home and Gluck was punished.

Soon after this incident, the older brothers suffered for their exploitation of
the land. There was a dreadful flood, and the wealth of the brothers was swept
away. With no material resources to speak of, and obviously no inner resources
to sustain them, Hans and Schwartz turned to alcohol for consolation. They instructed Gluck to melt down a gold drinking mug, which they intended to mix
with copper and sell as pure gold. In the melting pot, the cup turned into the little gentleman, who introduced himself as the King of the Golden River, and told
Gluck to pour him out. Gluck did so, and the King made the following pronounce-
ment:

Whoever shall climb to the top of that mountain from which
you see the Golden River issue, and shall cast into the stream
at its source three drops of holy water: for him and for him
only the River shall turn to gold. [7]

Then the King ran away.

When Hans and Schwartz returned, and found the gold gone, they beat Gluck
into telling them what had happened. "They beat him again till their arms were
tired and staggered to bed." Next day, they competed over who would first cast

the holy water into the source, and they made such a racket that Schwartz was jailed for disturbing the peace. Hans stole a cupful of holy water and set off for the mountains. On his way, he scorned in sequence a dog, a child, and an old man, each of whom begged water. Reaching the brink of the chasm from which the Golden River ran, Hans hurled the stolen holy water into the torrent. As he did so, he turned to a stone. Schwartz then repeated the pattern, except that he purchased the holy water, and instead of a dog, saw his own brother in the path, begging water. Like his brother, he became a stone.

Finally, little Gluck set off with the holy water which he had neither stolen nor purchased, but which was freely given to him by the priest. He, too, met those begging water: an old man, a child, and a dog, and to each he gave water. "In three seconds the dog was gone and before Gluck stood his old acquaintance the King of the Golden River."

The dwarf picked a lily. "On its white leaves there hung three drops of clear dew." He ordered Gluck to cast the drops into the stream. The dwarf then evaporated. Gluck cast the three drops into the river and "stood watching it for some time very much disappointed." The river had not turned to gold at all! Instead,

> as Gluck gazed, fresh grass sprang beside the new streams,
> and creeping plants grew and climbed among the moistening
> soil. Young flowers opened suddenly along the river sides,
> as stars leap out when twilight is deepening, and thickets of
> myrtle and tendrils of vine cast lengthening shadows over the
> valley as they grew. And thus the treasure valley became a
> garden again and the inheritance which had been lost by
> cruelty was regained by love.
>
> And, Gluck went and dwelt in the valley, and the poor were
> never driven from his door, so that his barns became full of
> corn, and his house of treasure, and for him the river had
> according to the dwarf's promise become a river of gold. [8]

Aside from the subject matter, one interesting point about this story is the date (1841). Whereas the apparent turning point of Ruskin from criticism of art to social criticism occurs in the 1850's, this story clearly indicates that he had been deeply concerned about social injustice for a long time. Indeed, no transition occurred in his thinking from a criticism of art to consideration of the environment in which great art might flourish. Instead, he came increasingly to emphasize his love of undefiled nature and his innate regard for the dignity of labor. As for his regard for labor, it is not surprising to find that by the late 1850's, he was combining criticism of art with practical protests against machinery. [9]

His deep interest in the landscapes of Turner and the titles of his own lectures, chapters, and books (e.g., Sesame and Lilies, The Crown of Wild Olives, "Tree Twigs") indicate how close he was to nature. In Modern Painters (1846), he deals with Beauty of Mountains, Beauty of Water, Beauty of Vegetation, and Beauty of Sky. These studies he related to Greek mythology and to the basic elements of language in a way still new a hundred years later. Regarded as vague, poetic, or fantastical, his approach foreshadows that of Norman O. Brown, Theodore Roszak, or Marshall McLuhan—a kind of fictional non-fiction focussing on the underlying patterns of human history. His work forms one long footnote to what he wrote as a young man in the fantasy of The King of the Golden River.

The need for a closeness to nature in a pure state is found everywhere, from Ruskin's introduction to an edition of Grimm (1868), where he argues for a simplicity of beauty in tales for children (he later wrote that he would never again write anything "more rich in thought"),[10] to his lectures in 1883 on the "Art of England" where he observes in Lecture Four on Fairy Land:

> You never find a child make a pet of a mechanical mouse that runs about the floor—of a poodle that yelps—of a tumbler who jumps upon wires. The child falls in love with a quiet thing, with an ugly one—nay, it may be, with one, to us, totally devoid of meaning. My little—ever-so-many-times-grand-cousin, Lily, took a bit of stick with a round knob at the end of it for her doll one day;—nursed it with the most tender solicitude; and, on the deeply-important occasion of it having a new night-gown made for it, bent down her mother's head to receive the confidential and timid whisper—"Mamma, perhaps it had better have no sleeves, because as Bibsey has no arms, she mightn't like it."[11]

And later on, in the same lecture:

> Though you should put electric coils into your high heels, and make spring-heeled Jacks and Gills of yourselves, you will never dance, so, as you could barefoot. Though you could have machines that would swing a ship of war into the sea, and drive a railway train through a rock, all divine strength is still the strength of Herakles, a man's wrestle, and a man's blow.[12]

Anyone familiar with Ruskin is aware of his frequent references to nature, to cooperative living (such as Gluck's with his neighbors), and also, to his close awareness of the eminent writers and illustrators for children of his period, including John Tenniel, Randolph Caldecott, Ralph Crane, Charles Kingsley, Thomas Hughes, and particularly Kate Greenaway and George MacDonald—both of whom were intimate friends.[13] At twenty-two, or much earlier than most of these writers and/or illustrators, Ruskin had seen the possibilities of depth in the limpid simplicity of children's literature, for it was at that age that he had written The King of the Golden River. With his tendency to read his own subtlety and depth into the characters of the young women he admired, one would expect something out of the ordinary in a fantasy for the girl he would marry. Even his art training had conditioned him towards children's literature as a deep medium. His training (which he praised) began when he was around eight in copying Cruikshank's illustrations to an edition of Grimm.[14] It is unlikely that at the same time this brilliant child did not absorb the rich folklore for which the sketches were made—folklore which washes over and gathers up most of human experience.

As Ruskin's life developed, his ideas on how human beings should live were simply, as I have suggested, a more detailed representation of what he had already expressed in The King of the Golden River. Thus, in his General Statement of 1882 on St. George's Guild, which he had established, Ruskin writes:

> This Guild was originally founded with the intention of showing how much food-producing land might be recovered by well-applied labour from the barren or neglected district of nominally cultivated countries. With this primary aim, two intimate objects of wider range were connected: the leading one, to show what tone and degree of refined education could be given to persons maintaining themselves by agricultural labor: and the last, to convince some portion of the upper classes of society that such occupation was more honourable, and consistent with higher thoughts and nobler pleasures, than their at present favourite profession of war; and that the course of social movements must ultimately compel many to adopt it. . . .[15]

In additional passages left in manuscript form, Ruskin writes:

> Supposing for a single year, that the sums spent by the idle rich in dissolute pleasures and unproductive ostentation could be accurately registered, and, on the other side, the wages given to the poor for the most useful work, together with the number of persons who have perished or become exiles for actual want of bread, the submission of thoughtful and amiable persons to the present order of things would assuredly cease to be complacent. And although it is for the present impossible to obtain such a census and account (for all persons who spend money uselessly and selfishly, although they pretend to justify themselves by the false sophism that their extravagance supports the poor, confess the real verdict of their consciences by terrified indignation at any public scrutiny of their incomes and modes of expenditure).[16]

He goes on to say that novelists have done good in depicting the situation, but the lesson has been disguised by the excitement of the narrative or commercial interests of the writer himself. One wonders if this is why Ruskin (later, C. S. Lewis ackowledged this purpose) [17] chose a children's story as the best medium for a serious message.

In Education, Ruskin favored the kind of education which the King of the Golden River gave Gluck, that is one which stimulated a wisdom of heart through developing a love of natural beauty and an appreciation of man and his work. This he points out again and again.[18]

Though, as Peter Quennell observes, the Guild was more theoretical than practical, [19] Ruskin had planted a seed in the imaginations of other people, so that his Golden River did become a reality at Yellow Creek, Tennessee, where, in 1893, a Ruskin Commonwalth was founded. The story of this colony can be followed in the issues of its newspaper, The Coming Nation (1893-1902), a complete file of which is in the Draper Collection at the University of Wisconsin Library.

The colony was founded by Julius Wayland, who writes in The Coming Nation on December 2, 1893:

> One of the reasons I love John Ruskin's writings is that he leads your mind off to pastures of restful thoughts, away from his profound philosophy and yet never wastes a moment of your time. . . . How few people who have seen in print those two words, John Ruskin, have any conception of the great, loving, wise spirit they stand for. If they only did know! What a world of happiness that would be.

Most of the colonists were garment workers or mill workers, refugees of the depression of 1893 in President Cleveland's adminstration, when factories closed all over the country. Colonists entering the commune were asked to contribute $500 per family, which was refundable if the family decided to leave. Workers received equal wages regardless of skill. They were paid in scrip printed on the presses of The Coming Nation and redeemable at the Commonwealth Store. [20]

If, for instance, a workman wanted to buy a lemon costing half an hour, and gave the store clerk a ten-hour bill, he received nine and a half hours' change. Coffee was seven hours a pound, tea was one hour, a cut of tobacco sold for two hours. Three sticks of candy were half an hour and a pair of pants was priced at thirty-seven hours. Coffee, incidentally, was cereal coffee, made in the colony. Like Ruskin, who once opened a tea shop for the sale of pure tea,[21] colonists were concerned with the goodness and purity of the food for their fellow man and at the same time, were opposing the importers of coffee from Brazil. Soon, a large quantity of pure food was collected in the huge, barnlike building, still standing, in which food was stored. Gluck would have been delighted.

An unbound copy of Ruskin's Fors Clavigera or Letters to the Workmen and Labourers of Great Britain, used in the Ruskin Commonwealth, consists of Letters I-XXIX, with printers' marks and other marked passages. Much of it was serialized in the issues of The Coming Nation, and long passages were undoubtedly read to audiences in the large Theatre of Commonwealth House (seating capacity: 700), where the colonists held their meetings. The edition may have been printed in the colony. [22] In Letter IX, one finds the following passage noted on Education:

> But in my first series of lectures at Oxford, I stated, (and cannot too often or too firmly state) that no great arts were practicable by any people, unless they were living contented lives, in pure air, out of the way of unsightly objects, and emancipated from unnecessary mechanical occupation. (p.123)

"No, my friends, believe me," Ruskin writes in Letter IV, "it is not the going without education at all that we have most to dread. The real thing to be feared is
getting a bad one." (p. 42) And what is a good one? It is knowing that there are
three Material things essential to Life and three Immaterial things. The Material
things are Pure Air, Water, and Earth. The Immaterial are Admiration, or "the
power of discerning and taking delight in what is beautiful in visible Form, and
lovely in human Character"; Hope, and Love. (Letter Five) In the same Letter,
he speaks of the smoke in the air, caused by industrial waste. (p. 64) Education
must be directed to labor with the hands as well as with the mind. (In 1872, at
Oxford, Ruskin himself had led a trash collection and clean-up campaign.) [23]

In conformance with Ruskin's ideas, children at the Workers' School in Ruskin,
Tennessee were taught a trade, such as printing, and also to paint, sculpture,
or to play a musical instrument. [24] For older workers, an experienced art teacher
was available, and the Ruskin Cave, the original center of colony life, afforded a
plentiful quantity of fuller's earth for modelling. In fact, a painting and two
busts of Ruskin were made by colonists and set up in the Ruskin Theater in Commonwealth House . . . somewhat ironically, it seems in retrospect, between the
masks of comedy and tragedy. (The Theater in Commonwealth House can still be
seen, with its raised stage bounded by a low, walnut fencing, and above, a high
proscenium arch framed with a hand-carved walnut grillwork.)

When not on tour, the Ruskin Band played in the Theater. Here, the Glee Club
performed, and there were piano recitals on the square, rosewood, Hale piano, [25]
including original compositions such as "Salut de Ruskin" and "The Village Where
Labor Is King." Also, programs of dancing—a Joan of Arc drill, for instance—
were presented. Joan was a symbol for the freedom of women in the Commonwealth, who had equal rights with men (something Ruskin believed in) [26] including
the right to vote, some twenty-five years before women's suffrage became an
amendment to the Constitution of the United States. The Coming Nation regularly
ran a "Women's Department" column, in which women's liberation was strongly
urged. A song, "Temporary," was composed and danced to a soft-shoe routine:

> We're a temporary lot and we've temporary got
> And we're wearin' a temporary buskin.
> We're temporary bro't to a temporary plot
> Which we've named after John Ruskin.
> Flip flop, rum-te-doodle-doo—
> Let your flapper rattle on th' ground.
> Double shuffle that old ruffle
> Happy as you walk around.

Though there was a chewing gum factory for the making of Tolu chewing gum
and a tailoring industry for the cutting and sewing of all-wool trousers, very little
manufacturing was done in the colony to produce the kind of smog Ruskin had
noted in Fors Clavigera and later in his Storm-Cloud of the Nineteenth Century. [27]
Much of the livelihood was gleaned from farming. The truck gardens provided a
supply of vegetables and fruits to be dried, canned, or cold-stored in Ruskin

Cave, and even furnished a large surplus, which was sold by truckster's wagon in the surrounding country. An experimental attempt to raise bananas failed because boys filched the ripe fruit. Flower seeds were saved and advertised for sale in the columns of The Coming Nation. On May 30, 1899, the colonists enjoyed a special treat: 152 quarts of strawberries from their own patch, ice cream (the ladies had cranked out 30 gallons of it and stored it in a recess in Ruskin Cave) and 10 square yards of Lady Baltimore cake.

By then, Ruskin was indeed a treasure valley. It had become a small village of around 300 people. Besides such professional people as a publisher, a doctor, a sculptor, and teachers, there were several artisans who were contributing their services to the experiment, including a carpenter, machinist, barber, shoemaker, baker, butcher, cooper and blacksmith.

Although antipathy to the colony was not strong, occupants of neighboring Dickson tended to be suspicious of the goings on in Ruskin. For one thing, the appearance of the colonists was unkempt. Old photographs indicate that many did not brush or cut their hair. [28] Clothes were ragged and often very dirty. Some of the colonists went barefoot. (Though Ruskin himself was a man of some tonsorial elegance, he made Gluck a waif, and frequently expressed a great admiration for the beauty of the ragged, barefoot, uncombed youths he saw in Italy.) Neighboring Dicksonites, however, were displeased when they saw, out in the fields, male Ruskinites working stripped to the waist, while their female companions were working in pantaloons. There were rumors that the dark recesses of Ruskin Cave were occasionally employed for uses other than the storage of food.

But along with the seeds which the Ruskin farmers planted were the seeds of dissension. Like Ruskin himself, the colony was somewhat schizoid, and the most serious opposition to its perfect plans came from within. A few of the colonists began to rebel bitterly against Julius Wayland, founder of the colony and publisher of The Coming Nation, whom they regarded as a dictator. (Like the King of the Golden River and Ruskin himself, [29] Wayland was rather dictatorial.) In the summer of 1895, after several quarrels, Wayland left the colony, abandoning his newspaper press. [30] For awhile, the colony went on as before, but the dissensions continued.

One serious difficulty centered on Education. The majority felt that if a child were educated to the age of ten, knew a trade and one of the arts, he was well equipped for life. They did not want to contribute money for the establishment of anything beyond the Workers' School and formed a resentful and hostile audience on the occasion of the cornerstone laying of the Ruskin College of the New Economy, June 18, 1897. Although the noted labor sympathizer, Henry Demarest Lloyd gave an impressive speech at the cornerstone laying, [31] the College never materialized.

As the valley grew in prosperity, some Hanses and Schwartzes joined up, so that gradually they gained a decisive vote in the affairs of Ruskin. Some objected to providing for the children of large families or supporting the lazy or ill. Some wanted the glory of being leader. Finally, and very suddenly, a group of the colonists succeeded in having the property sold at forced sale. Colony assets of over $100,000 brought about a tenth that amount. Instead of the comfortable sums the quarreling colonists hoped to receive, only the lawyers were enriched. Each colonist discovered that he had sold his dream of a treasure valley for less than thirty silver dollars.

A remnant of the loyal believers struggled on with the Ruskin experiment for two years at the edge of the Okefenokee Swamp in Ware County, Georgia. Here they tapped pine forests, planted a pecan grove, made brooms. They tried Yankee farm methods, but found them out of place in Georgia, especially some thirty years after the Civil War. Old residents of Wayland have even asserted that as their horses died, colonists hitched their women to the ploughs. [32]

Soon, colonists fell ill of malaria, typhoid, or malnutrition. When the colony finally broke up, large houses sold for as little as ten dollars. Boards were carried away or rotted into the swamp. In July, 1902, the last of the colonists wandered away with the colony's old rat terrier mascot, "Ruskin." Today, nothing is left of the experiment there, except a board sign, "Ruskin," some six miles from Waycross.

Still, the headline, Principles Never Die! was correct, as it appeared in The Coming Nation, August 5, 1899, in Ruskin, Tennessee, when the colony there was dying. True, Wayland had deserted the practical experiment with a utopia, but, like John Ruskin, he had turned to a more general application of this theories. In Girard, Kansas, he had founded another sociaist newspaper, The Appeal to Reason, and had asked his managing editor to get a young writer, Upton Sinclair, to do a story to be serialized in it on the stockyards of Chicago. . . . (The reader scarcely need be reminded that this book, The Jungle, first serialized in The Appeal, is one of the most powerful socialist novels ever written.) [33] Also, Eugene Debs, who, as a young man, had become interested in socialism through selling subscriptions to The Coming Nation, had gone to work for The Appeal. [34] Few could begin to measure the ramifications of the experiment.

Probably Ruskin himself never knew the difficulties his utopia was experiencing. Old and ailing, he had nevertheless managed to send the Tennessee group an autographed copy of his Works. In January, 1900, The Coming Nation reported a total eclipse of the sun and also the death of "the man sent from God whose name was John—Ruskin."

Ruskin Cave, Tennessee, has now become a small capitalist resort, its history totally unknown to most of the dancers who jump about on the floored-over "bottomless" lake, which once supplied power for the printing press, and water for laundry and the communal canning of food. But with growing interest in ecology and Worship (a central tenet of Ruskin and of Gluck, as well, whose holy water came freely from nature and the priest), "treasure valleys" in John Ruskin's primal sense, are springing up in many places. It is difficult to avoid the suspicion that Ruskin's early childhood reading  somehow was related to all this. Possibly a study of other great writers would suggest the books read in childhood are more influential than most of us realize.

---

[1] E. T. Cook, The Life of Ruskin, Vol. I (New York, 1911), p. 31, 219.

[2] Ibid., p. 218.

[3] Charles E. Goodspeed, Yankee Bookseller (Boston, 1937), p. 218.

[4] Several editions are available in England and America, and it is also widely anthologized.

[5] Mss., John Ruskin, "The King of the Golden River," (1841), p. 3. Yale University Library, New Haven.

[6] Ibid., pp. 4-5.

[7] Ibid., p. 22.

[8] Ibid., pp. 40-41.

[9] J. A. Hobson, John Ruskin, Social Reformer (London, 1898), pp. 221-225.

[10] Cook, Vol. II, pp. 146-147.

[11] John Ruskin, The Art of England Lectures Given in Oxford (Kent, 1884), Lecture IV, "Fairy Land". From The Works of John Ruskin, eds., E. T. Cook and Alexander Wedderburn, Vol. XXXIII (London, 1908), pp. 329-330.

[12] Ibid., p. 346. Curiously, like Shakespeare before him, Ruskin makes frequent mention of Hercules. A play, "Hercules," with strong socialist overtones, was produced in Ruskin Cave in Tennessee.

[13] Peter Quennell, John Ruskin The Portrait of a Prophet (London, 1949), pp. 266-270; 299.

[14] Cook, Vol. I, p. 31.

[15] John Ruskin, "General Statement explaining the Nature and Purposes of St. George's Guild," (1882), p. 45. From Cook and Wedderburn, op. cit., Vol. XXX (London, 1907).

[16] Ibid., "Additional Passages Relating to St. George's Guild," p. 155.

[17] C. S. Lewis, The Last Battle (Penguin: New York, 1969). In an Afterword, the Editors write that Lewis insists that the proper reason for writing a children's story is "because a children's story is the best art form for something you have to say."

[18] Cook, Vol. II, pp. 361-373.

[19] Quennell, pp. 261-264.

[20] The writer of this paper has some of this scrip, inherited from her father-in-law, John Albin Butler, a laborer from Shelton, Connecticut, who joined the Ruskin experiment, and became one of the printers of The Coming Nation. She also has material from her late husband, Jerome Butler, born in Ruskin. An account of prices of specific items may be found in Robert Corlew, A History of Dickson County (Nashville, Tenn., 1956), p. 141 or in the manuscript files of the University of Tennessee Library.

[21] Cook, Vol. II, p. 226.

[22] In the writer's possession. Of the many books on socialism sold in the colony, some were printed on the presses of The Coming Nation. I have been so far unable to locate this particular edition.

[23] Cook, Vol. II, pp. 225-226.

[24] John Albin Butler, for example, was a printer on The Coming Nation and also flutist in the Ruskin Band. Though information on the colony comes mainly from the writer's late mother-in-law, Annie Ennis Butler, several trips have been made to collect available information in Ruskin, Tennessee, and one to the site of Ruskin, Georgia, near Waycross.

[25] Information furnished by Lillian Lee Corbett of Waycross, who located the piano used by the colonists in the home of Mrs. E. A. Barber, near the site of the old Georgia colony.

[26] Ruskin's ideas on women's suffrage are expressed most fully in Sesame and Lilies (1865).

[27] John Ruskin, The Storm-Cloud of the Nineteenth Century, pp. 31-40. In Cook and Wedderburn, op. cit., Vol XXXIV.

[28] Some of the original photographs are in the possession of the writer.

[29] As Quennell observes in writing of St. George's Guild, "a reader reluctantly arrives at the conclusion that, had Ruskin's Utopia ever materialized in real life, at its best it might have resembled that benevolent and harmonious tyranny which the Jesuit Fathers once imposed upon the Indians of the New World, while at its worst, under the pressure of circumstance, it might have acquired some of the ugly traits of later dictatorial regimes." (p. 264)

[30] In 1912, Julius Wayland, disillusioned in his fight for social justice, commited suicide. In the summer of 1964, the writer of this paper interviewed Wayland's son, Walter Wayland, in Girard, Kansas. Confirmation of statements of various observers of the colony, as well as corrections and new material, grew out of this interview.

[31] The speech, published by the colony as a monograph, is in the possession of this writer.

[32] Related to the writer by Hilton Blackburn, Walter Cribb, and other citizens of Waycross.

[33] In a letter to this writer dated September 4, 1964, Upton Sinclair confirmed that Wayland's managing editor, Fred Warren, did indeed make contact with Sinclair to write The Jungle, which was first serialized in Wayland's paper.

[34] See, for instance, Debs: His Life, Writings, and Speeches (Girard, Kansas, 1908), and for Debs' association with The Coming Nation: Ray Ginger, The Bending Cross: A Biography of Eugene V. Debs (Rutgers, N.J., 1949), p. 173.

TAP-ROOTS INTO A ROSE GARDEN

Alison White

The taproot maintained by writers and readers into their "first world" goes also into a submerged literature, for some of the world's most influential books are below visibility.  Unremembered for themselves they continue doing their work upon minds that may cast them aside but cannot cast them out.  Even though the books themselves are left  behind in the nursery, the marks they make on a reader's sensibility are lasting.  Their stratum is basic, and one who reads of Death's twilight kingdom or the Chapel Perilous may carry into his perception unrecognized images from North Wind and Golden River allegory, or from the hazards and heavens of the children's Kingsley, Ingelow, or Andersen.  Mr. C. S. Lewis has testified to the influence of George MacDonald "Curdie books"; Auden alludes to a "world of Beatrix Potter."  And through the dream-like sequences of the <u>Waste Land</u> and its companion poems the world of childhood is, like the Elizabethan world, used to evoke glimpses of lost kingdoms.

In the "first world" of <u>Burnt Norton</u> in Eliot's <u>Four Quartets</u>, an enclosed rose-garden figures prominently.  It is autumn, but the roses are blooming, the pool is filled with water come out of sunlight, and behind a "door we never opened". . . "the leaves were full of children,/Hidden excitedly, containing laughter."  The insistence of <u>first</u>:— "Through the first gate, "  "Into our first world, " and again, "into our first world" thrusts the mind back to the <u>time past</u> which according to <u>Burnt Norton</u>'s opening oxymoron contains its precipitated self.  In its backward search for a rose garden of the "first world, " the reader's mind may encounter a symbolic enclosed garden of the "submerged" literature of childhood— <u>The Secret Garden</u> (1911) , a Yorkshire idyl written by Frances Hodgson Burnett, earlier the author of <u>Little Lord Fauntleroy</u>.  This novel has as its last scene the reunion of a father and son, brought about by the telepathic summons of a bird and the child's dead mother.  As in <u>Burnt Norton</u> it is autumn in the rose-garden.  The leaves are "full of children/ Hidden excitedly, containing laughter."  The father

> turned into the Long Walk by the ivied walls . . . he knew
> where the door was even though the ivy hung thick over it—
> but he did not know exactly where it lay—that buried key. . .
> no human being had passed that portal for ten lonely years—
> and yet inside the garden there were sounds.  They were the
> sounds of running scuffling feet seeming to chase round and
> round under the trees, they were strange sounds of lowered
> suppressed voices—exclamations and smothered joyous cries.

It seemed actually like the laughter of children who were trying not to be heard but who in a moment or so—as their excitement mounted—would burst forth. . . Was he losing his reason
and thinking he heard things which were not for human ears?
Was it that that the far clear voice had meant?

Once the memory has spanned the garden of <u>Burnt Norton</u> and that of Mrs. Burnett's
Yorkshire rose-garden, other parallels suggest themselves. Eliot's "door we never
opened into the rose-garden" recalls the insistent, repeated image of a child looking for the garden door:

> . . . if she could find out where the door was, she could
> perhaps open it and see what was inside the walls, and what
> had happened to the old rose-trees . . . nobody would ever
> know where she was, but would think the door was still
> locked and the key buried in the earth.

and, at the end of the tale, of the father summoned from Lake Como:

> He thought that as he sat and breathed in the scent of the
> late roses and listened to the lapping of the water at his
> feet he heard a voice calling. It was sweet and clear and
> happy and far away . . . "In the garden," it came back like
> a sound from a golden flute. "In the garden!"

In <u>Burnt Norton</u> a bird is the summoning voice: "Other echoes inhabit the garden
. . . Quick, said the bird, find them, find them." In <u>The Secret Garden</u> a bird
lives in the rose-garden, leads the children to it, shows them the hidden key and
the overgrown door in the wall. To the most perceiving of them, however, and to
the brooding master of the house, it is the ghost of the garden's dead mistress who
used the bird's voice in calling the children, her own voice only to her husband.
"Happen she's been in the garden," says the boy Dickon, "an' happen it was her
set us to work, an' told us to bring him here."

The "deception of the thrush" (<u>Burnt Norton</u>) recalls two passages in the story
where secretiveness and pretense in respect to the garden are rationalized:

> "If tha' was a missel thrush an' showed me where thy nest
> was, does tha' think I'd tell any one? Not me," he said.
> "Tha' art as safe as a missel thrush."

and

> ". . . If we called it our garden and pretended that—that
> we were missel thrushes and it was our next . . ."

The children's first entrances into the secret garden suggest:

> Into our first world
> There they were, dignified, invisible,
> Moving without pressure, over the dead leaves.
> (Burnt Norton)
> (Dickon) began to walk about softly, even more lightly
> than Mary had walked the first time she had found herself
> inside the four walls . . . There were neither leaves nor
> roses on them now and Mary did not know whether they
> were dead or alive, but their thin gray or brown branches
> and sprays looked like a sort of hazy mantle . . . She
> moved away from the door . . . She was glad that there
> was grass under her feet and that her steps made no sound.

In the garden of Burnt Norton "water out of sunlight" fills the drained pool. Twice
in The Secret Garden water and sunlight are doubly yoked, as here: "It is the sun
shining on the rain and the rain falling on the sunshine." There is a pool also, and
the formality of the garden suggests Burnt Norton's "empty alley" and "box circle"
where the surface of the pool "glittered out of heart of light." Mary and Dickon
passed "through the shrubbery gate . . . down winding walks with clipped borders
. . . evergreens clipped into strange shapes, and a large pool with an old gray
fountain in its midst . . . and the fountain was not playing."

All of these images in Burnt Norton are natural, accessible to any reader who can
see or imagine rose-gardens in autumn and hear children laughing among the leaves.
But to many a reader the evocativeness of these images is intensified by their con-
noting also the symbolic, subjective use to which they were put in one of the first
novels he encountered in his life. The Secret Garden and other children's books
of its lyric intensity do their work early in preparing the reader's mind for the experience of poetry. To enforce its implications of spiritual waning and gradual
regeneration through the "Great Magic," The Secret Garden introduced rose-garden,
prophet bird, water out of sunlight, and children as symbolic properties. Such a
complex of images can carry over from childhood's "first world" of reading, to the
adult's encounter with such poetry as Burnt Norton. For him the images are then
not merely natural, generalized, drawn out of random experience. And Eliot's
poem gains in implication through such use of a set of images the more highly subjective by virtue of this allusiveness.

# THE AMBIGUOUS LEGACY OF WILHELM BUSCH

Der zweite schmeckt schon etwas besser
Der Frosch wird bunt und immer grosser

R. Loring Taylor

Wilhelm Busch stands at the headwaters of the twentieth century comic strip. Stephen Becker (<u>Comic Art in America</u>), Martin Sheridan (<u>Comics and Their Creators</u>) and Colton Waugh (<u>The Comics</u>) have recorded the influence of Busch on the earliest American comics, the "yellow journals." Following Busch, comics entered American life as a record of pranksters. Shortly after the success of the earliest "yellow journal" pranksters, in 1897, Rudoph Block, comic editor of the <u>New York Journal</u>, suggested to Rudolph Dirks that he work up an imitation of Busch's <u>Max und Moritz</u>, which had been translated by Charles Timothy Brooks in 1871. Dirk's creation was called <u>The Katzenjammer Kids</u> (from the German term for hangover—cat howling). Colton Waugh pursues the development of <u>The Katzenjammer Kids</u> down to the courtroom, where it suffered an unnatural mitosis, dividing into itself and its twin, <u>The Captain and the Kids</u>.

These three books, together with an occasional <u>Nachwort</u> in subsequent translations of Busch's comic material, virtually exhaust the critical attention that had been paid in English to Busch's work. Many of Busch's writings have not even been translated, including his important five page autobiography, <u>Von mir über mich</u>, his sayings and fairy stories, <u>Ut öler Welt</u>, his poetry, collected under the title <u>Schein und Sein</u>, and the elaborate fantasies of his later years, such as <u>Edwards Traum</u>. Although historians acknowledge the importance of Busch as the ancestor of American comics, there has apparently been little concern with the origin and significance of the German prototypes. Such oversights emphasize the fact that virtually the only attempt to set the American comic strip into the perspective of the grand European traditions of art, etching, book illustration and political satire emerges as a byproduct of the search for the origin of the mysterious phenomenon, the speech bubble.

German criticism of Busch, on the other hand, amply makes up for the deficiencies of criticism available in English. Since Busch's death there have been at least two doctoral dissertations and thirteen book-length studies devoted to his life and work. Some of this material is summarized in Bettina Hurliman's <u>Three Centuries of Children's Books in Europe</u>. Miss Hurliman establishes Busch's place in the development of German children's literature, indicating, for example, the relationship between Busch's cartoons and <u>Strumpfelpeter</u>. She also demonstrates a relationship between Busch's cartoons and subsequent American comics, although she finds the differences of greater significance than the similarities. In addition, she mentions Busch's work in other media, pointing out the enormous number of oil paintings he did, but she leaves virtually unexplored the relationship of this other work to his comic material. Although such an inquiry might lead outside her subject, its omission is disappointing because through Busch's other work one could trace the influences of prior artistic traditions and German thought and expression contemporary with Busch on the development of the medium of the comic strip, with its particular characterestics and constraints. Although the comic strip is now generally regarded as a peculiarly American institution, its continental background could be clarified by a translation of the German criticism which explores the relationship between Busch's comic and serious work.

From 1909 to 1913, shortly after Busch's death, there was a flurry of activity, mostly biographical. The most valuable of these works was an appreciation by his three nephews, Otto, Adolphe and Herman Nöldecke. This book supplements the earlier biographical work of Daelen with anecdotes about Busch as well as with a number of his sayings. Two academic studies appeared in 1910: O. F. Volkman's Wilhelm Busch der Poet: Seine Motive und Seine Quellen (Leipzig); and Fritz Winter's Wilhelm Busch als Dichter, Knustler, Psycholog und Philosoph (Univeristy of California, Berkeley). These studies opened the door to an investigation of literary sources such as the German Märchen and artistic sources such as Franz Hals and the Dutch naturalists. Finally in 1913 appeared Albert Vanselow's thorough edition and bibliography, Die erstdrucke und erstausgaben der Werke von Wilhelm Busch: ein bibliographische Verzeichnis. Subsequent editions of Vanselow have been issued, including an important edition in 1943 which includes much explanatory material by Otto Nöldecke. But after Vanselow's first edition, criticism was silent for close to twenty years.

In the early thirties interest once again began to be directed toward Busch. This interest incresed steadily throughout the decade, culminating in a book each year from 1937 to 1941. One cannot avoid the feeling that the interest was symptomatic of the gathering German self consciousness during these years. Karl Anlauf called Busch "der Völkische Seher" (1939)' Fritz Schweynert called Busch "Die Dichter der Deutschen" (1941).

Roelf Deknatel's book, Wilhelm Busch der Lachende Philosoph des Pessimismus, is the exception that proves the rule. Published in 1940, it is an exhaustive examination of Busch's debt to Arthur Schopenhauer. It is curious how many books from this era describe Busch as a "philosoph," particularly in light of his relationship to Schopenhauer, since it is now generally considered that Schopenhauer's contribution was to literature and art rather than to philosophy. In any case, Schopenhauer's importance to Busch, according to Deknatel, lay in providing certainty in the form of a metaphysical explanation for what the Germans call schadenfreude. Schopenhauer suggests that man is in a "no-exit" situation: the demands of the will are infinite; they can never be met in any real situation. Man is a comic figure, doomed to endless frustration and compromise. Deknatel proposes that Busch, as spokesman for the German, responds to this comedy with tragic intensity. He rides the will as a surfer rides an impossible wave, knowing all the time that he is doomed. The form of this belief goes back to the old German myths of the Voluspa and Wagner's Götterdämmerung. Busch's comedy, defined by these myths, becomes serious romantic irony. One's laughter is an act of faith in the exhilarating futility of life.

Deknatel's book was a rigorously academic exercise, published in Holland, and therefore just outside the stream of propaganda that might have exploited Busch. But by attributing these ideas to Busch, Deknatel is suggesting that Busch fits into the tradition of ideas leading from Schopenhauer to Nietzsche down through the architects of the Third Reich. Busch's "comedy" appears from this point of view as a member of the same family as the comic sequences in Nietzsche's Also Sprach Zarathustra, in which the "Übermensch," after being ridiculed and rejected by the populace, acquires a motley collection of disciples, including the priest who has been out of work since God died. There is a possibility that the German government may have exploited Busch in the same way that it exploited Nietzsche—by ignoring a level of irony and thereby treating figures which are comic in the Schopenhaurian sense as serious representations of the archetypal will.

Following Noldecke's re-edition in 1943 of Vanselow's complete Busch, criticism was silent for nearly fifteen years. Whether Germany during this period was embarrassed at the kind of attention it had paid to Busch or was simply too exhausted to publish anything is difficult to determine. The first criticism to appear after the war came from the aesthetic distance of Switzerland. Some of this work was new, some recapitulated earlier work (further studies of Schopenhauer's influence. . .), and some represented attempts of people like Friedrich Bohne to return to earlier doctoral-candidate enthusiasms.

In the early sixties Busch began appearing once again in the United States. In 1962 Arthur Klein edited a two volume selection of Busch's cartoons for Dover Books. The translation and supporting apparatus of this edition are significant, for they illustrate the kind of tidying up that was considered essential for Busch to continue to be regarded as suitable material for children. Klein introduced the first volume by re-issuing the Charles T. Brooks' classic Victorian translation of Max und Moritz. Klein himself translated several pieces including Die Fromme Helene.

The cover of this edition illustrates the intention of the editors. Drawings are selected from Busch's cartoons which portray Busch's realm as a state of vacant but happy fluidity in which children, animals and gingerbread cookies exchange identities or blur and blend into each other with joyous abandon. Since all these creatures look approximately alike, the transformation from one to the other does not result in a loss of identity, but is rather an assertion of identity at the level of projection. The children's world portrayed here is meaningful in the sense that the children's world portrayed in Blake's Songs of Innocence is meaningful. But in the context in which these pictures occur, Busch's handling of the Verwandlung theme is sinister and terrifying. People are drowning or freezing to death or being baked in ovens or ground up in mills. Such transformations serve to demonstrate the fragileness of identity and the inhuman ease with which nature can destroy it. The transformation of the child into the state of nature is eventually as incomprehensible as that portrayed by Wordsworth in the Lucy poems. Der Eispeter provides the clearest example. After the bereaved parents carry the frozen body of their son back home, they set him by the fire to thaw out, whereupon he melts into a pool of water.

Another difficulty with Klein's editorial policy is a tendency to render Busch's ironic figures with excessive literalness. Thus, for example, he translates Die

<u>Fromme Helene</u> as <u>The Hypocritical Helen</u>, losing the sardonic intensity of the German original, which means simply, <u>pious</u>. To call Helene "hypocritical" is true in one sense, but it is like leaving the recognition scene out of a production of Sophocles' <u>Oedipus Rex</u>. Busch's art depends on stock figures. But Busch will intensify the conventional tone of such figures until it becomes undermined or exposes its unacknowledged nature. Thus <u>Die Fromme Helene</u> is an expose of piety, not hypocrisy, because Busch is showing how piety becomes hypocritical. Helene's motive in having the affair with the minister is not at first hypocritical: she wants to raise herself to a higher spiritual plane than that afforded by her husband. Her disgust with her husband's obscene behavior is genuine, but he is usually too drunk to notice. In turning to the minister Helene is renouncing her old ways, is experiencing a conversion. That this conversion is dependent on a self deception as extreme as her earlier deception of others is the ironic conclusion of the piece.

A similarly excessively literal interpretation of Busch's stock figures leads Arthur Klein into some embarrassing confrontations. Klein gives a dark hint of unacknowledged problems in a note in the back of his first volume:

> They (Klein's notes) do not attempt to offer a biography of that cryptic, strange, and to some extent sick personality: Wilhelm Busch.

This vague suggestion is further clarified by one of Klein's singular achievements as a translator, leaving out the entire fifth chapter of <u>Plisch und Plum</u>. Mr. Klein explains his decision in a footnote:

> This short chapter is omitted here because it unfortunately embodies some of the anti-Semitism which tainted the work of Busch from time to time. There is no need for reproducing such occurrences in this day and age.

The image of Busch thus expurgated for the modern reader raises a number of intriguing questions. The first is the difficulty of determining the audience of comics. If comics are to be expurgated for children, who is to be the real reader of comics? Next there is the problem that if one begins to apply this kind of attention to Busch it is hard to know where to stop. Busch has something to offend everyone, and a version of Busch thoroughly expurgated by every group who had a reasonable right to expurgate some passage or other would be slim pickin's. A translator associated with the Black Panther movement would eliminate certain passages; translators sympathetic to the society for the prevention of cruelty to animals would eliminate others; the Catholic League would perpetuate its ban on such entire pieces as <u>Pater Filucius</u>, which were written in the service of Bismark's <u>Kulturkampf</u>; certain educators would object to the disrespect for authority; child psychologists would object to the wanton cruelty taken for granted throughout the pages. Taking all these matters into consideration, one is forced to conclude that Busch would never be considered appropriate material for appearance on <u>Sesame Street</u>. Indeed, there is in the United States a line of speculation about Busch that has become concerned with his "Germanness" in order to shed light on certain forms of pathological behavior. Critics of this persuasion may be censoring Busch for the very reason that Nazi Germany approved of him. But both such readings may be dependent on some excessively literal reading of Busch's stock figures.

A comparison between the gemütlich Bauer and the expurgated Jew in Plisch und Plum will serve as an illustration. The Fittig Eltern are introduced in a scene laden with schmalz so thick one could slice it. They are sitting hand in hand in front of their cottage while the sun sets behind some trees. Papa Fittig is described as treu und friedlich; Mama is sehr gemütlich.

The first appearance of the Jew, on the other hand, is unpromising enough:

> Kurz die Hose, lang der Rock
> Krumm die Nase und der Stock
> Augen schwarz und Seele grau
>
> Short the pants, long the coat
> Crooked the nose and the cane
> Eyes black and soul grey

This is the classic stage Jew. But there are some peculiarities about Busch's handling of the theme. Every other one of Plish and Plum's antics occur in spite of the two boys' efforts to prevent disaster. But in this instance the boys encourage the dogs to run out and bite the passerby. The harrassment the Jew receives takes place with the boys' full knowledge and sanction. However, when the father comes out, the boys ostentatiously direct their attention to a bug crawling up the wall, thus declining knowledge of or responsibility for the foregoing action. The behavior is not at all like that of the earlier pranksters, Max and Moritz. It resembles more closely that of the average respectable German citizen, who has been portrayed by George Grosz as walking comfortably along behind blinders saying, Ich will von Politik nichts wissen. The only concrete objection to the Jew is that he wants to be paid for his torn trousers.

It may at first seem surprising that this mild avariciousness is considerably exceeded by the good Papa Fittig himself, whose sole response to the dogs was indignant outrage until Phineas Fogg appeared to purchase them for some incredible amount of money. Papa Fittig declines in our estimation throughout the story, and the final culminating view of Papa Fittig returning home, smugly self satisfied with the money he did nothing to earn, echoes the closing picture of the Jew walking on down the street clutching the payment for his trousers. In eliminating the fifth chapter from his translation of Plisch und Plum Arthur Klein has eliminated not only antisemitic elements but also some very harsh comments about certain pretensions and moral voids among the Germans themselves.

The difficulties in interpreting Plisch und Plum lie at the heart of certain weaknesses in Busch's medium. The comic strip depends on stock figures which will retain their identity throughout a number of episodes. This situation differs from the novel, where a character is expected to change or develop. Busch drew his stock figures from types which had already been articulated in the culture around him. In moving into Busch's cartoons they carried their connotative value with them. Busch's stock characters rarely develop, even in such pieces as the Jobsiad, which are parodies of Bildungsroman. What happens instead is an intensification of connotation.

The differences between Max und Moritz and Plisch und Plum illustrate the dimensions of development sanctioned by the medium. I was first introduced to Max und Moritz by my father, who was fond of reciting snatches of Charles Timothy Brooks' classic Victorian translation which he had read as a child. The ending of the first prank lodged particularly in his attention. Several chickens, upon eating bits of bread fastened together by strings in the form of spokes of a wheel, somehow became wrapped around a branch and hanged themselves. Brooks describes the situation as follows:

> Each laid quickly one egg more
> Then they passed to the other shore

There is a sense to this account of duty being accomplished, after which the blessed pass on to their final reqard. The German version, on the other hand, reverberates with quite different implication. Under a picture of several chickens laying their eggs and a rooster laying what appears to be a peanut there is the caption,

> Jede legt noch schnell ein Ei
> Und dann kommt der Tod dabei

In this account death has become the personified abstraction of the medieval manuscripts, who appears with his summons like an unwanted guest interrupting people at their accustomed tasks. The flavor of medieval Germany, which so pervades Busch's work, was preserved intact into the nineteenth century by the Märchen, of which Grimm's collection is the most famous example. Busch was himself very interested in the ability of children's literature to preserve medieval forms intact. Before he even began cartooning he considered making collections of fairy stories, and he finally finished these to his satisfaction only shortly before his death. Busch also preserved such medieval forms as the bestiary in a series of animal alphabet works for children.

But there is a sense in which the medieval Anschauung, with all its apparatus of devils and witches, was not an artificial reconstruction for Busch. Busch was born in an old farm house whose style had remained the same for centuries. His mother was, according to his description, quiet and pious, and his father was a grocer who took long walks through the town and the forest. Busch grew up with all the trappings of the farm—the pigs wandering occasionally inside, the stubborn donkey, the well with its trough outside in the long grass. In his autobiography, Von mir über mich, Busch mentions an early childhood memory of discovering his baby sister lying in this trough, her body framed by the water. Busch's subsequent handling of the Verwandlung theme, including his portrayals of death by drowning and freezing, appear to return to this incident. As Busch subsequently went to Antwerp to study art, he discovered a world similar to that of his childhood, portrayed by Franz Hals and the Dutch naturalists. In imitating these painters and engravers, Busch was copying a world which was real for him.

But by the 1860's, for an increasing number of Germans, this world was vanishing. Bismark and the Prussians were seizing Germany and thrusting it headlong into the twentieth century. Within a generation Germany was moving from a peasant to an industrial society. Much of Germany had not participated in the movements which France and England had employed to consolidate their national identities and bring a cosmopolitan society into focus. In differing ways, both France and England recorded the transition between a court and a bourgeois society in novels and caricature. Both these forms demanded a highly self-conscious audience. But the new order in Germany could not support such a literature, and, for the most part, the old petty courts would not. Therefore, in order to find meaning in the new situation, Germany had to cling to symbols of its former identity. A great deal of German emotional and intellectual life consisted of mulling over traditional visual images or religious symbols. In this process the same forms satisfied the most simple and the most sophisticated modes of thought. People of all ages, literate as well as illiterate, read fairy tales and comics. Grimm's fairy tales and Goethe's Faust are framed of quite similar material. Such material can retain its essential form throughout fluctuations in tone or attitude as well as variety in sophistication of handling, just as a comic hero can retain his identity through a number of contexts. The realism of Busch was for this generation of Germans an object of sentimental fantasy.

Plisch und Plum was the product of Busch's studying for seventeen years the audience that had welcomed Max und Moritz. Arthur Klein has described the differences between these two works.

> Plisch und Plum was first published in 1882, about 17 years after
> Max und Moritz and about five years after Die Fromme Helene.
> Plisch und Plum, in terms of drawing and text, represented a more
> mature and developed Busch, one who had behind him successful
> years of planning and executing picture stories for book publication.
>
> It is conceivable that, since Max und Moritz, the most successful of his works in terms of continuing total sales, had been built around a mischievous or unruly pair, Busch may have set out to double the dose—two pairs, one of boys, the other of dogs. They begin as disruptive demons, thorns in the side of the Established Order. However, the passing years in some respects had developed a milder and gentler mood in Busch. So Paul and Peter and their two dogs are not made to suffer grim ends.

There is something not quite satisfying about this explanation. The new "milder and gentler" Busch portrays one drowning and several beatings. Indeed, one is at first struck by how little development there has been in 17 years. The circular pattern of vengeance characterizing the earlier work is even carried out, with Kaspar Schick drowning in the very puddle in which he tried to drown the pups. And there are few images in Busch so sadistically perverted as that of the very proper Madame Kümmel pouring kerosene over the puppies' genital organs, then passing into a sexual-anal

83

swoon over their anguished attempts to rub themselves off in the dirt.

Perhaps the most apparent difference is an intensification of the sentiment that apparently appealed to the original audience. But in this process certain contradictions emerge. Max and Moritz, under the immediate influence of Strumpfelpeter, are heartless pranksters deserving chastisement. They began by killing some chickens; Paul and Peter, on the other hand, began by rescuing some puppies. The latter boys are therefore much more deliberately objects of sympathetic attention. They are sentimental rather than rebellious heroes. But, strangely enough, they often find themselves chastized in a similar manner. Therefore one's attitude toward this punishment becomes ambiguous; the boys often appear to be punished unfairly.

A similar attitude characterizes one's attitude toward Papa Fittig. The Kitsch-like quality of the picture of domestic bliss in which the Fittig _Eltern_ are introduced appears a striking contrast to the caricature figures that are the objects of the humor of Max and Moritz. The uncle and the school teacher are good examples of the latter. Both seem to engage in pointedly anachronistic behavior. This behavior is obvious from the start, and one's attitude toward it does not change markedly during the course of the pranks. The actions of Papa Fittig, on the other hand, expose or undermine the _treu und friedlich_ image he originally presents. His suspicion of the dogs the children have recently rescued and his tendency to contribute to any confusion by a liberal application of the lash, arouse the reader's disenchantment, since the reader is now sympathetic toward the children for their selfless bravery in rescuing the puppies. By the time one reaches the closing scene showing Papa Fittig marching home clutching the money he has received for the pups, one's disenchantment with the triumph of bourgeois virtue should be complete, unless, of course, one believes in bourgeois virtue.

Busch's work, then, has developed simultaneously in two directions. In appealing to the public, Busch has become increasingly sentimental; but in an increasing contempt of the public to which he was appealing, Busch developed an irony which undermined the sentiment which was getting thicker all the time. The resultant ambiguity of tone bears a superficial resemblance to such picaresque novels as _Lazarillo de Tormes_, in which a figure with whom one would normally be sympathetic, a blind beggar, turns out in fact to be grasping and malicious. The difference between ambiguity in Busch and that of the picaresque novel is that the complexity in the picaresque novel is inescapably embedded in the subject, whereas one may read such a piece as _Plisch und Plum_ with either sentiment or irony, and one's reading will be perfectly coherent. There are, to be sure, occasional pieces in Busch in which a combined response is inescapable. Noteworthy in this respect is the vignette of the "_grossmütterchen_" who "tat alles für seiner kleiner Herr." The drawing portrays the "dear old thing" wisking away the chamber pot. But in most of Busch's pieces the tone is uncertain, ambiguous or optional. Once sentiment has asserted its appreciation, further realism becomes a mask or disguise. This dilemma can be traced back from _Plisch und Plum_ to the earliest of Busch's successful comic productions, _Max und Moritz_, in which it is impossible to determine whether one should regard the gruesome ending as a triumph of righteousness or a parody of the vindictive excesses of righteousness.

The problem of the weakness of the valence bonds connecting complexity of attitude to the raw visual image or icon was a characteristic of German literature throughout the century. This disassociation culminated in the brief and unpopular movement called German expressionism. Walter Sokel, in <u>The Writer in Extremis</u>, ably describes many of the features characterizing this movement—an anti-intellec-tualism, a rebellion against authority, a tendency to establish obtrusive rhetorical stances, the creation of mythical super heroes of impossible characteristics who often offset some feeling of lugubrious self pity or a sense of unworthiness. Walter Sokel has suggested that these features were in part caused by a disassoci-ation between the intellectual and society more extreme than that experienced in either France or England:

> . . . the German adolescent did not see himself as part of society and was more prone to resort to violent anarchic rebellion in his daydreams and fantasies.

The expressionist, then, was prone to engage in wild compensatory fantasies, tem-pered by a delicate and sophisticated irony.

However, one of the main suppositions of expressionism is that form can be dis-associated from content. In expressing this assumption the movement becomes the self conscious culmination of a feature which had characterized German literature to some degree throughout the century. But there is a self destructiveness about this assumption. Since irony or complexity of tone was one of the main moral wea-pons of the German intellectual, the ease with which it could be overlooked created an odd impotence in his position. As the forms of his outrage were smugly absorb-ed by the objects of his outrage, his complexity of response became an evanescent byproduct of his creative energy, and his sophistication remained locked within his fantasies.

German expressionism was the transitional phase or <u>seive</u> through which nine-teenth century German thought, including Grimms' fairy tales, the speculation of Nietzsche and Schopenhauer as well as that of Busch passed into the twentieth century. The assumptions of expressionism made it feasible for the Nazis to de-tach the irony from such figures as Nietzsche's <u>Übermensch</u> and treat them as se-rious and literal if debased archetypal representations of the Schopenhaurian will. The Busch criticism of the late thirties was devoted to exploring the peculiar "Germanness" of Busch's work. But during the peak of this sort of enthusiasm the "comic" medium which Busch had helped to develop was proving particularly well adapted to articulating self closed archetypes of an insatiable will. The <u>Über-mensch</u> publicly promoted by the German government was paralleled in the United States by an underground cult of super heroes.

American "funnies" had evolved for three generations under heavy competition or selective pressure. The subterranean fantasy life represented by the rapid evo-lution of comic super heroes moved from Harold Foster's and Burne Hogarth's ren-ditions of Tarzan through Prince Valiant to Buck Rogers (in which the setting moved from constraint to decoration), culminating in the epitome of comic strip characters, the refined sterility of Superman (in which the setting served only to measure its own irrelevance, and the only threat to existence came from one's own identity).

Although Superman was conceived by two people still in high school, his debt to Schopenhauer's interest in Eastern thought remains uncanny. Superman is pure disembodied will, unencumbered by any sophistication or complexity of tone. Reality exists for Superman only as a yardstick to measure its negligible effect on him. He is frustrated by it only when he faces the problem of finding a place to undress. Superman has no motive for his actions, unlike Batman, who is conduting a personal crusade against criminals who killed his parents, or Plastic Man, who is waging a vendetta against his former associates who abandoned him at the scene of a crime. He has no lusts or desires (unlike Freud's id), no drive for power (unlike Adler), although he may inspire lust for power. Schopenhauer suggests that to articulate an object of desire is to debase the infinite expectation of the will. What Schopenhauer defines as the will Krishna of the Bhagavad-Gita defines as pure being—the raw material of the universe. Following Krishna's doctrine, Superman seeks no fruit for his action, although Western heroes from Achilles onward have always struggled for some goal. Superman's strength comes from within his own nature. He does not have to say magic words or lift weights or study science. He is not dumb (like strong men in the Ajax tradition), but neither is he smart, because he doesn't have to be. Superman's power exists, in an absolute sense. But Superman does not behave like a strong man. His strength is more than accident. It is a relativistic illusion. From the perspective of his own planet he is perfectly normal. No wonder editors rejected Superman for five years. They were confusing realism with purity of archetype. And their ears were not close to the ground-swell of public demand.

Superman has the tonal opacity of a mickey mouse balloon. Yet one can see how he evolved from the complex comic creations of Busch. The prankster fulfills a set of fantasy expectations analogous to those met by the super hero. In many societies the prankster is a social magician, one who is adept at setting aside the laws of nature. The primary constraint to the will in the nineteenth century was the dignity of figures of authority. The brittle authority of such figures as the schoolmaster is sufficiently exposed or eroded by Max and Moritz that it can never recover, no matter what fate is eventually mated out to the pranksters.

Analogies between Max und Moritz and Superman can be established along a number of dimensions which Walter Sokel considers characteristic features of German expressionism—anti-intellectualism, rebellion against authority, tendency to establish exaggerated rhetorical stances, compensatory fantasies centered around some hero of impossible characteristics. But perhaps the most important similarity between Max und Moritz and Superman (as the ultimate representative of his genre) is an apparent meaninglessness which is shared by both of them. Without the constraints of the social or physical world, neither the prankster nor the superman can exercise the will that each represents, since every articulation of some constraint serves only to express its irrelevance. (When one discovers that Superman can fly faster than a speeding bullet, one does not ask what caliber.) The figure representing the will remains, therefore, within a realm of disembodied fantasy or self-enclosed romantic irony.

Although the fantasy image of the will acknowledges no exterior constraints, the insatiable demands of the will create a situation in which the will must collapse of its own being. This situation is symbolically portrayed for both Superman and Max und Moritz by some fetch of their essential identities. For Superman it is kryptonite, from his home planet; for Max und Moritz it is the farmer or the miller, earthy characters devoid of artificial dignity and thereby impervious to the threat of their antics. It is at first surprising that, for both heroes, the effect of confronting their fetches is absolute annihilation. Superman collapses into something having the power of limp rhubarb, which Max and Moritz are ground up by the mill and spat forth as harmless chunks of kid stuff, which are used as duck or chicken feed, carrying the fable back to the beginning prank in which Max and Moritz fed to the chickens the bread which entangled them in their doom. Both comics, then, enact a Hegelian account of the old Germanic myths. The will expands its demands insatiably until it collapses of its own weight in some sort of Götterdämmerung

The comic medium which Busch had helped to develop owed its success in generating stock and archetypal fantasy figures to the ease with which complexity of tone could be detached from the subject. This characteristic emerges from the assumption central to expressionist doctrine that form can be disassociated entirely from content. This assumption forces moral outrage, the stance of the artist as prophet and teacher, into the circular and self closed sterility of romantic irony. By some species of evolution the productions of the comic artist will tend to drift in the direction of being taken at their most literal or sentimental level, and there is a poignant irrelevance about the artist's original complexity of intent. Looking backward through the spectacle of a generation of Germans laughing at the "solution" to the "Max und Moritz problem"—shoving the social misfits into ovens and mills—it is now virtually impossible to reproduce Busch's original intent. At the risk of drifting into McLuhanesque mysticism, one cannot help being struck by the ease with which the medium of the comic strip eliminates complexity which is irrelevant to it.

In the 1890's Busch stopped work on his cartoons and turned his hand to some long-delayed projects, which had probably been exerting quiet influences on his comic productions. He turned, for example, to writing children's stories and fairy tales, an enthusiasm he had begun before doing any of his comic pieces. He also pursued his former interest in sketching and oil painting. His landscapes remind one of the movement of Van Gogh from naturalism to expressionism, while his devotion to self-portraiture, in an age obsessed with the genre, was probably exceeded only by his younger contemporary, the Norwegian expressionist painter Edvard Munch.

One of the most important productions of this period was a series of poems exploring the relation between appearance and reality (Schein und Sein), a subject of interest to one who saw his realism become the raw material of fantasy. One poem entitled Beruhigt, meaning soothed, reassured or assuaged, is of particular interest in clarifying the relationship of expressionist doctrine to the comic strip.

    Zwei mal zwei gleich vier ist Wahrheit.
    Schade, dass sie leicht und leer ist,
    Denn ich wolte lieber Klarheit
    Über das, was voll und schwer ist.

Emsig sucht ich aufzufinden,
Was im tiefsten Grunde wurzelt,
Lief umher nach allen Winden
Und bin oft dabei gepurzelt.

Endlich baut ich eine Hutte.
Still nun zwischen ihren Wanden
Sitz ich in der Welten Mitte,
Unbekümmert um die Enden.

Two times two equals four is truth.
Too bad that this fact is so light and empty
For I would dearly love clarity
About something that is complete and difficult.

Diligently I sought to discover
What grew in the deepest ground
I have run around in all kinds of winds
And often been tumbled about.

At last I built myself a hut.
Quietly now between its walls
I sit in the middle of the world
Unconcerned about the end.

The poet is here proposing the gloomy prognosis that the rupture between form and content is irreparable. Mathematics, which is equivalent to pure form, will always remain void and empty, while the subject one desperately wants to express will always elude expression. The solution is to build a fantasy world which will protect one from an awareness of the disjuncture between the mind and the object of knowledge. One senses a delicate irony here, an awareness that the comfort can only be maintained as long as one has the energy to maintain the walls of the illusion in good repair, but since the irony is a by-product of the mind which saw the original necessity for the walls, its debilitating influence on the desperation which maintains the walls is minimal.

Perhaps Busch's most extravagant venture into expressionism was a fantastic piece written, apparently, for children. Edwards Traum is the record of a person who dreamed he was travelling through the realm of mathematics. Like Alice in Wonderland, this is a very special form of fantasy. In the name of the irrational, both books carry one into the meaningless realm of the purely rational. Both works attempt to make mathematics accessible to human experience, and very little adult literature makes such demands on the imagination. There are, of course, differences. Dodgson was a successful scholar and teacher of mathematical logic, whereas Busch was an unsuccessful engineering student, so there is a vindictiveness about Busch's treatment of the subject. Busch was, in a sense, paying off an old score, and his final conclusion is not complimentary to those who spend their lives in the land of mathematics. But, by an ironic twist that characterizes the fate of many of Busch's works, Edwards Traum can be read as serious science fiction, as speculation about life in a post-Einsteinian fourth dimension. Busch was as aware as anyone of the dubious role fantasy plays in human life, but this awareness served only to enable him to articulate fantasies with increasing efficiency.

In conclusion, Busch's contribution to the origin of the comic strip enables us to explain many of its peculiar characteristics. One would have expected that the comic strip would have emerged from the traditions of caricature well developed in England from Hogarth to Rowlandson, in France by Daumier and Lautrec and in Spain by Goya. But this tradition seems to have contributed surprisingly little to the comic strip. Most of this caricature was prepared for some self conscious society which delighted in observing itself in a mirror. The direction of its productive development was an increasing realism, brought into focus by moral outrage.

The comic strip, on the other hand, seemed to have bubbled up from some depths of its own, virtually oblivious to the extreme social self consciousness of the great European caricaturists. The goal of the comic strip was not to portray life but to offer an alternative to life. It was an ideal medium for expressing aggressive, sentimental or compensatory fantasies. The irony is that these were the very objects of Busch's satire.

---

EXCERPTS FROM EDWARDS TRAUM

Some people have an unfortunate habit. They like to tell us their dreams, which are usually nothing other than the dubious entertainments in the children's and servant's quarters of the mind, after the father and master of the house have gone to bed.

However the wise say that all people (except the ladies) are lacking something.

This saying could be useful to us. Since all of us do not have great assets but have at the same time a few little shortcomings with which we annoy others, we should be tolerant of our fellows who find themselves in similar situations.

Thus our friend Edward, as considerate as he usually was, began one day as follows. . .

The clock struck ten. Our dear little Emil had long since been put to bed. Elisa got up, gave me a kiss and said, "Good night Edward. Do come to bed soon." But not until much later, after I had frittered away my time as usual, comfortably meditating on the limits of the incomprehensible, did I take my last puff on the butt of my Havana, swallow the dregs of my drink, stand up, yawn in satisfaction at my solitude and make my way to bed.

For a long time after I had gone to bed I lay on my left side, staring into the light of the candle. Just at the stroke of 12 I blew it out and turned to lie on my back. Before my inner eye, as on a crowded tapestry, stood the image of the flame I had just extinguished. As I observed it closely and attentively something eerie began to happen, without my knowing quite how.

My spirit, my soul, or whatever you want to call it, in short, just about everything that I have in my head started to draw itself together. My whole self became smaller and smaller: first like a medium sized potato; then like a Swiss pill;
then like the head of a pin; then smaller and still smaller until I could shrink no
further. I had shrunk down to a point.

Just at that moment I was swept away as if by the noisy howling of the wind.
As I tumbled backwards I turned around and found myself staring into my own
nostrils.

Then I sat down on the corner of the night stand and thought about my destiny.

I was not only a dot; I was a thinking dot. Not only was I one and two, I was
here and there and now and then. I created my own time and space according to
my needs, as if these were merely byproducts.

Suddenly I sprang up and began to move freely in a motion like a hovering fly—
flfsht to the rose, flfsht to the carnation and then away again—skimming from
flower to flower on sunny summer days.

At first I began to drift toward my former body.

There he is: eyes closed; mouth hanging open; a fine figure of a man.

Then I drifted over Elisa.

"Look," I cried out, "at the way the master appears when he is sleeping."

Here, my love, you could see how much I had altered in my dream to my own
disadvantage because I dared to express a thought so fresh and risky that I
would prefer not acknowledge it if I were waking and in full command of my facul-
ties.

Then I paused for a moment over Emil's little bed.

His tiny hand was resting under his cheek; the empty baby bottle way lying by
his side.

"What a handsome boy," I thought. "And just like his old man."

I can recognise the expression on your faces, my dear friends, and the condescension embarrasses me. Perhaps I must agree that you are right.

But even though, as I mentioned, my five senses were almost left at home on
account of the dreamlike isolation of my being, it still appeared to me that I noticed things around me with an unusual clarity just as on those occasions when
the moon appears to be shining through the window even though it has already
descended. It was a fact of experience, without doubt or ambiguity, which probably could not be explained to many people.

However the truth of the matter is really very simple. One needs only to contemplate it further.

In order to test whether I was still flexible I flew over in front of the mirror.

Right! There I was! A fine shivering little churl of microscopic tidiness.

"How," I exclaimed, "is it possible that you can shed your old self and still
have something left? Why not ZZZzzzzz. . .

Here a voice suddenly interrupted me with the words, "Edward, don't snore
like that."

Only someone who has been disturbed by chance in the middle of his noon nap
by a squawking foghorn can form a vague impression of how much these words
(which one would imagine could have lasted for eternity) brought to a halt. Prob-

90

ably only three seconds elapsed before I came to myself.

The interruption, however, did not please me. With little consideration for wife and child, I decided to continue my journey.

With my mind now working like a telegraph, I took a sidestep through the wall (this was easy for me now) and at once found myself in friendly territory within the land of numbers. Before me lay a beautiful little city all of figures.

Strange. But in a dream even little curlicues can come to life.

Morning came. A few anonymous figures passed me like farm workers going about their chores. They were multiplying, but only just so far, as if they did not want to rise too high or get too far ahead.

Now I noticed numbers like civil servants riding the morning subway. These were much more aware of status, and there was much talk among them of a certain Zero, who got in the way of all sorts of honest hard-working people. If one who did not deserve it received a promotion, people claimed that this could be attributed to the old intriguer Zero, as sure as two times two equals four.

The wealthy quarters were inhabited by fancy numbers of power and position who could trace their family trees back to the oldest ABC books. A certain X was the most highly sought after of them all, but he was so shy that every day approximately a thousand fools asked about him before one wise man could ever meet him. There were other figures one could almost call pushy. Two such, whom I met on the promenade, introduced themselves to me over and over. First Mr. A, then Mr. B; then Mr. B and again Mr. A. Finally they asked with conceited expressions whether they might after all be the same because $A + B = B + A$.

It was all the same to me, I replied politely. But I knew only too well that, looking at the matter from certain directions, something was not quite right.

But such small oversights could probably only happen in a dream.

---

BIBLIOGRAPHY

Altemark, Joachim. Der Larm womit der Musikant uns Stort: Nachdenkliches über das Verhaltnis Wilhelm Busch zur Musik. H. Buske, Hamburg, 1962.

Anlauf, Karl. Der Philosoph von Wiedensahl, der Volkische Seher. Buchergilde, Gutenberg, Berlin, 1939.

Bohne, Friedrich. Wilhelm Busch und der Geist Seiner Zeit. Bernhard Vopelius, Jena, 1931.

_____ . Wilhelm Busch: Leben, Werk, Schicksal. Fretz and Wasmuth, 1958.

Cremer, Hans. Die Bildergeschichten Wilhelm Buschs. G. H. Notte, Dusseldorf, 1937.

Dangers, Robert. _Wilhelm Busch, der Kunstler_ und der Weise. Gebr. Fretz, Zurich, 1956.

Deknatel, Roelf. _Wilhelm Bush der Lachende Philosoph des Pessimismus_. M. Wyt en Zonen, Rotterdam, 1940.

Ehrlich, Josef. _Wilhelm Busch der Pessimist: Sein Verhältnis zu Arthur Schopenhauer_. Francke Verlag, Bern und Munchen, 1962.

Flugge, Gerhard. _Wilhelm Busch_. Bibliographisches Institute, Leipzig, 1967.

Hofmiller, Joseph. _Von Dichter, Malern und Wirtschausern_. A. Langen, G. Müller, München, 1938.

Marxer, Peter. _Wilhelm Busch als Dichter_. Juris, Zurich, 1967.

Nöldecke, Herman, Adolfe und Otto. _Wilhelm Busch_. L. Joachim, Munchen, 1909.

Schweynert, Fritz (pseud. Peter Scher). _Die Dichter der Deutschen: Wilhelm Busch_. J. G. Cotta, Stuttgart, 1941.

Vanselow, Albert. _Die erstdrucke und erstausgaben der Werke von Wilhelm Busch: ein bibliographisches Verzeichnis_. A. Weige, 1913.

Volkman, O. F. _Wilhelm Busch, der Poet: Seine Motive und seine Quellen_. Leipzig, 1910.

Winther, Fritz. _Wilhelm Busch als Dichter, Kunstler, Psycholog und Philosoph_. The University of California Press, Berkeley, 1910.

# THE TIN-TIN SERIES: CHILDREN'S LITERATURE AND POPULAR APPEAL

John Rodenbeck

One of the continuing questions in a democracy is whether or not high artistic quality can ever be combined with genuine mass popularity. Tocqueville's answer more than a century ago was negative; and, "Pop Culture" notwithstanding, there seems little reason to question the fundamental soundness of his judgement now, when the vastly accelerated commercialization of American culture seems in fact to have made him more right than ever. If the outlook for a truly popular yet truly humanizing art in America is therefore rather gloomy in general, the outlook from the point of view of those who are interested in children's literature may be gloomier still in particular. Trapped in an imposed passivity our children constitute the largest and most uniform single audience in the country. It has become vitally important therefore, to try to find some model for children's literature that would hold out the possibility of surmounting the dilemma of art in a democracy. There may be such a model for us in Belgium.

Three years ago the world sales of a series of children's books published in nine languages passed beyond the twenty-five million mark. The author of this series, an anglophile Belgian artist in his sixties, has been called a genius; his work has been praised in Parliament, in a front-page article in The Times Literary Supplement, in Newsweek, The Sunday Times, The Daily Mail, Time and Tide, and The Listener, ample testimony to its impact within the English-speaking world. And yet this series is virtually unknown and virtually unobtainable in the United States.

Its hero is a boy of indeterminate age, always accompanied by a small white dog named Snowy in the English version and Milou in the original French; generally he is accompanied also by one Captain Haddock, a bumbling blackbearded sea-captain with an almost metaphysical gift for invective and a pronounced weakness for alcoholic drink. The boy-hero's name is Tintin: and in contrast not merely with Captain Haddock but with nearly all the adults who appear in his adventures, he is a miracle of cool-headed competence. But Tintin's numerous adult admirers (Henri Peyre, King Baudouin, André Malraux, Brigitte Bardot, and Madame Chiang Kai-Shek) have not been resentful of his moral superiority.

His occupation given as "journalist," Tintin began his fictional life in 1929. His "father" was Georges Rémi, an artist now much better known under the name of Hergé. At the age of sixty-four Georges Rémi has become admired, imitated and very rich. When Tintin's adventures began in the weekly supplement to a Brussels daily, however, the future Hergé was working in its process and photographic department. His real ambition, an ambition frustrated by the immediate success of his creation, was to be a painter. He attempted eventually to satisfy it in the middle nineteen-sixties when Tintin momentarily became too much for him. He now regards himself chiefly as a collector, much to the relief of his readers, who had seen his long-delayed and temporary desertion of the draughting board for the easel as a threat to the whole structure of French literature.

The fact that Tintin's adventures are narrated through strip cartoons in color is probably why they have had no success in the United States. The American parents who buy books for their children are likely to be the same parents who find the very idea of "color comic books" appalling, though they probably allow their children to watch the morally dubious and aesthetically vulgar animations on American television until their eyes pop out. The Golden Press, which tried unsuccessfully to introduce the Tintin series several years ago, apparently has no further plans for a second try. Certainly the failure of the series in the U. S. is a pity. As an anonymous front-page reviewer for The Times Literary Supplement remarked, "The real strength of Tintin is not so much that he exemplifies a sensible moral outlook as that the books are works of high quality and even beauty, put together with obvious enjoyment and brimming over with intelligence and life."[2] They are clearly worthy of serious critical consideration not merely as an international phenomenon but also as works of art.

The creator of Tintin has described the plot line of his adventures as "linear," episodic, adorned with as many gags (in, of course, the French sense) and as much suspense as possible. To take one example: The Red Sea Sharks, like all of Tintin's adventures, runs to precisely sixty-four pages including the title page. This length, one fascicle, is dictated by the economics of publishing but has the effect of imposing an almost Joycean "closed field," restricting the scope of each adventure to roughly predetermined limits. Each page is slightly larger than a sheet of typing paper, though considerably heavier, and usually holds four strips of three color frames. The last frame on each page provides either a gag or a point of suspension to the onward movement of the story, while the first frame on each page provides what we might call relief. A succession of pages thus creates a kind of emotional oscillation, rather as if one were riding an aesthetic roller coaster. And one suspects that it is in large part this roller-coaster effect that endears the adventures to children. The plot line meanwhile serves merely to provide opportunities for this effect and to spread it over the largest possible background of land- and seascape, in Europe, Africa, Asia, or the Americas.

The Red Sea Sharks begins with Tintin and Captain Haddock encountering an old acquaintance, who reappears thereafter in only one frame. This encounter leads them on, however, into investigating the machinations of an international armaments combine apparently controlled by a mysterious American named Dawson. From Europe their investigation takes them next to a fictitious country in the Middle East, where another old acquaintance has just been overthrown as ruler with weapons supplied by the combine. They are nearly killed several times, but eventually find themselves on a raft in the middle of the Red Sea, having in the meantime picked up an airplane pilot who has deserted from the criminals. By chance they meet a pleasure-cruising yacht, which turns out to be owned by one Rastapopoulos, the real master mind behind the combine. Rastapopoulos rescues and entertains them, then hands them over unsuspecting to the crew of the Ramona, another ship in the combine's fleet who plan to kill Tintin, Captain Haddock, and the pilot but instead simply abandon them when the Ramona catches fire. Finally, now in control of the burning ship, the castaways put out the fire, release a cargo of intended slaves, and are attacked by one of the combine's submarines, only to be rescued at the last moment by the U. S. Navy. Meanwhile the ingenious Rastapopoulos escapes again to fight another day.

A plot like this one finds its best analogy in the plot of a good opera, the function of which is to provide what Gian-Carlo Menotti has called meditative moments, occasions for the effective singing of arias. And like the plot of a good opera, it has minor moral significance. The real moral vision of the Tintin series resides instead almost wholly in the self-respecting character of Tintin himself and in the moral judgments the reader is invited to make, from Tintin's point of view, upon each of the characters he meets. We encounter, not only the bad and the good among these characters but also the bumbling, the stupid, the greedy, the naive, the misled, the silly, the innocent—a wide variety of human types.

The striking visual beauty of the Tintin books can be exemplified by a page from another adventure, The Crab with the Golden Claws. On page twelve Tintin and Captain Haddock, in trouble at sea again, float on an overturned life boat, while a small airplane makes strafing runs at them. Suddenly the next page is devoted to a single picture, rather than to the usual four strips of small frames: from a vantage point deliberately placed level with the rolling surface of the sea, as if to make one share the sensation of a castaway, the reader sees the plane about to sweep almost directly over his own head, while in the background Tintin and Captain Haddock sit on their overturned boat, looking dismayed. The sky is pastel blue, the sea is green with white flecks and crests, the plane is ochre against the sky where the sun strikes its edges, shadowy beneath, and its engine housing is actually rounded (incredibly enough in an age of publishing short-cuts) by subtle gradations of color from pearl to dark gray. The dramatic composition of this picture is faultlessly effective and the extra-ordinary care devoted to printing the color values is worthy of an art book. One suspects, in fact, that though the picture works very well to enhance the drama of the story, it represents really an act of creative gusto on the part of the author and his staff.

Such meticulousness and gusto constitute the endearing aesthetic overplus of the Tintin books, an overplus that admirers of Tintin delight to discover exemplified in small features: the wonderful imitations of medieval manuscripts and the clever use of the Cyrillic alphabet in The Scepter of King Ottakar; the attempt to spell out "Tintin" and "Haddock" in Arabic on a poster in the background of one frame in The Red Sea Sharks; the brilliant green cloth and the decorative nails in the background of another full-page picture in The Crab with the Golden Claws; the subtle distinctions in drawing made between the shapes of the Andes and the Himalayas; the absolutely authentic motor cars that roar and put-put through all the adventures; the mere arrangement of frames by size and colors upon a page.

One always returns, however, to the character of Tintin as the greatest source of the books' appeal. To a child Tintin (who cannot be more than fourteen) must naturally stand for what he himself would like to be. One notices for example that Tintin is absolutely and almost mysteriously autonomous. He lives alone in his own simple flat. There is no hint of anything parental in his relationship with Captain Haddock, who in fact seems much more childish than Tintin. Furthermore there is only one woman of any importance in all the Tintin adventures, Bianca Castafiore, an aging opera-singer who, though plenteously bosomed, offers not the remotest suggestion of a mother surrogate. In a couple of instances Tintin establishes friendly relations with other boys, a Peruvian and a Chinese, but one notices that they are in many ways essentially reflections of Tintin himself. Tintin seems to realize, in other words, the wish for total and perfect self-sufficiency.

Tintin is always treated by adults as an adult, whether they wish to do him harm or good. He is taken seriously and without any condescension by everyone he meets. Though he is often threatened and sometimes feels ridiculous, he is never humiliated and never reduced in his independence. Though the world he lives in is an adult world, he understands and navigates within it much better than any of his elders. Identifying himself with Tintin, the young reader must therefore feel the unusual satisfaction of finding that here the situations that prevail within his prolonged babyhood are not merely altered but reversed, though it should also be pointed out that Tintin is never in the position of becoming anything like a quasi-parental tyrant. The independence of others is respected just as much as his own, even though Tintin stands over all, made superior to them not merely by his greater resourcefulness and energy for good but also by his knowledge and intelligence. He is after all, we are continually reminded, just a boy, smaller and weaker physically than any of his foes, and therefore he must depend on brains instead of brawn.

One would guess, in fact, that it is specifically the disparity of Tintin's physical smallness and mental largeness in relation to the adult world that accounts in considerable part for his appeal to children: he satisfies them as a simultaneous reflection of both childhood reality and childhood dream, which the author keeps always securely balanced against each other, allowing neither reflected element to predominate. Balance is the secret of Tintin's morality, a balance that can be seen as resting upon the creative intelligence so much admired by the critic of the Times Literary Supplement, an intelligence that led Olivier Todd to title his Listener article on Tintin "Tintin, Milou, and European Humanism" and to claim that the Tintin adventures are a supreme example of "the best aspects of European humanism, measure, equilibrium, a taste for justice, generosity, and an unmaudlin liking for human beings."[3]

The world of Tintin offers satisfactions to the most sophisticated adult. A world utterly without the imposed, philosophically naive design of absolute cause and effect, it is subjected to no general thematic conceptualization and therefore remains very real as well as morally humanistic. The headlong series of loosely related incidents that I have summarized from The Red Sea Sharks, for example, is adorned not only with gags (again, in the French sense) but with accidents and reminiscences, (as, I take it, is life itself), which the linear narrative and oscillating aesthetic effects make no attempt to define for us as a "lesson for a child." The world of Tintin thus reaches out of the epistemological innocence of children to touch something highly adult and highly sophisticated in the best sense of those words. In contrast with this world, the worlds offered to us by the novels that grown-ups customarily read have continued to be made up for a hundred years out of essentially nineteenth-century ideal solipsistic structures masquerading as reality. Only in the last two or three decades has the novel been able consciously to break out of its nineteenth-century epistemological molds and get back to something like the episodic vigor and the artistic freshness of, say, a Henry Fielding. It has done so, sometimes at the expense, unfortunately, of its own traditional humanism, by returning deliberately to the great literary tradition that Fielding saw his work as belonging to, and to which the Tintin books quite equally belong. This is the tradition not of the "story" but of the "tale." It includes the Odyssey, the Satyricon, the Golden Ass, A Thousand and One Nights, Tom Jones, Moby Dick, the Arthur Gordon Pym of Poe, as well as the tales of Isak Dinesen. It would be pleasant to think that American children could be as easily introduced as their European cousins are to this humanizing tradition, as well as to a little realism, a little "sensible morality," and a great deal of visual beauty.

---

[1] Reported in Newsweek, (February 22, 1970) p.

[2] "The Epic Strip: Tintin Crosses the Channel," TLS, (December 5, 1958), p. 698.

[3] The Listener, (October 3, 1957), p. 513.

# PHILOSOPHY AND FANTASY

Laurence Gagnon

As the snows of mid-December had all but buried any hope of prolonged activity, the Rat and the Mole had taken to sitting by the fireplace during the short winter days, sometimes quietly smoking or drinking tea but mostly just dozing. Occasionally a trickle of ideas could be discerned flowing from their frozen streams of consciousness—evidently the result of some momentary mental thaw. It was during such brief periods as these that they turned to philosophy, for the discussion of philosophical issues always had a therapeutic use for them, namely, as a sedative.

The Rat: But I do think that philosophy and fantasy have something in common.

The Mole: Well, certainly philosophy tends to be fantastic, for many philosophers make bizarre and even preposterous claims—"foolosophers," Erasmus called them. Then again, many fantasies are philosophical, that is, they can be construed as having something important to say about "man and the world" which is not a matter of scientific law or theory. But regardless of which way one were to take your claim, Ratty, it would be misleading for you to suggest that philosophy and fantasy share a particular property in the way different red things may be said to share the same property.

The Rat: Blinking How in the world did you arrive at those conclusions from what I said?

The Mole: Nonchalantly By a process of inference.

The Rat: Hmm . . . Look, Mole, I know that you believe you understand what you think I said, but I'm not quite sure you realize that what you heard wasn't all of what I meant to say. Let me explain . . . Sometimes philosophers are daring enough to employ a certain type of conceptual technique which is, as a matter of fact, commonly used by writers of fantasy. This kind of conceptual procedure is simply the fabrication of an imaginary world that is logically possible but, as far as we know, not physically possible.

The Mole: In other words . . .

The Rat: In other words, a description of the "essential" features of such a hypothetical world would include some statements about certain creatures, entities, events, or states of affairs which, while not logically self-contradictory, would, nevertheless, be contrary to some set of scientific laws, if the statements in the description were taken literally as making assertions.

The Mole: For instance . . .

| | |
|---|---|
| The Rat: | Well, for example, suppose we began to describe the essential features of the hobbit-world in J. R. R. Tolkien's trilogy, The Lord of the Rings. No doubt we would disagree over what we would consider to be a "complete" list of the necessary features of that imaginary world... |
| The Mole: | No doubt. |
| The Rat: | But we probably could agree on some points. In particular, if we were to describe that world to someone who had not read the trilogy, we would have to mention the imaginary age during which that world existed because, unlike some other fantasies, The Lord of the Rings is placed in a definite "historical" setting. We would also have to mention that men lived in that world. Now if we removed ourselves from the spirit of the fantasy for a moment and construed the sentence, 'Some men lived during the Third Age of Middle-earth', as an assertion of some fact, then we could see, first of all, that we could make such an assertion without contradicting ourselves and, secondly, that in making it, we would be saying something contrary to certain laws of paleontology, anthropology, and archaeology. According to such sciences, all members of the species Homo sapiens have lived at some time during the Cenozoic era. But the Third Age of Middle-earth did not occur during the Cenozoic era or, for that matter, during any other era. |
| The Mole: | I see . . . But you said that some philosophers have used this conceptual technique. How are you going to prove that, Ratty? |
| The Rat: | Why should I try to prove it? Why should I attempt to give a deductive argument for my thesis in order to convince you that what I say is true? |
| The Mole: | Oh, I don't know really. It just seemed to be the natural thing to ask, since you are playing the philosopher. |
| The Rat: | Hmm . . . Anyway, I don't see how I could prove it, if I wanted to. About all I can do is show you that some philosophers occasionally employ at least a portion of the same procedure that any creator of fantasy must use. |
| The Mole: | Wait a second! You're going a bit fast for me. To begin with, do you mean to say that if a particular work is a fantasy then it is about an imaginary world which is logically possible but not physically possible? |
| The Rat: | Yes, for I wouldn't call a piece of writing a fantasy, if it were not about that kind of possible world. |
| The Mole: | I see . . . Well, then how are you using 'fantasy'? How do you define it? |

The Rat: I am using 'fantasy' in a very general way such that some writings called 'fairy-tales', some labeled 'science-fiction', and, perhaps, some designated 'dream-stories' will fall under the concept of fantasy. Of course, you could make as many subdivisions under this general heading as you think are required for the purposes of literary criticism.

But I see no advantage in attempting to define 'fantasy' just for the sake of clarity of meaning, even supposing that it would be possible to capture all of its slithery features in a net of words. For of what use would a definition be to you, if you were not also given some kind of procedure for applying or not applying the defined expression? So what is important is not my telling you what I think 'fantasy' is synonymous with, but rather, how I think you can go about applying 'fantasy' to this or that case.

The Mole: Stretching So what application-procedure do you envision for 'fantasy'?

The Rat: I know that two conditions are necessary for calling something 'a fantasy', and I think that the two conditions I am going to mention are also jointly sufficient conditions.

The first is the special type of imaginary world we have already talked about. Now concerning this condition, we should note that in almost every fantasy there is, so to speak, a blending of what is physically impossible with what is physically possible; where you find fire-breathing dragons, you almost invariably find a few rather ordinary men.

Furthermore, the fantasy-world as such cannot be distinguished from other types of imaginary worlds on the basis of features which are physically possible but, perhaps, not actual in that world. The differences which separate the England of The Once and Future King from that of Lady Chatterley's Lover are not to be found in such things as this: that while air and water pollution were only a possibility in the former, they were an actuality in the latter. The differences are more radical than that. They are largely the result of the fact that magic has a place in the world depicted by T. H. White, while it has none at all in that described by D. H. Lawrence. Do you catch my meaning?

The Mole: Yawning Like a cold. But what about the second conditon?

The Rat: Well, the second condition is that there be some explicit rendering of the personality of at least one of the characters in the tale. For it would be hard to imagine a fantasy in which we were given no information about any of the characters' behavioral, conceptual, or emotional patterns or tendencies. In addition, I maintain that any story might justifiably be called 'a fantasy' which gives us some explicit indication of the personality of one or more of the characters and which is also about a world that is conceivable but physically impossible.

| The Mole: | Therefore, something counts as a fantasy if and only if it satisfies your two requirements? |
|---|---|
| The Rat: | Yes. _Sigh_ |
| The Mole: | Good, that clarifies things a bit. But let's return to this supposed connection between philosophy and fantasy. What do you make of the case of a philosopher who makes use of the particular kind of possible world you have been describing and who also goes to the trouble of developing the personality of some of the characters in that world? Is he doing philosophy or creating a fantasy? |
| The Rat: | You needn't make the distinction into such a dichotomy, Mole. After all, the man may be doing both at the same time. According to my criterion, he is certainly creating a fantasy. His work, considered as a fantasy, is subject to the strictures of literary criticism. His style has committed him to that much. If, for example, his work fails to enchant its readers, it cannot be considered a good fantasy; for, as Tolkien rightly remarks, a fantasy should be enchanting. _Changing position in his chair._<br><br>Now he may also be doing philosophy. If he is fabricating a fantasy-world in order to make certain philosophical points or if we have good reasons for supposing that he is, then part of what he communicates to us through his work will be subject to philosophical scrutiny. His purposes or the purposes we justifiably suspect him to have will leave him and his work open even to this onslaught. In some of his philosophical essays, O. K. Bouwsma attempts to create such a philosophical fantasy. |
| The Mole: | _Shaking his head to keep awake_ Huh? Oh, yes! Ah . . . Ratty, would you be a little more specific. How about giving me a few examples of a philosopher who has used the device of imagining a fantasy-world in order to make a philosophical point? |
| The Rat: | Now don't get impatient, Mole. I could mention Plato's _Republic_ as an example. Remember the ring of Gyges, the ring which, when turned a certain way, made the wearer invisible? |
| The Mole: | Yes, vaguely. |
| The Rat: | Well, Glaucon used the idea of such an imaginary ring in his futile attempt to show Socrates that a man will be unjust, whenever he thinks he can "get away with it." |
| The Mole: | Now I remember. But I was hoping that you would give me a more recent example. |

| | |
|---|---|
| The Rat: | All right, in <u>An Essay Concerning Human Understanding,</u> in the section where John Locke is exclaiming how wonderfully suited to our needs are the faculties we possess for "discovering the qualities and powers of substances," he imagines a man who sees things a hundred thousand times more acutely than you could, if you were looking through the most powerful microscope made. Locke argues that such a man would not be able to communicate with other men concerning visible objects and properties, since his visual experiences would be so utterly different from everyone else's. |
| The Mole: | <u>Yawning</u> Excuse me, Ratty. Then in the third part of David Hume's <u>Dialogues Concerning Natural Religion,</u> there is Cleanthes' rather humorous use of a world in which books reproduce sexually. Something or other was supposed to be proven by it, but I've forgotten. Anyway . . . <u>Suppressing a yawn</u> . . . It must be getting late! Anyway, I'd like an example of a contemporary philosopher who takes fantasy-worlds seriously. |
| The Rat: | Fair enough. Let's see, besides O. K. Bouwsma, there is P. F. Strawson. In the second chapter of <u>Individuals</u>, Strawson constructs a No-Space world in which there are conscious beings whose only sensory experiences are auditory. |
| The Mole: | Sort of like the one-dimensional world that Mister Square dreams he visits in E. A. Abbott's <u>Flatland</u>, isn't it? Auditory sensations were the primary sensory experiences of the inhabitants of Lineland, as I remember. |
| The Rat: | That's right. But Strawson's objective is not the elucidation of certain geometrical concepts. Instead it is the determination of the kinds and amount of sensory experiences that are needed by conscious beings in order for them to be able to recognize a particular item in their experience as something they have encountered before. |
| The Mole: | <u>Fighting to keep his eyes open</u> In general what do you think are the <u>advatages of employing fantasy-worlds in philosophical</u> and literary pursuits? |
| The Rat: | Hmm . . . I think that you'll realize what the advantages are, when you consider the various motivations for using fantasy-worlds as conceptual tools. <u>First of all, through the construction of</u> such worlds and the elaboration of <u>their histories, one can reinterpret the concepts we ordinarily employ in organizing</u> our manifold experiences. In C. S. Lewis' <u>Out of the Silent Planet</u>, our ordinary notion of space is given a radical reinterpretation, although this is by no means the main point of the story. |
| | <u>Secondly, fantasy-worlds can serve as</u> a means whereby we can <u>ascertain what structural or functional analogies there are</u> between <u>different parts of our experience or between our experience as a conceptually organized whole and some part of it.</u> These are the types of things that Strawson especially looks for in his No-Space world. |

Then again, such worlds can be utilized in testing the tensile strength of concepts, so to speak. In other words, in such worlds we are allowed to see just how far it is possible to break down the connections between various concepts or between certain concepts and types of experiences without completely destroying the chosen concepts. The fantasy-world in Lewis Carroll's Alice in Wonderland is constructed for at least this purpose.[1]  Mole, wake up!

The Mole:    Waz-zu-ween . . . vy Dozes

Realizing that the discussion had achieved its end, the Rat placed a quilt over the Mole and, securely wrapping himself up in another, proceeded to dream about one-dimensional creatures whose eyes were like microscopes and who were imagining a strange world in which rats and moles conversed about philosophy and fantasy. A half-burnt log in the fireplace hissed quietly, as if to express its relief.

--------

[1] Donald Rackin, "Alice's Journey to the End of Night," PMLA (October, 1966), pp. 313-326.

# DEATH IN CHILDREN'S LITERATURE[*]

Francelia Butler

C. S. Lewis, whose "Narnia" fantasies for children are one expression of his religious philosophy, observed that "a children's story is the best art form for something you have to say."[1] Like a parable—or sometimes, an epitaph—the limpid simplicity of the form makes it easier to see into the depths, even of death.

Once upon a time, children and adults shared the same literature and together understood what there was to be understood about death. That time was from the beginning of literature up until the end of the seventeenth century, when a separation began to take place between the literature of adults and that of children. From then on, the treatment of death became part of a larger problem—the commercial and psychological exploitation of children through a special literature aimed at them alone.

Indications are that the separation might have begun with the "Warnings to Apprentices," published by commercial interests in the seventeenth century. These bear a striking resemblance to the warnings to little children, the "death-bed confessions" of children who disobeyed moral "laws" and reformed too late. Numerous books of these confessions were published in England and America by the Puritan merchant class in the late seventeenth and eighteenth centuries. These deathbed confessions and other dire warnings to children were continued in the hundreds of Sunday School tracts which grew out of the Sunday School movement begun by Robert Raikes. Raikes, a wealthy shipowner, acknowledged that he began the Sunday Schools to keep working children from depredations on Sundays.[2] These tracts distorted goodness itself by getting children to do the right things for the wrong reasons. Raikes' family ties with John Newbery, who is considered to be the "father" of children's literature, could be one indication that the establishment of children's literature as a separate field had an economic basis.

As a result of the separation, so little good literature for children has been produced that the whole field is not even considered worthy of investigation by most departments of the Humanities.[3] This neglect by scholars has resulted in a lack of respected criticism and has led to an indiscriminate lumping of all books for children, classical and commercial, into the category, "children's literature." There is no clear demarcation, as there is in adult literature, between books of real literary merit and books which were designed to sell or those which were written for propaganda purposes. The few great books written primarily for children have been mostly by writers with such deep emotional

---

* An address at the Thirtieth Annual Session, The English Institute, Columbia University, September 9, 1971.

problems that they have been afraid to express themselves openly to their peers and hence have written simply and honestly to children as their equals.[4]

Before the seventeenth century, children learned about death in literature shared with adults. They heard Bible stories, fables, legends, ballads, folk tales, or folk plays or read them themselves. Death could be seen in proper perspective because in this literature all the convictions, fears, and hopes of people about many things were gathered up and transmitted.

For the most part, this literature encouraged hope for life after death in some form. Stith Thompson's Motif-Index of Folk Literature abounds with references to restoration to life, either by magical reassemblage of the body's dispersed members, or by administration of the water of life, or by medicines, or in various other ways. Men may come back as women or women as men. People may become children, dwarves, monsters, princes or princesses, stars or angels or gods. They can return to earth as fish, horses' heads, donkeys, cows, bulls, oxen, calves, buffalo, swine, wild boar, goats, cats, dogs, lions, wolves, rabbits, foxes, deer, seals, bears, hyenas, jackals, elephants, monkeys, rats, otters, ducks, owls, hawks, eagles, swallows, cuckoos, doves, pigeons, ravens, quails, partridges, herons, cranes, geese, peacocks, parrots, snakes, lizards, crocodiles, tortoises, or frogs. Or they may come back as bees, butterflies, fleas, weevils, bedbugs, salmon, goldfish, sharks, whales, leeches, scorpions, crabs. Again, they may turn into trees, roses, lilies, lotus, grass, straw, herbs, bramble-bushes, tobacco plants, peanut plants, eggplants, musical instruments, dishes, fountains, balls, wind, stones, salt, smoke, rainbows, minerals, meteors, hills, flour vats, hoes, hoe-handles, mussels, or currants. Or, after a variety of transformations, they may return to their original human form.[5] In any case, the possibility of coming back as an eggplant or a fish, for instance, should sharpen one's interest in ecology. The hopeful note in folk literature is that people do tend to come back.

In North American Indian tales, as Jaime de Angulo's beautiful crystallization suggests,[6] life and death are closely related, are at times interchangeable states.[6] However, in some American Indian tales, people stay dead:

> Nearly all North American Indian tribes offer some explanation of the origin of death. The most widespread tale is that of an early controversy between two characters, either animal or human. One character wants people to die and be revived, the other wants death to be permanent. The second character wins the controversy. Often, a little later, a close relative of his, such as the son, dies and the parent wishes the decision reversed. His opponent reminds him, however, that he himself has already decided the matter.[7]

A similar matter-of-fact acceptance of death is occasionally found in European folktales, as in Grimm's story, "The Death of Partlet," a story left out of most Grimm collections. As the story ends in Grimm,

Chanticleer was left alone with his dead Partlet. He dug
her a grave and laid her in it, and raised a mound over it, and
there he sat and mourned her till he died too. So they were
all dead.[8]

Children themselves seem to begin with this same simple acceptance of death.
In the still very active oral tradition, in the skip-rope rhymes jumped by children
from the age of six on, and chanted much earlier, children treat death quite matter-of-factly:

> Little Miss Pink
> Dressed in blue
> Died last night
> At quarter past two
> Before she died
> She told me this:
> When I jump rope
> I always—miss. [9]

By writing the American Field Service, which solicited the rhymes from foreign
lycées, and also through writing foreign embassies in Washington, I have made
a collection of these rhymes. One contributed by the New Zealand Embassy goes:

> There was an old woman and her name was Pat,
> And when she died, she died like that,
> They put her in a coffin,
> And she fell through the bottom,
> Just like that.[10]

Restoration to life is the general rule in children's play, however. "Bang bang,
you're dead!" is only a figure of speech.

One of the many stories of restoration to life in the Grimm collection is the
famous "Juniper Tree" story. In this story, a little boy who has been murdered
by his jealous stepmother and made into a tasty stew for his father, comes back
as a bird to reward his loving father and little sister and to drop a millstone on
his stepmother's head. As a bird, he sings about what has happened to him:

> My mother made a stew of me,
> My father ate it all.
> My little sister wept to see
> Marlene, my sister small,
> Then gathered my bones in her silken shawl,
> And laid them under the Juniper tree.
> Sing, hey! What a beautiful bird am I.[11]

After the stepmother's death, the bird becomes a little boy again and rejoins his family. When the stepmother dies, however, she dies for good; for the wicked, death often provides irreversible retribution. It brings death or rigidity, turns one to a statue or a stone.

Andrew Lang's Fairy Books of various colors date back to the nineteenth century, but they have always been loved by children and furnish an excellent cross section of the folk tales from all parts of the world. In these volumes, there are at least a dozen stories of special interest which relate to death. In The Orange Fairy Book, there is a story from India entitled, "The King Who Would See Paradise."[12] The theme here seems to be that though Paradise may be one's lot eventually, one should not hasten the process, but prepare for the end by performing as perfectly as possible one's duties while on earth. The Pink Fairy Book contains a Spanish story which should comfort the women's liberationists who deplore the beautiful Cinderellas in fairy tales who always marry aristocracy and money. In "The Water of Life," a sister, wiser and more courageous than her brothers, fetches the magic water and restores not only her brothers, but "a great company of youths and girls" who have been put under an evil spell and turned to stones.[13] Another folk tale which should delight women's liberationists appears in The Brown Fairy Book. In this story, purportedly from ancient Egypt, a brave and clever princess overcomes three fated terminations of her lover's life. "My wife," the lover says, "has been stronger than my fate."[14] The Red Fairy Book contains a Rumanian story which attempts to explain death. People feel impelled to follow a mysterious Voice and are never seen again. When the source of the Voice is finally located, it turns out to be nothing but a vast plain. After that, people don't bother to follow the Voice anymore, but simply die at home.[15] The Crimson Fairy Book has a more cheerful story—one of a prince who seeks immortality and gets it. In this Hungarian tale, the Queen of the Immortals and Death himself fight over a youth. The Queen wins.[16] The Yellow Fairy Book has a North American Indian story which combines elements similar to those in the story of Pygmalion, and the Orpheus and Eurydice legend. When an Indian's wife dies, he makes a wooden doll just like her and dresses it in her clothes. The doll comes to life, but the husband is under a prohibition not to touch her until they have returned to their own village. He can't wait and she becomes a doll again.[17] In The Violet Fairy Book are two Swahili stories in which animals, in one a gazelle and in the other, a snake, sacrifice their lives so that human beings may live.[18] The Lilac Fairy Book contains another Swahili tale—this one about a clever monkey who professes to keep his heart in a safe place at home, when he travels. This idea of an external heart or soul is not infrequent in folk tales. It is a means of safeguarding one's immortality by keeping it stashed away—not putting all one's organs in one's body, so to speak. The other tale has to do with a fish who achieves immortality. A tree arises from his buried bones. This tale is unusual because, even in Christ's use of them in the New Testament, fish are expendable . . . one of the innocuous animals that ends up as food for people and the act of killing fish is blotted out, some way.[19]

Though there are a variety of approaches to the subject of death in these stories, all in all the approach is not morbid. Generally in folk tales, the magic potion which conquers death is love. One sees this in the German folk tale, "Briar Rose," or essentially the same, the French story, "The Sleeping Beauty." As G. K. Chesterton observes in his essay, "The Ethics of Elfland,"

> There is the terrible allegory of "The Sleeping Beauty,"
> which tells how the human creature was blessed with all
> birthday gifts, yet cursed with death; and how death also may
> perhaps be softened to a sleep. [20]

Nor does this death-conquering love have to be sexual. Stravinsky's ballet, "The Firebird," has acquainted many westerners with the Russian folk tale of "Prince Ivan, the Firebird, and the Gray Wolf." Murdered by his evil brothers, "Prince Ivan lay dead on that spot exactly thirty days; then the gray wolf came upon him and knew him by his odor:

> Then the gray wolf sprinkled Prince Ivan with the water of
> death, and his body grew together; he sprinkled him with the
> water of life, and Prince Ivan stood up and said: "Ah, I have
> slept very long!" [21]

In the legends enjoyed by children, the hero has power, even over death. In the Norse legend of "Thor's Unlucky Journey," Thor is challenged to a wrestling match with Utgard-Loki's old nurse, Eli, who, unbeknownst to him, is Old Age or Death: "It was a marvel," said Utgard-Loki, "That you withstood so long and bent only one knee." [22]

In Caxton's version of Le Morte d'Arthur, from which many children's versions, including Lanier's Boy's King Arthur, stem, Arthur commands Sir Bedivere to throw Arthur's sword, Excalibur, into the water. Bedivere throws the sword far out, and sees an arm and hand reach above the water, take the sword, brandish it three times and vanish. Then Sir Bedivere takes the dying King on his back and carries him to the waterside. Here a barge is drawn up, with many fair ladies in it, all of them wearing black hoods. At the King's command, Bedivere puts him on the barge, and the barge moves away:

> Than sir Bedwere cryed and seyde,
> "A, my lorde Arthur, what shall becom of me, now ye go frome
> me and leve my here alone amonge myne enemyes?"
> "Comforte thyselff," seyde the kynge, "and do as well as thou
> mayste, for in me ys no truste for to truste in. For I muste
> into the vale of Avylyon to hele me of my grevous wounde.
> And if thou here nevermore of me, pray for my soule!" [23]

Roland, in all versions of the Charlemagne cycle, blows a note of defiance in the face of death. Here is a version for children:

> Count Roland's mouth was filled with blood. His brain

had burst from his temples. He blew his horn in pain and anguish. Charles heard it, and so did his Frenchmen. Said the King:

"That bugle carries far!"
Duke Naimes replied:
"'Tis that a hero blows the blast!" [24]

When The Cid dies, in a current children's version of this Spanish legend, the embalmed body of The Cid leads a victorious charge against the enemy:

It was The Cid himself who led the charge, mounted upon Babieca, his sword Tizone gleaming by his side! This was too much for Yusuf and too much for his army. The legends were all true! This Cid was really a demon from hell! Here he was, raised from the dead, charging relentlessly down on them! [25]

Best known of the many retellings of the Robin Hood story for children is probably that of Howard Pyle. Here, too, Robin Hood seems to be in control, even of his death:

His old strength seemed to come back to him, and, drawing the bowstring to his ear, he sped the arrow out of the open casement. As the shaft flew, his hand sank slowly with the bow till it lay across his knees, and his body likewise sank back again into Little John's loving arms; but something had sped from that body, even as the winged arrow sped from the bow.[26]

Universally, in folk plays, which are shared both by children and adults, there is an element of wonder, of fantasy, in the ritual death so often portrayed and inevitably followed by restoration to an even more vigorous life.[27] Fertility symbol or whatever it may be, this death and resurrection is accepted both by audience and the players—and these plays continue in some sections of the world.[28] In the mummers' play of St. George, for instance, St. George may kill the Turkish Knight (there are many versions of the play), but then the Doctor invariably enters with a special medicine:

It will bring the dead to life again.
A drop on his head, a drop on his heart.
Rise up, bold fellow, and take thy part. [29]

Also, in the Punch and Judy shows, which in their present form probably date to the eighteenth century but which may date back to the fertility rituals in Greek and Roman mimes, Punch literally triumphs over Death, or the Devil.[30]

One finds in folk drama the concept of life as a journey towards death, a journey in which children and adults move on together, the morality, "Everyman," being the notable example of this theme. In such plays, the traveler is guided by the various tenets of his faith, his deeds being the mileposts of his progress. Thus, he takes the same path as he takes later in Bunyan's Pilgrim's Progress, particularly in the second half. Here Christiana, with her four small sons, James, Joseph, Samuel, and Matthew, pass through worldly experience such as a good "supper," story telling, games, music and dancing, marriage, and even sightseeing in a heavenly museum until they reach the gates of the Celestial City, where Christiana goes on before. Several versions of this book were published for children in the eighteenth and nineteenth centuries as well as adaptations.[31]

The strong dramatic element in life as a journey is found in many folk tales, including those among Indians in the Middle American area, where "The underlying theme is that the soul on its way to the afterworld is confronted by dangers and difficulties which must be overcome."[32] Some of these, such as going between clashing rocks or over a body of water, are reminiscent of the Greek or Roman epics. The idea of life as a journey toward death peeps through most notably, perhaps, in children's literature in the nineteenth century in Louisa May Alcott's Little Women, where Meg, Jo, Amy, and Beth (who is about to die) go on a pilgrimage from cellar to attic—a more realistic journey than that in Bunyan—and later receive small copies of Pilgrim's Progress, in colored bindings, under their pillows as Christmas gifts.[33] Andersen's "Little Mermaid" also must make a journey from sea to land and undergo much suffering—must die that others may love—before she wins an immortal soul. Nor is it enough purgation for Tom, the chimney sweep in Charles Kingsley's The Water-Babies, to be brutally beaten by his Master and maltreated by everyone in contact with him. Even after he drowns and becomes a water-baby, he still must undergo a long Jungian journey and spiritual purification—must help someone he doesn't like (his old Master, Grimes).[34]

Besides folk tales and folk drama, another form of literature for children which has ancient roots is the fable. Though there is currently no satisfying popular edition, there are several bowdlerized editions of Aesop published by various companies every year. We know that Caxton's translation of Aesop was read both by children and adults, and John Locke repeatedly recommends Aesop for children.[35] Here the relation of all aspects of human experience is quite complete—including sexual experience—complete enough to make spicy reading for Playboy. (But this shouldn't bother us if we have seen the rhymes chanted today by children themselves and recorded in the seventy-fifth volume of the Journal of American Folklore.) To return to the subject, here is one of the "death" fables from Caxton's Aesop:

> Many one ben whiche haue grete worship and glorye/
> But noo prudence/ ne noo wysedom they haue in them whereof
> Esope reherceth suche a fable/ Of a wulf which found a dede
> mans hede/ the whiche he torned vp so doune with his foote/
> And sayd/ Ha a how fayr hast thow be and playsaunt/ And
> now thow hast in the neyther wytte/ ne beaute/ yet thow arte

withoute voys and withoute ony thought/ And therefore men
ought not only to behold the beaute and fayrenesse of the body/
but only the goodnes of the courage/ For somtyme men gyuen
glorye and worship to some/ whiche haue not deseruyd to
haue hit/. [36]

Alas, poor Shakespeare and Milton, who were limited to reading like this, instead of having the benefit of such current and expensive emptiness as Michael
Is Brave (a frightened little boy learns courage by showing a little girl how to go
down a slide), or any of the other hundreds of commercial books (we shan't call
them literature) by one-message tacticians in the Puritan tradition, who—no matter how they may try to sugar coat the message—talk down to children. Sir
Roger L'Estrange's Aesop, which came out two years after Locke had recommended
Aesop for children's reading, states specifically in the preface that it is designed
for children and has nothing unsuitable for childish ears.[37] Yet it is just as
explicit about all areas of human experience as is Caxton's.

A newly published book for little children, Life and Death, by Herbert Zim and
Sonia Bleeker, also is explicit, but the focus is on factual and scientific information:

> Long ago people had the idea that death was like a long
> sleep. Children think so too. This belief is far from the
> truth. A sleeping animal or a sleeping person is alive. He
> breathes, his hearts beats, he moves, dreams, and will react
> to a touch or a poke. Someone who is dead does none of these
> things.[38]

Later on, the book candidly tells the child:

> After burial a body, which is composed of nearly three-
> quarters water, soon changes. The soft tissues break down
> and disappear first. Within a year only bones are left. [39]

Such man-in-the-white-coat treatment lacks warmth and beauty and is certainly
not sufficient for initiating children to the subject of death. In many commercial
books for children now, there is a paucity of imagination, a lack of philosophical
reflection, something missing. Their spiritual nihilism is in itself a moral message in the Puritan tradition. Truth, these books imply, can only be determined
by scientific testing. Zim and Bleeker stand for no philosophical truth. Instead,
they indifferently display various beliefs on a kind of religious lazy Susan:
"There is no way," they say, "to know if these beliefs are true or not. They are
beyond our power to test or experiment." [40]

Too many current books for children on death tend to be slight or frighteningly
inhumane and impersonal. The inadequacy of these books as literature for children on the subject of death is commented on by Sheila R. Cole in a recent article
which appeared in The New York Times Book Review. Miss Cole summarizes her

observations as follows:

> All of these stories were written with a didactic purpose: to give a child a way of looking at death and living with the knowledge of it. All of them try to diffuse the finality and fearfulness by presenting death as just another natural process. But to most adults in our culture, death is more than just another natural process. It is an occasion surrounded with mystery and deep emotions. Presenting it to a child as just another change we go through is less than candid. Adults often present a prettier reality to children than actually exists. But to give easy answers to a child's questions about death is to deny reality and to diminish both life and death and, ultimately, to turn our children from our counsel.
> —"For Young Readers: Introducing Death" (September 26, 1971), p. 12.

In the nineteenth century, the neurotic writers of the classics for children expressed at least some honest emotion. Freud wasn't around yet, and they felt safe in exploding their problems—homosexuality or other—into childish rhymes and fantasies. Filled with guilt, these writers were constantly aware of death. In Lear's limericks, supposedly light rhymes designed both for children and adults, death is a leading topic, as Alison White has pointed out.[41] There was, for example, "The Old Man of Cape Horn, / Who wished he had never been born/ So he sat on a chair till he died of dispair." Professor White surmises (as Elizabeth Sewell suggested earlier in The Field of Nonsense) that "in his limericks Lear, like all of us, is trying to get used to death, to dull its sting."[42]

Perhaps Professor White's explanation will also serve for the grim death jokes which critics have noticed in Alice in Wonderland:

> "Well!" thought Alice to herself, "after such a fall as this, I shall think nothing of tumbling down stairs! How brave they'll all think me at home! Why, I wouldn't say anything about it, even if I fell off the top of the house!" (which was very likely true.)[43]

Children themselves have many grimly comic—"mini-dramas"—about death:

> Look, look, mama!
> What is that mess
> That looks like strawberry jam?
> Hush, hush, my child!
> It is papa
> Run over by a tram.

> Ushy gushy was a worm
> A little worm was he
> He crawled upon the railroad track
> The train he didn't see.
> Ushy gushy! [44]

Besides Lear and Carroll, two other writers of the nineteenth century who seem to have given vent to their emotional problems in their writings for children were J. M. Barrie and Oscar Wilde. In Fifty Works of English and American Literature We Could Do Without, a book published a few years ago, J. M. Barrie is accused of making Peter Pan the vehicle for his triple theme of incest, castration, and homosexuality.[45] Barrie is also criticized for his treatment of death in the play. Say the authors:

> It's not enough, however, for Barrie to betray children.
> He betrays art. He does it brilliantly. That superb piece of
> engineering (the engineering, however, of an instrument of
> torture), the scene where Peter Pan appeals to the children
> in the audience to keep Tinker Bell alive by clapping to signal
> their belief in fairies is a metaphor of artistic creation itself.
> . . . Peter Pan blackmails the children, cancels the willing-
> ness of the suspension of disbelief, and disrupts the conven-
> tion on which all art depends when he threatens to hold the
> children morally responsible for Tinker Bell's death unless by
> a real act—an act done in the auditorium, not on the stage—
> they assert their literal belief in what they know to be an
> artistic fiction.[46]

In Barrie's defense, one can say that he is asking the children to do what many fairy tales do—that is keep the protagonists alive through an act of love.

All five of Oscar Wilde's famous fairy tales for children have death as their theme. In the best known of the tales both "The Selfish Giant" and the little boy he loves die. The little boy is identified as Jesus. "The Happy Prince" (a statue) persuades a swallow to pluck the ruby from the Prince's sword, the sap-phires from the Prince's eyes, and the gold leaf from his body and give it to the poor in the city. By the time these acts of charity have been accomplished, it is too late for the swallow to fly South for the winter.

> "I am glad that you are going to Egypt at last, little
> Swallow," said the Prince, "you have stayed too long here;
> but you must kiss me on the lips, for I love you."
> "It is not to Egypt that I am going," said the Swallow.
> "I am going to the House of Death. Death is the brother of
> Sleep, is he not?"
> And he kissed the Happy Prince on the lips, and fell
> down dead at his feet.

113

At that moment a curious crack sounded inside the statue,
as if something had broken. The fact is that the leaden heart
had snapped right in two.[47]

The saddest of Wilde's stories is "The Nightingale and the Rose." A little nightingale sees a student weeping for a red rose. The student's girl has said she
would dance with him if he brought her such a rose. The nightingale seeks a
rose for the youth, and is told by a tree that the only way such a rose can be ob-
tained is for the nightingale to build it out of music and stain it with her own
heart's blood. The nightingale must sing to the tree all night, with her breast
against a thorn (an old English belief, by the way, as to how nightingales sing).
The thorn must pierce her heart, and her life-blood must flow into the tree.
"Death is a great price to pay for a red rose," cried the Nightingale:

> So the Nightingale pressed closer against the thorn, and
> the thorn touched her heart, and a fierce pang of pain shot
> through her. Bitter, bitter was the pain, and wilder and wilder
> grew her song, for she sang of the Love that is perfected by
> Death, of the Love that dies not in the tomb. . . .
> "Look, look!" cried the Tree, "the rose is finished now;"
> but the Nightingale made no answer, for she was lying dead
> in the long grass with the thorn in her heart.[48]

The Student finds the rose outside his window and presents it to the girl, but
she spurns it as the Chamberlain's nephew, meanwhile, has sent her some jew-
els. Disgusted, the Student throws the rose down in the street, and a cart-
wheel runs over it.

> "What a silly thing Love is," said the Student as he walked
> away. "It is not half as useful as Logic, for it does not prove
> anything, and it is always telling one of things that are not
> going to happen, and making one believe things that are not
> true. In fact, it is quite unpractical, and, as in this age to
> be practical is everything, I shall go back to Philosophy and
> study Metaphysics."
> So he returned to his room and pulled out a great dusty
> book, and began to read.[49]

Cynically, the Student throws away the emotional and picks up the scientific.
"The Devoted Friend" also has as a theme the unawareness of human beings of
the sacrifices of those who love them. Trusting little Hans gives his life for
his false friend, the Miller. Lastly, and grimly humorous, is "The Remarkable
Rocket," the story of an egocentric rocket who explodes into the sky with a
dreadful racket and then fizzles out. But nobody notices.
Even though these stories sound like dreams recounted on a psychoanalyst's
couch, they do have the ring of honesty, which can be tested by comparison with

the Puritan educational propaganda for children, in which death is a punishment for sin. Closely related in theme to the "Warnings to Apprentices" of the late seventeenth century, numerous deathbed confessions of young children stemmed from James Janeway's A Token for Children: Being an Exact Account of the Conversions, Holy and Exemplary Lives, and Joyful Deaths of Several Young Children (1671). These continued to be printed in small American towns during the eighteenth and nineteenth centuries. The Connecticut Historical Society in Hartford has a number of these little books[50] and several are listed in the A. S. W. Rosenbach catalog of Early American Children's Books.[51] Their reflection is seen in The New England Primer, many editions of which contained these verses:

> Tho' I am young yet I may die,
> And hasten to eternity:
> There is a dreadful fiery hell,
> Where wicked ones must always dwell.[52]

As if the poor American Indian children had not suffered enough, even they were subjected to these deathbed confessions, and in 1835, Triumphant Deaths of Pious Children was translated into Choctaw by Missionaries of the American Board of Commissioners for Foreign Missions.[53] What is more, these deathbed confessions of children merged imperceptibly with the nineteenth century Sunday School literature, so that we have, for instance, An Authentic Account of the Conversion, Experience, and Happy Deaths of Ten Boys, designed for Sunday Schools, and published in New Haven (1820).[54]

As mentioned before, one of the acknowledged purposes of the Sunday School literature was to keep working children off the streets on Sunday.[55] Here is a quotation from one of the early nineteenth century Sunday School booklets published for children by the American Tract Society in New York. Since I have not located it elsewhere, I am quoting from a copy in my own collection:

> Why should you say, 'tis yet too soon
>     To seek for heaven, and think of death?
> The flower will fade before 'tis noon,
>     And you this day may lose your breath.
>
> Then 'twill for ever be in vain
>     To cry for pardon and for grace;
> To wish you had your time again,
>     Or hope to see the Savior's face.[56]

This gloomy literature allied itself easily with the sentimental attitude toward death of the mid-nineteenth century, famous examples being Hans Christian Andersen's stories of "The Little Fir Tree," "The Steadfast Tin Soldier," and "The Little Match Girl." Then there is the death of Little Eva in Harriet Beecher Stowe's Uncle Tom's Cabin. Often, in the sentimental literature, the child does not die for his own sins but for the adultery of adults—his parents—and the trend here is found in adult literature as well, as in Mrs. Wood's East Lynne.[57] Always quick to penetrate hypocrisy, Mark Twain in Tom Sawyer has the boys, supposedly dead, return to witness their own funeral and to hear themselves eulogized as saints by those who hated their humanity while they were alive in the town:

> First one and then another pair of eyes followed the min-
> ister's, and then almost with one impulse the congregation
> rose and stared while the three dead boys came marching
> up the aisle, Tom in the lead, Jose next, and Huck, a ruin
> of drooping rags, sneaking sheepishly in the rear!  They had
> been hid in the unused gallery listening to their own funeral
> sermon!  (Tom Sawyer, Chapter 17)

Thus, the boys have the double satisfaction of getting back at their parents or parent-figures and, at the same time, of witnessing their own "death" and resurrection.

In our own time, one of the best known instances of death as a punishment for a mistake (or at least, death as closely associated with the mistake or sin) is that of the death of the good Thorin in Tolkien's Hobbit.  Thorin's greed for the great jewel, the Arkenstone, to which he feels rightly entitled, leads to a fight.  Though the quarrel is resolved, Thorin dies and the Arkenstone is buried with him.  Thus Thorin (and possibly the readers) learns the worthlessness of material things.

One of the most notable recent treatments of death in children's literature is that of E. B. White in Charlotte's Web.  White makes an interesting blend of fantasy and realism: when the little spider dies, she lives on through her 500 offspring, through the memory of the extraordinary web-writing she did above the stable door, and through the love of her friend, the pig Wilbur.  White is to be commended for facing a subject which most writers for children now avoid—though not all children are content, I find, with the prospect of a selective immortality for those with children or extraordinary ideas or (short-lived) friends.  Still, such lines as these have beauty, pathos, and above all, sincerity:

> Nobody, of the hundreds of people that had visited the Fair,
> knew that a grey spider had played the most important part
> of all.  No one was with her when she died.
> (Charlotte's Web, Chapter 21)

This same kind of immortality was treasured by Ben Jonson in 1603, who wrote a well-known elegy to his little boy who died of plague at the age of seven: "Here doth lie / Ben Jonson his best piece of poetry."  At the same time his "best piece of poetry" was all too mortal.  This and other elegies on children have been anthologized recently in Sister Mary Immaculate's book, The Cry of Rachel.[58]

For the fullest treatment of death in children's literature, we must return to the nineteenth century, to the fantasies of George MacDonald, most notably to

<u>At the Back of the North Wind</u> and <u>The Golden Key</u>. George MacDonald (1824-1905) was a Scottish preacher influenced by Paracelsus, Boehme, Swedenborg, Blake, Wordsworth, Novalis, and negatively, by Calvinism. He in turn exerted an influence on Lewis Carroll, Ruskin, C. S. Lewis, Charles Williams, and J. R. R. Tolkien. Since most of his family died of tuberculosis, including four of his own children, MacDonald (who also suffered from the disease) was understandably preoccupied with the subject of death.[59]

To some extent, his writings combine the various attitudes toward death, for they embody a simple acceptance of death and fear of death and the conviction finally that death is "more life." [60] He believed that child-like qualities are eternal; he believed that all life goes through a mystic evolution, each step of which on the way up is attended with sacrifice; and one is tempted to conclude from his fantasies that he believed that through love, faith, and the imagination one can create one's own Paradise and make it real.

Robert Lee Wolff, Professor of History at Harvard, has long been fascinated by MacDonald's writing, and has written a book on it published by Yale University Press. Professor Wolff compares MacDonald's views on death to those of Norman O. Brown in <u>Life against Death</u> (1959) and comments:

> Here in the sixth decade of the twentieth-century we find a classical and learned student of comparative mythology making all of George MacDonald's choices:  not intellect but pure emotion, not grown-ups but children, not people but animals, a bi-sexual God, and the eager welcoming of death as an essential part of life. [61]

Might a reader then ask the question E. R. Eddison asks in the introduction to his fantasy for adults, <u>A Fish Dinner in Memison</u>:

> But to the mind developed on the lines of the Mahometan fanatic's, the Thug's, the Christian martyr's, is it not conceivable that (short, perhaps of acute physical torture) the 'slings and arrows of outrageous fortune' should be no more painful than the imagined ills of a tragic drama, and could be experienced and appraised with a like detachment? [62]

At any rate, so death is treated in MacDonald's <u>At the Back of the North Wind</u>. Diamond, a poor, Christ-like child, makes friends with the North Wind, a mother figure (as the wind is, one remembers, in some nature tales for children such as those of Thornton Burgess). She is all of life, including death. Shortly before Diamond dies, North Wind tells him:

> "People call me by dreadful names, and think they know all about me. But they don't. Sometimes they call me Bad Fortune, sometimes evil chance, sometimes Ruin; and they have another name for me which they think the most dreadful of all."

"What is that?" asked Diamond, smiling up in her face.

"I won't tell you that name. Do you remember having to go through me to get into the country at my back?"

"Oh yes, I do. How cold you were, North Wind! and so white, all but your lovely eyes! My heart grew like a lump of ice, and then I forgot for a while."

"You were very near knowing what they call me then."

(At the Back of the North Wind, Chapter 36)

But one must be careful not to be too explicit about meanings in MacDonald's fantasies about death. He is not like Whitman, who flatly states that "to die is different from what any one supposed, and luckier." [63] Rather, his fantasies have a vague quality like that in mystical treatises such as the fourteenth-century Cloud of Unknowing. And what they say is all the more effective because it is not pinned down. One must simply make the leap of faith into his stories. As W. H. Auden says in his Afterword to MacDonald's Golden Key,

But to hunt for symbols in a fairy tale is absolutely fatal. In the Golden Key, for example, any attempt to "interpret" the Grandmother or the air-fish or the Old Man of the Sea is futile: they mean what they are. The way, the only way, to read a fairy tale is the same as that prescribed for Tangle at one stage of her journey. [64]

And Auden quotes the following passage from the story:

Then the Old Man of the Earth stooped over the floor of the cave, raised a huge stone from it, and left it leaning. It disclosed a great hole that went plumb-down.

"That is the way," he said.

"But there are no stairs."

"You must throw yourself in. There is no other way." [65]

My own feeling is that the vagueness of MacDonald's fantasies is not a deliberate artistic accomplishment but an accident induced by an imperfect fusing of his own thought with his reading in Paracelsus, Boehme, and Novalis. I think he wrote the fantasies because he needed deeply to believe them, but that ultimately he did not altogether trust them. The despondent silence of his last five years might serve as evidence. But I also believe that he wrought better than he knew, and that the blurred picture he produced was intuitively good, for it frees the imagination of the reader.

How far can the imagination of the reader extend? In the same introductory essay referred to before, E. R. Eddison also wrote,

It may be asked, Why not suicide, then, as a way out? Is not that the logic of such an other-worldly philosophy? The answer surely is that there is a beauty of action (as the North-men knew), and only seldom is suicide a fine act. [66]

Following Eddison's thinking, is there "beauty of action" in the near suicide of the Little Prince in Antoine de St. Exupéry's French fantasy for children? In this work, which Martin Heidegger is said to have regarded as "one of the great existentialist books of the century," [67] the Little Prince deliberately goes out to meet the snake which he knows will return him to the earth, cause his death:

> There was nothing there but a flash of yellow close to his ankle. He remained motionless for an instant. He did not cry out. He fell as gently as a tree falls. There was not even any sound, because of the sand. [68]

The supreme act of giving is his death. It washes over him like a great wave and returns him to the cycle of nature. His courageous act of faith is not unlike the leap demanded of Tangle in The Golden Key. And it bears a striking symbolic resemblance to the leap demanded of all human beings in a strange Vietnamese folktale, "The Well of Immortality." In this folktale, the God Nuoc comes to earth and stations himself at the bottom of a deep well. He calls up that those who have the faith to leap down to him will become immortal. But people hesi-tate. Instead of leaping, they dip their fingers and toes and the tops of their heads in the water. And this is all the immortality they get—their nails and hair continue to grow after death. [69]

After the disturbing reaches of the fantasies of MacDonald or of St. Exupéry, it is rather a relief to turn to the old-fashioned Christian Platonism of C. S. Lewis' Narnia series, concluded in the seventh book The Last Battle:

> "The Eagle is right," said the Lord Digory. "Listen, Peter. When Aslan said you could never go back to Narnia, he meant the Narnia you were thinking of. But that was not the real Narnia. That had a beginning and an end. It was only a shadow or copy of the real Narnia, which has always been here and always will be here: just as our world, England and all, is only a shadow or copy of something in Aslan's real world. You need not mourn over Narnia, Lucy. All of the old Narnia that mattered, all of the dear creatures, have been drawn into the real Narnia through the Door. And of course it is different; as different as a real thing is from a shadow or as waking life is from a dream." His voice stirred everyone like a trumpet as he spoke these words: but when he added under his breath "It's all in Plato, all in Plato: bless me, what do they teach them at these schools!" the older ones laughed. It was so exactly like the sort of thing they had heard him say long ago in that other world where his beard was grey instead of golden. [70]

How is it best to introduce a child through literature to the idea of death? Folk literature, the amalgam of human experience, and some of the great fantasies seem to indicate that the honest and warm human approach is best—not talking down to the child because of his age, for death knows all ages, but simply telling him what we know, what we don't know, what we fear, and what we hope. We find this approach in folk literature, which, as Tolkien might put it, is the very bones of the stock of human experience,[71] in which there is frequently a close and friendly relationship between life and death. The predominant attitude toward death is simple acceptance, combined very often with a belief that death is not final, that it is to be accepted, even actively embraced with the sure knowledge that through love, a resurrection will occur.

---

[1] See the editorial Afterword, "About the Author of This Book," to any of the Penguin Books in the Narnia Series (Middlesex, England, 1965).

[2] Edna Johnson, Evelyn R. Sickels, and Frances Clarke Sayers, Anthology of Children's Literature (Boston, 1970), p.1155. And see all of J. Henry Harris, Robert Raikes, The Man and His Work (Bristol, 1899?).

[3] Indeed, the Chairman of the English Department of one of the greatest Ivy League Schools has written me that "for various reasons" his Department cannot teach children's literature, but that he deplores the level at which it is taught throughout the country.

[4] Yet generally historians of children's literature seem to feel that the separation is a good thing. Some, however, seem not as positive and stress the profit motive.

[5] Stith Thompson, Motif-Index of Folk Literature, Vol. II (Bloomington, Indiana, 1956), pp. 402-517.

[6] Jaime de Angulo, Indian Tales (New York, 1969). First edition, 1953.

[7] The Standard Dictionary of Folklore, Mythology, and Legend, Vol. I (New York, 1949), p. 300.

[8] Grimms' Folk Tales, tr., Eleanor Quarrie. The Folio Society. (London, 1965), p. 189. For the matter-of-fact acceptance of death by primitive man, see Paul Radin, Primitive Man as Philosopher (New York, 1957), pp. 97-113. First published, 1927

[9] For "Little Miss Pink," see Francelia Butler, The Skip Rope Book (New York, 1963).

[10] The New Zealand rhyme may also be found in Brian Sutton-Smith, The Games

of New Zealand Children, University of California Folklore Studies, No. 12 (1959), pp. 73-88.

[11] Grimm's Folk Tales, p. 25.

[12] Andrew Lang, ed., The Orange Fairy Book (New York, 1968), pp. 24-28. First published, 1906.

[13] Andrew Lang, ed., The Pink Fairy Book (New York, 1967), pp. 184-190. First published, 1897.

[14] Andrew Lang, ed., The Brown Fairy Book (New York, 1965), p. 244. First published, 1904.

[15] Andrew Lang, ed., The Red Fairy Book (New York, 1966), pp. 182-185. First published, 1890.

[16] Andrew Lang, ed., The Crimson Fairy Book (New York, 1967), pp. 178-191. First published, 1903.

[17] Andrew Lang, ed., The Yellow Fairy Book (New York, 1966), pp. 149-151. First published, 1894.

[18] Andrew Lang, ed., The Violet Fairy Book (New York, 1966), pp. 127-147; 263-269. First published, 1901.

[19] Andrew Lang, ed., The Lilac Fairy Book (New York, 1968), pp. 42-53; 209-215. First published, 1910.

[20] Gilbert Keith Chesterton, Orthodoxy (New York, 1908), p. 89.

[21] Aleksandr Nikolaevich Afanasiev, "Prince Ivan, the Firebird, and the Gray Wolf," in The Twelve Dancing Princesses and Other Fairy Tales (New York, 1964), pp. 122-123.

[22] Johnson, Sickels, and Sayers, p. 447.

[23] The Works of Sir Thomas Malory, ed., Eugene Vinaver (London, 1954), p. 871.

[24] Johnson, Sickels, and Sayers, p. 534.

[25] Robert C. Goldston, The Legend of the Cid (Indianapolis, 1963), p. 154.

[26] Howard Pyle, The Merry Adventures of Robin Hood (New York, 1968), p. 295. First published, 1883.

[27] Sir Edmund Chambers, The English Folk-Play (London, 1969), pp. 50-59; 200-210. First published, 1933.

[28] One has only to consult the English Folk Dance & Song Society for a current calendar of performances in English villages.

[29] Chambers, p. 8.

[30] George Speaight, Punch & Judy A History (London, 1970), pp. 8-10. First published as The History of the English Puppet Theatre (London, 1955).

[31] Incidentally, in Bunyan's tale, the role of women as guides to children is extolled because of the good relationship of women to Christ, as well as the role of gracious old men: "Indeed, old men that are gracious are best able to give advice to them that are young, because they have seen most of the emptiness of things."—John Bunyan, The Pilgrim's Progress (Penguin: Middlesex, Eng., 1965), p. 321. Many reprints, as well as other versions of Pilgrim's Progress for children were published in America in the nineteenth century. See, for instance, A. S. W. Rosenbach, Early American Children's Books (New York, 1971). First published, 1933. There have also been several versions in the early twentieth century, such as Mary Godolphin's Pilgrim's Progress in Words of One Syllable (McLoughlin Brothers: New York, 19--).

[32] The Standard Dictionary of Folklore, Mythology, and Legend, p. 300.

[33] Louisa May Alcott, Little Women (Boston, 1919), Chapters I and II.

[34] Charles Kingsley, The Water-Babies. University Microfilms (Ann Arbor, 1966), p. 222. First published, London, 1863.

[35] The Educational Writings of John Locke, ed., James L. Axtell (Cambridge, Eng., 1968), pp. 259, 271, 298, 349, 364.

[36] Caxton's Aesop, ed., R. T. Lenaghan (Cambridge, Mass., 1967), p. 98.

[37] See, for instance, Sir Roger L'Estrange, Fables and Storyes Moralized. Being a Second Part of the Fables of Aesop . . . (London, 1699). In his introduction, L'Estrange writes, "Now This Medly, (such as it is) of Salutary Hints, and Councels, being Dedicated to the Use, and Benefit of Children, the Innocence of it must be preserved Sacred too, without the least Mixture of any Thing that's Prophane, Loose, or Scurrilous, or but so much as Bordering That way." He then includes stories that would be considered too gross for Playboy. (The writer of this paper examined this copy at Guildhall Library, London.)
Unfortunately, a current edition of L'Estrange (New York, 1967) is so badly bowdlerized that it constitutes merely a poor sample. The publishers nevertheless avoid acknowledging that L'Estrange intended the book for children.

[38] Herbert S. Zim and Sonia Bleeker, Life and Death (New York, 1970), p. 20.

[39] Ibid., p. 46.

[40] Ibid., p. 55.

[41] Alison White, "With Birds in His Beard," Saturday Review (January 15, 1966), p. 27

[42] Ibid.

[43] The Annotated Alice. By Lewis Carroll, with an introduction and notes by Martin Gardner (New York, 1960), p. 27. Here also Gardner refers to William Empson's comments in Some Versions of Pastoral on the numerous death jokes in Alice.

[44] Rhymes familiar to Gertrude and Bruce McWilliams of Southend-on-Sea, England, now of Pound Ridge, New York.

[45] Brigid Brophy, Michael Levey, and Charles Osborne, Fifty Works of English and American Literature We Could Do Without (New York, 1968), p. 109.

[46] Ibid., p. 112.

[47] The Best Known Works of Oscar Wilde (New York, 1927), p. 519.

[48] Ibid., pp. 523-524.

[49] Ibid., p. 524.

[50] In the Albert C. Bates and Maria E. Hewins Collections, Library of The Connecticut Historical Society, Hartford.

[51] A. S. W. Rosenbach, Early American Children's Books (New York, 1971), pp. 18, 31, 82, 133, 196. First published, 1933.

[52] For instance, in The New England Primer, published by Ira Webster (Hartford, Conn., 1843).

[53] Rosenbach, p. 285.

[54] Rosenbach, p. 126.

[55] Johnson, Sickels, and Sayers, p. 1155. And all of J. Henry Harris, Robert Raikes. The Man and his Work (Bristol, 1899?).

[56] A New Picture Book. Series 1 No. IV. American Tract Society (New York, 19--). Arnold Arnold, in Pictures and Stories from Forgotten Children's Books (New York, 1969), shrewdly observes that "the manipulative school of child literature has its counterpart in our own day" in "psychologically manipulative" stories which "tend to be written according to formula and confining, anti-literate, age-grouped vocabularies." p. 2.

[57] Peter Coveney, Poor Monkey: The Child in Literature (London, 1957), pp. 136-149.

[58] Sister Mary Immaculate, C. S. C., The Cry of Rachel: An Anthology of Elegies on Children (New York, 1966).

[59] Robert Lee Wolff, The Golden Key: A Study of The Fiction of George MacDonald (New Haven, 1961), pp. 4, 9, 48, 138, 146, 373-375, 388.

[60] George MacDonald, The Golden Key (New York, 1967), p. 71.

[61] Wolff, pp. 379-380.

[62] E. R. Eddison, "A Letter of Introduction to George Rostrevor Hamilton," A Fish Dinner in Memison (New York, 1970), p. xxviii.

[63] Walt Whitman, "Song of Myself," Part 6.

[64] George MacDonald, The Golden Key. "Afterword" by W. H Auden, p. 85.

[65] Ibid., p. 57.

[66] Eddison, p. xxix.

[67] Curtis Cate, Antoine de Saint-Exupéry (New York, 1970), p. 465.

[68] Antoine de St. Exupery, The Little Prince (New York, 1943), p. 89.

[69] Ruth Q. Sun, Land of Seagull and Fox: Folk Tales of Vietnam (Rutland, Vermont, 1967), pp. 19-20.

[70] C. S. Lewis, The Last Battle (Penguin: Middlesex, Eng., 1969), pp. 153-154. First published by The Bodley Head, 1956.

[71] J. R. R. Tolkien, "On Fairy Stories," The Tolkien Reader (New York, 1966), pp. 19, 30, 31.

# WHAT FINNISH CHILDREN READ[*]

Taimi M. Ranta

During the Strategic Arms Limitation Talks in Finland, the foreign reporters exclaimed over the abundance of well-stocked bookstores and libraries there and the general interest in reading. As a matter of fact, in spite of its sparse population, Finland is reputed to have more bookshops per capita than any other country in the world. In Helsinki, for instance, even a one-day tourist from a cruise ship anchored in Helsinki harbor cannot miss seeing the Academic Bookstore. This modern copper-and-marble structure, designed by the world-famous Finnish architect, Alvar Aalto, houses one of the largest bookstores in Europe. It is not only a business enterprise but a center of culture. Its section of books for children and young people is enviable. But a wide range of books is also available for purchase all over the country, and people from all socio-economic levels take pride in book ownership.

Though this vital interest in books is not a recent development, since Finnish people have long been known as book lovers and book owners, outsiders are frequently so astonished by the vitality of the Finnish passion for books that they assume it must be a current fad. Reading is a way of life. One sees people of all ages reading on streetcars and buses, on park benches during lunch breaks or while watching children play in recreation areas. Last summer, I saw a young woman reading while she pushed a perambulator in a city park.

Finns also like to discuss what they have read. When I was visiting friends at their summer residence a short distance from Helsinki, one of the young daughters of the family wanted to tell me about a book she had enjoyed reading. So, there we sat on the pier, our feet dangling in the water, while she related the story. Almost immediately the story sounded familiar, yet its title was <u>Kadun Hauskin Talo</u> (The Street's Happiest House). It turned out to be <u>The Moffets</u> by the New Englander, Eleanor Estes. This child was but one of the coutless Finnish children who have shared their favorite books with me over the years.

No country in the world can boast a higher literacy level than Finland. When I was doing research on the methods and materials of teaching reading in Finland under church and state, an investigation which included a historical survey from the Middle Ages to the present and a modern field study, I discovered that during the centuries literacy has been considered indispensable for salvation and survival in Finland. The widespread literacy, which has been prevalent for some 300 years, has an interesting story, which can only be hinted at in this short paper.

---

[*] This article is a brief introduction to an extensive study which the writer began as a Fulbright scholar in Finland, and on which she has continued work for a number of years. Given at the Seminar on Children's Literature, Modern Language Association, Chicago, Illinois, December 27, 1971.

The church law of Sweden-Finland clearly prescribed in 1686 that everybody was to learn to read, and in addition he was to learn a considerable number of religious texts by heart. Every year the clergyman in charge of a parish would call the people of each village to a lukukinkeri, the name given to the general examination in reading conducted once a year by the minister in a rural community. At these examinations, observance of the decree was checked. Every inhabitant over seven years of age had "to read both from within and by heart," and the reading ability of each was graded by a system of crosses and parts of crosses and recorded in the church books, many of which still can be seen in church archives. It was not uncommon for those who had not learned to read to be humiliated in various ways such as by being put under the table. For punishment, some stubborn, indifferent, and rebellious ones were ordered to sit in the stocks or on a so-called bench of correction and repentance during Sunday worship services and large church festivals.

The illiterates were excluded from Holy Communion, which in the concept of the day meant that those concerned could not go to heaven. If even this formidable threat proved ineffectual, the illiterate person was refused the authorization to marry. During the centuries, countless Finns contemplating matrimony met the A B C book and learned to read. Also, men who could not read were labeled vagrants and were taken first into the armed forces. This was a very real threat because these people were involved in many wars in those days. As early as the beginning of the eighteenth century, literacy was made a condition for enjoying civic rights. Hence it is apparent that literacy has been a fundamental instrument of the church and state by which the individual is controlled.

In addition to the regular readers and supplementary readers, I found some library books available to the pupils at all the schools I have visited in Finland. The elementary school law of 1957 made every community responsible for supplying its elementary schools with additional library books, fiction, non-fiction, and special reference works. The more than 4000 public libraries all have children's sections, ranging from only a separate corner to a modern, well-lighted, well-equipped room. Some have special additional features such as the puppet theater of the Kallio Branch Library in a less-priveleged area of Helsinki. Various listings of books for children and young people help teachers and librarians in making their selections. Two examples for such aids to book selection are the annual Kirjavalikoima (Book Selection), published annually by the National Board of Schools of Finland, and the third edition of Nuorten Kirjoja (Books for Children and Young People), compiled by the very competent Vuokko Blinnikka, Kerttu Manninen and Kaija Salonen and published in 1969 by the Finnish Library Association (founded 1910). The publishing houses have been issuing colorful catalogs advertising their books for children and young people.

Nuorten Kirja (The Book of the Young), an organization concerned with "young people's literature as a cultural question," was formed at the end of World War II. Interested in raising both the quantitative and qualitative level of books for children and young people in Finland, it has been instrumental in sponsoring critical evaluation of children's books, in encouraging contests for writers of books for boys and girls, and in generally emphasizing the place of literature for young people in the total literary structure. The Topelius Award for the outstanding children's or young people's book of the year was instituted by the Werner Söderström Publishing House in 1946, and in 1947 and 1951 the Valistus Press and the Otava Press followed with the establishment of similar awards. The Rudolf Koivu Medal, named for an outstanding artist, has been made to an illustrator each year since 1949. From 1961 on, a special Anni Swan Award has been given every three years to the best book for young people. One of the winners of the Anni Swan Award has been artist-author Tove Jansson, who also won the Hans Christian Andersen Medal in 1966. Jansson's imagination has produced the books about the "Moomin" creatures, many of which are translated into English. Kauppiaitten Kustannus Press has been sponsoring contests for youthful writers in a popular series called Kontakti (Contact), in which one example is Umpikuja (Blind Alley) by a fifteen-year-old adolescent girl.

In 1957, the Suomen Nuortenkirjaneuvosto (The Council for Young People's Books of Finland) was established to take care of matters pertaining to international cooperative activity in the area of children's and young people's books. This organization cooperates with the International Board on Books for Young People (IBBY). Since 1964 the Scandinavian countries have organized biennial congresses on juvenile literature. The fourth such congress met in Helsinki in June, 1970. The Finnish section of IBBY, the Finnish Library Association, and other groups were responsible for the arrangements.

For some time a week has been designated annually as "literature week," but in 1958, 1962, and 1967, special "book days for young people" were observed. Illustrated, annotated book lists, called Kirja Airut (Book Messenger) were distributed to all school children. The slogan has been "Lue Enemmän, Lue Parempaa" (Read More, Read That Which Is Better). Rv. Sylvi Kekkonen, the wife of the President of Finland and an author herself, was the sponsor of events. Another such week is in the planning stage.

Finnish children have had their own treasures of children's literature. Theirs has been a rich heritage, including poetry, folk tales, legends, hero stories, proverbs, and riddles. The second and final edition compiled by Elias Lönnrot of the Kalevala, the national epic, was published in 1849. Aili Konttinen has a five-book series called Lasten Kultainen Kalevala (Children's Golden Kalevala), which delights Finnish children. Dr. Martti Haavio, prominent folklorist and recently retired member of the Finnish Academy, and A. Lindberg, a well-known illustrator, collaborated on an impressive volume in prose for youngsters that manages to capture the spirit and tone of the epic itself. This Kalevalan Tarinat (Stories of the Kalevala) has illustrations that are reminiscent of the ones in Jane Watson's The Iliad and Odyssey. Elias Lönnrot also compiled some 600 old lyric poems in his Kanteletar (Muse of the Kantele) in 1840. This collection gets its name from a stringed, zither-like instrument used in the accompaniment of the folk tunes. It contains many poems which the children have enjoyed over the years and memorized to this day.

There are a number of excellent collections of Finnish folk tales of varying levels of difficulty. The classic of all folk tale collections in Finland, enjoyed by the "young of all ages," is Suomen Kansan Satuja ja Tarinoita (Tales and Legends of the Finnish People) published in four volumes, 1852 - 1866. Although it was not meant for children originally, the work, now in one volume, has been appropriated by them. According to a reading inventory that I made in Finland, a sizeable number of youngsters in the intermediate grades mentioned this collection as a favorite book. Dr. Haavio rates these tales as incomparably superior to the prototype of the Grimm brothers. Two large Finnish folktale volumes by Merikoski (1947) and Roine (1952) are much easier to read, especially the former. Merikoski did for the Finnish stories much the same thing Joseph Jacobs did for the English ones, that is he made the "suitable" for the nursery.

Sakari Topelius (1818-1898) has been called the "story uncle" of the Finnish children, having written many stories, plays, and poems which have been loved by generations. Jorma Mäenpää, who has written a history of a hundred years of children's literature, has said that folklore and Topelius are the foundation of children's and young people's literature in Finland.

In the nineteenth century, the Finnish children had a procession of their own devoted writers. For example, there were Helmi Krohn, translator, editor of children's and young people's magazines, writer of biography, and girls' books; Arvid Lydecken, prolific children's author and poet and writer of mild adventure stories for boys; Jalmari Sauli, author of books for boys ages nine through four- teen; and Anni Swan, author of numerous fanciful stories and of books for girls ages eight through twelve. All of these writers were born in the latter third of the last century and lived until the 1950's and 1960's. Many new names have more recently appeared in the field of children's and young people's literature. Some of the prominent ones are Aili Konttinen, Tove Jansson, Annikki Setälä, Kirsi Kunnas, Rauha Virtanen, and Väinö Riikkilä.

An average of about sixty new books for children, written by native authors, have been published annually in Finland in recent years, but approximately fifty per cent of the books available to Finnish children in the 1960's were translated from English, Swedish, Norwegian, German, and other languages.

Judging from the answers which I received from the children, especially the fourth-grade boys and girls, on my questionnaire concerning their voluntary read- ing, Finnish children read an admirable amount, including folklore, adventure stories, and girls' stories, both Finnish and foreign, as well as the "standards" of Finnish literature for children and young people.

Finnish children for years have had in translation stories of King Arthur and Robin Hood, Alcott's Little Women, Barrie's Peter Pan, Burnett's Little Lord Faunt- leroy, The Little Princess, and The Secret Garden, Carroll's Alice's Adventures in Wonderland, Mark Twain's The Adventures of Tom Sawyer and The Adventures of Huckleberry Finn, DeFoe's Robinson Crusoe, Dodge's Hans Brinker and the Silver Skates, Grahame's The Wind in the Willows, Kingsley's Water Babies, Kipling's Captains Courageous, Jungle Books, and Kim, Milne's Winnie-the-Pooh and The House at Pooh Corner, Spyri's Heidi, Stevenson's Treasure Island, Swift's Gulli- ver's Travels, Tarkington's Penrod, Wyss's Swiss Family Robinson, and many other books from the lists of familiar classics for children and young people. Over and over again these and other beloved old favorites appeared on the child- ren's answer sheets.

More recently Benary-Isbery's <u>The Ark</u>, Brink's <u>Caddie Woodlawn</u>, DeJong's <u>The Wheel on the School</u>, Estes's <u>Ginger Pye</u> and <u>The Moffets</u>, Henry's <u>King of the Wind</u>, Lawson's <u>Rabbit Hill</u>, McCloskey's <u>Homer Price</u>, Means's <u>Shuttered Windows</u>, Norton's <u>The Borrowers</u>, O'Dell's <u>Island of the Blue Dolphins</u>, Wilder's <u>Little House in the Big Woods</u> and <u>Little House on the Prairie</u>, White's <u>Charlotte's Web</u>, and other works have been translated for Finnish children to enjoy. In August, 1971, <u>Jennifer, Hecate, Macbeth, William McKinley, and me, Elizabeth</u> by E. K. Konigsburg was to be released under a much simpler title that translates as <u>My Friend, the Witch Girl</u>.

In 1958 Valistus Press published Jorma Mäenpää's <u>Sata Vuotta Sadun ja Seikkailun Mailla</u> (A Hundred Years in the Lands of Story and Adventure), a general history of children's literature in Finland, which has given teachers in the elementary schools and others interested in this area of literture some background in the field. Then in 1966, Werner Soderstrom came out with <u>Nuorten Kirja Suomessa Ennen ja Nyt</u> (Books for Young People in Finland in the Past and Present) to which various people in literature for children and young people in one capacity or another contributed chapters. The overall editor was Irja Lappalainen. Forty-nine pages are devoted to literature for children and young people in the eight-volume work on <u>Suomen Kirjallisuus</u> (Finnish Literature). Kari Vaijarvi is currently working on a children's guide to literature that should prove very interesting and helpful.

In the second issue of <u>Aika</u> (Time) for 1971, Prof. Maija Lehtonen, who last year taught the first course in children's literature to be offered at the University of Helsinki, discussed children's literature in something of a "state of the art" message. She called her article <u>Taidetta-Tietoa-Toiveunta?</u> (Art-Knowledge-Wishful Dreams?) She asked the question, "What is Children's Literature?" Is children's literature that which is written for certain age groups or what the children really read? She observed that the subject of criticism in children's literature is a plaguing one. More carefully planned research obviously is needed in this area, and it should be recognized as on a par with research in other areas of literature. There should be opportunities for those interested to specialize in children's literature. She wondered if the time were ripe to establish in Finland an institute of children's literature such as those which have been established in a few countries. She recognized that there was no dearth of problems and disputable questions in the field of children's literature.

I can only conclude that those devoting talents, time, energy, and heart to the endeavor of bringing boys and girls more and better books, be they in the United States or Finland, share many of the same concerns.

# THE CHILD AS REBEL IN SONG AND RHYME

Harriet Korim Hornstein

   Children might sing a political song (or a religious or bawdy one[1]) with little comprehension of the words they are singing. Many Mother Goose rhymes that are sung as nonsense were originally intended as political satire. For example, it is supposed that Little Jack Horner won his political plum (a land grant from Henry VIII) for informing upon his old friend, the Abbot of Glastonbury, at a Christmastime trial; the Abbot was consequently hanged.[2] Yet generations of children have sung about Horner, thinking that he probably <u>was</u> a good boy. Children's apolitical delight in singing about political figures extends to this century. In 1956 a young child who did not know who Hitler was sang this corruption of an anti-Hitler rhyme she claimed to have "just made up":

> In 1954 Hitler went to war
> He lost his socks
> In the middle of the docks
> In 1954. [3]

   Topical rhymes and protest songs about specific personalities and issues might have little significance for children. But children do sing—with considerable understanding and feeling—many songs in which the issues are clear and anti-authoritarian. Children love good rebellious songs as only the powerless can. This is most obviously true of the children of oppressed minorities:

> The only place where we could say we did not like
> slavery, say it for ourselves to hear, was in these
> old songs. We could not read and the master thought
> he could trap us with no existence and we could do
> nothing about it. But we did—even as children—
> with the music. And it is our own; it came from
> ourselves. . . . In my time when I was coming up we had
> plays—ring plays of different types. And these old
> ring plays sometimes meant a whole lot to the people
> and what they had to say and what they wanted to do.
> We had a play—there used to be four of us would stand
> in a circle and skip across and swing one another. [4]

Two of the ring songs Bessie Jones describes above are "Where Ya Go Lily" and "Juba":

> Where ya go Lily, oh sometimes,
> I'm gonna rule our ruler, oh sometimes,

I'm gonna rule him with a hickory, oh sometimes,
I'm gonna rule him with a shotgun, oh sometimes.

The bitter words of "Juba" are chanted to the accompaniment of handclapping:

Juba this and Juba that
And Juba killed the yellow cat
And gives us double trouble, Juba.

You sift the meal, you give me the husk,
You bake the bread, you give me the crust,
You cook the meat, you give me the skin,
And that's where my mama's trouble begin.

Massa killed the big old duck
And give us all the bones to suck.
Massa killed the big old goose
And give us all the bones to chew.

My old massa promised me
When he died he'd set me free.
He lived 'til his head got slick and bald
He give up the notion of dying at all. [5]

In the nineteen-sixties black children were still singing about getting their freedom:

. . . in Mississippi we had a Freedom Day. One lady
brought her little son. He had a sign, say: I'M TOO
YOUNG TO VOTE BUT MY MOTHER WANT TO VOTE. A
policeman called him over and said, "If you don't pull
off that sign and throw it away, boy, I'm gonna throw you
in jail." The little boy remembered the song that we sing,
and he looked up to the policeman and said, "Mister, I
ain't scared of your jail, 'cause I want my freedom!" [6]

Howard Zinn writes in SNCC: The New Abolitionists that "For the first time in
our history a major social movement, shaking the nation to its bones, is being led
by youngsters." [7] Teenage activists (children by political or legal definition)
have had to defy parental authority and concern as well as police repression:

Ain't gonna let brutality turn me round,
Turn me round, turn me round,
Ain't gonna let brutality turn me round,
I'm gonna keep on walkin', keep on talkin',
Keep on marching 'til I'm free.

131

> Ain't gonna let my mother turn me round,
> Turn me round, turn me round,
> Ain't gonna let my mother turn me round,
> I'm gonna keep on walkin', keep on talkin',
> Keep on marching 'til I'm free. [8]

The last song shows children not only as members of an oppreseed group, but as an oppressed group. Even the child of wealthy, white parents might identify with the resolute defiance of that song as easily as with this older protest against parental control:

> I won't be my Father's Jack
> I won't be my Father's Jill
> I will be the Fiddler's Wife
> And have Music when I will. [9]

These lines lose some of their lightheartedness when one considers that they were written at a time when fathers usually decreed when and whom their daughters would marry.

The following American folksong protests parental authority over marriage, and pokes fun at other prominent adults:

> Mama sent me to the spring
> She told me not to stay
> Fell in love with a pretty little girl
> Could not get away
>
> CHORUS:
> Chawing chewing gum, chewing chawing gum
>
> First she gave me peaches nice
> Then she gave me pears
> Next she gave me fifty cents
> Kissed me on the stairs
>
> (CHORUS)
>
> I wouldn't have a lawyer
> Now here's the reason why
> Every time he opens his mouth
> He tells a great big lie
>
> (CHORUS)

I wouldn't have a doctor
Now here's the reason why
He rides all over the country
A-making the people die

(CHORUS)

I took my girl to the church last night
And what do you reckon she done
She walked right up to the preacher's face
And chawed her chewing gum

(CHORUS)

Mama don't 'low me to whistle
Poppa don't 'low me to sing
They don't want me to marry
I'll marry just the same

(CHORUS)  10

Although "children's songs" (like the Mother Goose rhymes) may have been composed by adults, the fact that some of these songs and rhymes are picked up and held onto so naturally by children would suggest that they are a valid expression of a child's sensibility. A far more valid expression of this sensibility, however, may be found in the songs, rhymes and poems composed by children themselves.

Some of the best examples of children's poetry, and many valuable insights about it, are contained in Kenneth Koch's Wishes, Lies, and Dreams (New York, 1970). Many other collections of creative writing by children—usually poems and stories written for teachers[11]—have been published, most of them in the last ten years. By contrast, children's folklore (the songs and rhymes shared by children through oral tradition) continues to go largely unnoticed and unrecorded by adults. The main exception to this in the twentieth century is the work of Iona and Peter Opie, whose Lore and Language of Schoolchildren (see Note 1) includes hundreds of the bawdy songs, topical rhymes, taunts, superstitious rituals of British children. Many of the following protest rhymes and poems are taken from these two excellent books.

The chief figures of authority in a child's life (excluding parents) are policemen and teachers, and these figures are the most frequent objects of children's ridicule and abuse. In 1885 English schoolboys used to shout from behind bushes at passing policemen:

There goes the bobby with his black shiny hat
And his belly full of fat
And a pancake tied to his nose. (Opie, p. 370)

133

A British taunt popular in the nineteen-fifties attempts to explain the paunch if not the pancake:

> No wonder, no wonder, the coppers are so fat,
> They go around the market and eat up all the fat.
> And what they can't eat they puts in their 'at. [12]
> No wonder, no wonder, the coppers are so fat.

Whereas the police are largely resented for keeping children out of places they want to be, teachers are resented for keeping them where they do not want to be. "A classroom is like a cage" [13] to many children, and the logical protest against forced attendance is projected or actual escape. One avenue of escape is sleep— either before school ("A dillar, a dollar, a ten-o-clock scholar") or during it. The following poem, "Sleepy Dream," describes a beautifully circular sleep-escape:

> I dreamt I went to school in my blue and white pajamas.
> I took three pink pillows and fell asleep during a social
>     studies lesson.
> My friends slept with me. Two to each pink pillow.
> No more pink pillows so poor Mrs. Weick must sleep on
>     that horrible social studies book.
> We dreamt we went to school in our blue and white,
>     orange and yellow, and psychedelic pajamas. [14]

A fourth grader composed a more desperate fantasy:

> I wish that school would not exist
> And it would ride away in a car . . . [15]

But the most popular means of escape is simply leaving school, or not going in the first place. British children's rhymes about minor holidays often end with the threat, "If you don't give us a holiday, we'll all run away." "'We never do get a holiday, and we never run away,' complained one child, rather perplexed" (Opie, p. 265). Better organized and more militant tactics resulted in the children of one English district winning a day off on Shrove Tuesday:

> . . . the children rode to school on poles, taking
> turns to carry each other. They then rushed into
> the schoolhouse in a body and locked the door against
> the headmaster, shouting out at the tops of their voices:
>     Barley, master, barley,
>     Barley in a spoon!
>     If you don't give us a holiday
>     We'll bar you out till noon! (Opie, p. 239)

When children play hooky or enjoy the legal respite of school vacations, they not only get away to do things they like; they get away from the things about school they do not like:

> No more classes
> No more books
> No more teachers' dirty looks.

Perhaps the thing children hate most about school is the physical punishment that is still practiced in many of our schools.[16] One protest rhyme long repeated by British children has a convenient pocket in which to tuck the appropriate name:

> Mr. _____ is a good man,
> He goes to church on Sunday.
> He prays to God to give him strength
> To whip the boys on Monday. (Opie, p. 363)

Through many of the songs and rhymes that they sing, children identify themselves as rebels. Sometimes children threaten militant action ("Barley, master, barley"); sometimes they express their contempt or boredom by chewing gum or falling asleep. "Where Ya Go, Lily" threatens violent revenge, as does this well-known parody of "John Brown's Body":

> Glory, glory, hallelujah,
> My teacher hit me with a ruler!
> I knocked her on the bean with a rotten tangerine,
> And her teeth came marching out!

In almost all these songs and poems, the real weapons are the irreverent words themselves, ridiculing an establishment that demands to be taken seriously.

---

[1] Children are most likely to parrot or garble the songs they are taught by rote and required to sing in school or church, (i.e., "Gladly, the cross-eyed bear"). Although children are often intensely aware of the content of "dirty songs," a contributor to Iona and Peter Opie's Lore and Language of Schoolchildren (Oxford, 1959) recalls a chorus of "dear little girls aged five to eleven" spontaneously breaking out into these words when an orchestra played "Men of Harlech" at a patriotic assembly:

> I'm a man that came from Scotland
> Shooting peas up a Nannie goat's bottom,
> I'm the man that came from Scotland
> Shooting peas away.

135

We are assured that "there was not a smirk on any child's face. They were bliss-fully unconscious of what they were singing and merely making a joyful noise" (p. 95).

[2] The rhyme is recited by Pete Seeger with all the sarcasm intact on _Dangerous Songs!?_ (Columbia, CS9303). A slight variation of the historical explanation on the Seeger record is included in William S. and Ceil Baring-Gould's _Annotated Mother Goose_ (New York, 1962), p. 62.

[3] Opie, p. 103.

[4] Bessie Jones, as quoted in _Freedom is a Constant Struggle_, ed. Guy and Candie Carawan (New York, 1968), p. 112.

[5] Ibid., p. 113, 116. Bessie Jones comments that "yellow cat" is cant for white man. Ruth Crawford Seeger in _American Folk Songs for Children_ (Garden City, New York, 1948) quotes only the first two lines of "Juba"—in which abbreviated form it is hardly a protest song. Unaware of the meaning of the song, she offers in her introduction a nonviolent version for those parents and teachers who might be troubled by Juba's unexplained cruelty to animals!
Julius Lester's _To Be a Slave_ (New York, 1968) includes this variation of "Juba," a more accurate description of the economics of slavery:

> We raise the wheat,
> They give us the corn;
> We bake the bread,
> They give us the crust;
> We sift the meal,
> They give us the skin,
> And that's the way
> They take us in.
> We skim the pot,
> They give us the liquor,
> And say that's good enough for the nigger
>
> The big bee flies high,
> The little bee makes the honey.
> The black folks make the cotton
> And the white folks get the money. (p. 114)

[6] Sam Bock, a SNCC fieldworker, as quoted in _Freedom is a Constant Struggle_, p. 46.

[7] Ibid., quoted p. 48. Many black revolutionaries today are in their teens. Chicago Panther leader Fred Hampton was nineteen when he was assassinated; Jonathan Jackson was seventeen when he was killed in San Rafael, California.

[8] Italics mine. "Don't You Let Nobody Turn You Round," is sung by the Staple Singers on What the World Needs Now is Love (Epic BN26373).

[9] Annotated Mother Goose, p. 54.

[10] This song, originally recorded by the Carter Family, is played and sung by The New Lost City Ramblers on Old Timey Songs for Children (Folkways FC7064).

[11] An interesting attempt to break this pattern is KIDS: A Magazine Written and Illustrated by Children for Each Other (Box 30, Cambridge, Massachusetts 02139).

[12] Opie, p. 370. The stereotype of fat, greedy policemen reflected in the epithet "pig" is at least as old as the "Keystone Kops." A three-year-old black child who has seen full-grown farm pigs did not mention fatness or greed in her explanation of this metaphor: "They're both scary."

[13] From a poem by fifth-grader Debbie Novitsky, Wishes, Lies, and Dreams, p. 98.

[14] "Sleepy Dream" by Robin Harold, Wishes, Lies, and Dreams, p. 136.

[15] Lisa Jill Braun, Wishes, Lies, and Dreams, p. 77.

[16] Jonathan Kozol's Death at an Early Age (Boston, 1967) describes routine use of rattans by Boston public school teachers.

# SENDAK CONFRONTS THE "NOW" GENERATION[*]

Julie Carlson McAlpine

There I was: front row center, stack of note cards and pencil in hand, cassette recorder on the floor before me with speaker precariously propped on top of my coat. "What would Maurice Sendak be like when facing an auditorium packed with the 'now' generation at the University of Connecticut on December 10, 1970?" I found myself wondering. He had already refused to deliver a formal . . . or informal . . . address. He would only answer questions from the audience.

I had already been favorably impressed the previous evening when I had my first encounter with him. Sendak had seemed to enjoy an informal Polish dinner in his honor and he had mixed agreeably with students, faculty and members of the community.

While waiting his appearance at the podium, I attempted—with some embarrassment—to keep my equipment and belongings from spilling over to the spaces occupied by the students beside me. But they seemed oblivious of my presence as they passed Sendak books back and forth and talked around and through me. I heard such comments as: " 'Where the Wild Things Are' is just great!" "Let's have him for lunch. Do you think he's doing anything for lunch?"

Materials anchored better, I ventured to ask the students near me who had already met Sendak at an informal Inner College bull session how he rated with them. They were very vocal. I was told that he ranked as one of the best speakers they had had at the University. He was smart, warm and easy to talk to. "Say, are you with the radio and television people?" one asked.

"Not exactly," I mumbled, omitting that I was faculty, always primed for an opportunity to ward off the "publish or perish" scare, and in this instance having a vague premonition that I was in for something special.

Then he appeared. Standing there one was struck by the fact that his strong face and manner commanded the attention which his small stature of itself never would.

The first question "Who was your inspiration?" was quickly eliminated. "Try another," he replied. This was but one example of Sendak's direct manner. In addition to the rich mixture of honesty in his answers and the depth of thought and feeling he expressed, one noted the liberal use of hand gestures and the facial features which would fascinate a sculptor.

One had the feeling that Sendak's candidness facilitated an easy two-way dialogue between the author/illustrator and questioners who represented a "mixed

---

[*] Given at the Seminar on Children's Literature, Modern Language Association, Chicago, Illinois, December 27, 1971.

bag" of student types. At one point he was asked if he liked young adults. His frank reply was yes—if they were interesting. About midpoint a question card with a smiling sunshine cartoon character sketched at the bottom was passed down front. It asked him for his honest reactions to being at the University. Sendak responded that he liked being there and found it quite a shift from his usual introversion. He was usually by himself, did not keep a journal and does not talk to himself. The visit was an opportunity to "air his head out" and he found that an interested audience stimulated him.

The questions and answers which follow are topically grouped and necessarily rephrased for smooth, concise reporting except where indicated by the use of quotation marks. The condensed dialogue ran the gamut from Sendak's own work to his reactions to the creations of others and publishing in general.

Q: In what ways was Blake a major influence on your work?
Sendak: His "Songs of Innocence" and "Songs of Experience" were the works which chiefly affected my work, especially my books done in the fifties. Not everyone realizes that he was both an author and an illustrator. He created the perfect illustrated book because he enhanced and compounded his verbal meanings in his images. The viewer undergoes a mystical experience just with the pictures if the words are taken away. "I think Blake is the mainstay of my background."

Q: Would you comment on "A Hole Is to Dig" ?
Sendak: When I met Ruth Krauss, a number of illustrators had turned down her work as being too way out, farfetched or silly. She is the only school I ever went to in the sense that everything I learned about making a book I learned from Ruth. She even moved around and posed for the dancing pictures I did for the book. We have done six books together, but that first one was the least interesting to me. The succeeding ones were "more experimental and fascinating for me."

Q: Reading "Where the Wild Things Are" proves that you can write a child's book without having deep sexual connotations.
Sendak: This is natural to be in a book for it is part of one's full humanity.

Q: The illustrations for "Where the Wild Things Are" are more important than the story. Have you thought of writing for older children?
Sendak: No, I don't intend to write for older people. I differ with the statement that the illustrations are more important. Words and pictures are equally important. I carefully selected the 384 words used. In a picture book pictures and words come first, then the illustrations. Also, I prefer writing for the preschool child because I can be freer and be myself. I find that my audience is ruthless in their criticism and has no hang-ups or prejudices.

Q:     Is it always necessary to have children escape from the mundane by creating fantasy?

Sendak:     Children are not always escaping from the mundane but from the horrific—all kinds of big strong feelings they have. Fantasy can provide an avenue of escapism.

Q:     Was there an experience in your childhood which triggered "Where the Wild Things Are"?

Sendak:     No, it symbolizes anxiety which is general to childhood. All experience this; it is not necessarily unique to me or was it set off by a particular incident in my life. As a child, I didn't go to art galleries or read the classics. I read comics and saw movies. I could perhaps say that "King Kong" was a major influence.

Q:     The child doesn't really win in the story.

Sendak:     Many interpretations are read into works. "Psychological jargon bores the hell out of me."

Q:     How long does it take you to do an illustration?

Sendak:     "That varies considerably." A "Wild Thing" illustration would take from one to two weeks. A "Higglety Pigglety Pop" illustration would take about two days. One for "In the Night Kitchen" could take one day. The "Wild Things" drawings would take the longest because they are technically the most difficult.

Q:     Why are fear and mystery so recurrent in children's literature?

Sendak:     "It's the fundamental shape of the story." Children enjoy a little anxiety and heart failure as long as they know that all will end all right.

Q:     Would you elaborate on your illustration of Jarrell's work.

Sendak:     "The Animal Family" had some images that couldn't be in art medium. I just did landscapes without characters as introductions to chapters to prepare the reader. My illustrations and layout physically created a "house" for his story.

Q:     What kind of environment did you grow up in?

Sendak:     I grew up in Brooklyn in the thirties. My parents were low middle class. Our neighborhood was pleasant; I remember trees, a candy store, our front stoop. I had an older brother, the sensitive one, and a sister, the brain of the family, of whom I was jealous. My childhood was average and undramatic. I was the spoiled one!

Q:     What is the setting for your creation?

Sendak:     My ideas take a long time to jell. At one time I may have four or five ideas. Book ideas come from an outer source not usually consciously because I will it. When my dog Jenny was near death, I had to put her in a book. While I'm not writing all the time, I am illustrating and "tuning in."

Q:         Were you a doodler as a child?

Sendak:   Yes, I drew. I was a withdrawn child. My brother wrote and I illustrated—and made things. We did a book, "They Were Inseparable" about a twin brother and sister who were madly in love. When my mother found out about it, she confiscated it, for it suggested incest in her mind.

Q:         Why doesn't Jenny go back to her owner in the story? Is it because your dog died?

Sendak:   Essentially yes, but Jenny in real life really would abandon her owner if the food was not good—or if the food were better elsewhere.

Q:         Is there any reason why many of your characters look like you?

Sendak:   I'm often told this. Also, I'm asked if there's any meaning why many characters' names begin with M—like Max.

Q:         What kind of drawings do children seem to like?

Sendak:   I've noticed that they'll reject peer drawings. Perhaps they feel that they can do as well. Children look at a picture as an adult never does—it's as if they were looking at two separate pictures. A child sees the subtleties and detail.

Q:         Did you go to art school? Did formal training make any difference?

Sendak:   I went to the Art Students League for two years—and it made no difference. "I learned nothing from school at all." It was a waste of time and an agony. (When later asked how he would change schools, Sendak said he had no idea.)

Q:         Do you think photographic illustrations can be successful in a children's book?

Sendak:   I take my own photographs and work from them, but photographs haven't been used originally as yet. I think they can be.

Q:         Do you think realism is the best approach to writing?

Sendak:   Fantasies or dreams interest me most.

Q:         Do you ever work with children?

Sendak:   "I would never work with a child." I recall my own childhood with its emotional upsurge which is nonverbal. "You have to find the form and shape for it."

Q:         Can an unknown break into publishing?

Sendak:   Although the field is inundated with books—many of them lousy—there is a need for original writing. And some publishing houses have a warm "care and feeding of young plants" attitude toward their new writers.

Q:         Do you feel as if you've really grown up?

Sendak:   Yes, in the sense that my work gets better. Presently I feel that my writing comes first and it's harder to do than illustrating. In fact, since illustrating is becoming so easy for me, it may lose its challenge and I might give it up. Fundamen-

141

|          |                                                              |
|----------|--------------------------------------------------------------|
|          | tally, I feel I haven't changed for I still react and respond the same way as when I was younger. |
| Q:       | What adult literature would you like to illustrate?          |
| Sendak:  | I'd like to do Kafka. Actually, there isn't much adult fiction which can be illustrated. |
| Q:       | Would you comment on Meindert DeJong?                        |
| Sendak:  | I love Meindert DeJong's writing, but illustration for his age group is not so important. It is more decorative. |
| Q:       | Could you illustrate Lear?                                   |
| Sendak:  | Again, I love Lear's work. I couldn't illustrate it.        |
| Q:       | What do you think of Shultz?                                 |
| Sendak:  | "Peanuts" is essentially original, but is now oversold. The idea and drawing are good, while line and word choice are fine. There is adult sophistication in his work. |
| Q:       | Would you like to illustrate Barrie?                        |
| Sendak:  | "Peter Pan" is a bore.                                       |
| Q:       | Would you like to illustrate Tolkien?                       |
| Sendak:  | I'm not interested.                                          |
| Q:       | Would you like to illustrate Andersen?                      |
| Sendak:  | Andersen is not for me to illustrate. Upon rereading his work, I find I dislike it. His tales are watery, weak, sadistic and sentimental. |

Sendak was asked what he would like to illustrate. He replied, "Grimms Fairy Tales" which is exactly what he's working on at the moment. He commented that he didn't feel like doing another book of his own for about four or five years. He also wants to illustrate his father's first book. Sendak mused that he had copied and learned from his father, rather than the other way around. But eternally "The child is father of the man."

Sendak's revealing answers to youth's questions raise several points to ponder. I would propose two for consideration.

Is his work simply a release of his own hangups—or is he expressing feelings common to all children? On the one hand, he has mentioned that he was a withdrawn child obsessed with his emotions. On the other hand, he states that all children are looking for an escape from the big strong feelings inside of them. His readership enjoys a little anxiety and heart failure as long as they know all will turn out well in the end.

Is his work entirely new— or is it a fresh restatement of the gothic novel for children of the twentieth century? Sendak has said that fantasies and dreams interest him most and he is drawn to the strange, eerie works of Kafka and Jarrell. He suggests that his books and illustrations dare to expose deep feelings in imaginative ways. Yet, an analysis of gothic novels and their illustrations may well show that Sendak may be a gothic writer responding to a recurrent need expressed in terms of our times.

# WHAT'S LEFT OUT OF BIOGRAPHY FOR CHILDREN[*]

Marilyn Jurich

Biography is hard to write. Resurrection may be more difficult than creation. The biographer "assays the role of a God, for in his hands the dead can be brought to life and granted a measure of immortality." [1] Not only must he revive persons— and particularly one person—but he must breathe back past times—not so much a panorama of ceremonies and battles, but the trivia that are significant to most people.

Biography for children is especially difficult to write because it is supposed to re-create and at the same time provide a guide to success, to encourage the child "to make something of himself" by giving him a believable model who "made it." [2] Thus, the biographer is supposed to be a psychologist or a moralist or both. At the same time, he is dealing with a necessarily imperfect subject about whom the young reader wants to know as much as possible. As Richard Ellmann writes, "More than anything else we want in modern biography to see the character forming, its peculiarities taking shape. . . ." [3]

In the preface to <u>Literary Biography</u>, Leon Edel cites that difficulty besetting all biographers: keeping a perspective somewhere between sterile objectivity and shrieking subjectivity. If one interprets the facts, may not he be inventing new facts? In straining to be truthful, there is always the danger of inventing the facts beforehand out of one's own prejudices. De Voto, in 1933, attacked this "intuitive" form of biography: "Biography," he wrote, "is different from imaginative literature in that readers come to it primarily in search of information." [4]

Yet that very information, Andre Maurois believes, should in modern biography contain a moral lesson, if only to prove something about life, its difficulty, its frustrations, its end result of becoming what we did not choose. He feels that a special lesson is contained in exceptional lives. "Great lives show that, in spite of all, it is possible for a man to act with dignity and to achieve internal peace." [5]

Many of these exceptional lives, particularly as they are presented to the child, are made into heroes whom the child cannot only admire but extravagantly worship. For children, biographies are often like those for adults in Victorian times, when Carlyle pronounced that "it was in great men's actions, fully as much as in their pronouncements, that lessons of great wisdom could be read." [6] Indeed, psychologists or child experts frequently tell us children must have ideal beings after whom to pattern their behavior.

---

[*] Given at the Seminar on Children's Literature of the Modern Language Association, Chicago, Illinois, December 27, 1971. This paper is an excerpt from a larger study by Professor Jurich.

It seems to me, however, that there is need today for more biographies of ordinary people—not the Victorian type of biography which was written to affirm middle-class values, but biographies enabling a child to identify with the figure in the biography and so endure—something of the kind of thing one finds in drama in Brecht's Mother Courage. Thus, I do not altogether agree with Harold Nicolson, who believes that "the life of a nonentity or mediocrity, however skilfully contrived, conflicts with primary biographical principles." [7] We are no longer a compla cent Victorian audience. We find it more difficult, perhaps, to define "nonentity" or "mediocrity." Further, since ideals as absolutes can never exist, in past or present, one might suggest that hero making is ethically wrong simply as a false-hood. The effects of hero worship might also be questioned. What happens when the child finds he cannot become even close to the ideal? Does he destroy himself or the society that seemingly prevented the attainment of this end? What happens when the hero is discovered to be an ordinary man or even a fraud? Does the child become so disillusioned that he gives up the possibility of positive change, or does he decide that, after all, the dishonest way "to the top" still gets you there—or gets you there more easily? I believe that the anti-hero is a legitimate subject of the biographer who works for children, that passivity or even outright failure can be interesting, imaginative, and even inspiring.

According to children's writer, Jean Karl, one of the attributes that makes a children's book distinct is "outlook." She finds that "A children's book looks at life with hope, even when it is painting the most disastrous of circumstances. . . It does not believe that everything is always fine. But it is willing to hope that something can be done, that life can be better." [8] Such an outlook means not only that certain subjects would necessarily be considered improper, but certain portions of the lives of eminent people might be excluded. If the subject's weaknesses or failings were included, the reader might question whether the contribution was, in fact, worth it. Other lives might be censored, not because their examination leads to existential despair, bur because their "sexual irregularities" might inspire to youthful orgy. According to Lillian Hollowell, the editor of a well-known anthology of children's literature, the complete lives of a Brahms or a Shelley "do not bear close inspection." [9] She is eager to maintain, however, that " A good biographer neither distorts nor suppresses; he may give a partial life, but he portrays his subject truthfully, noting both virtures and shortcomings." [10] One may ponder on whether exclusion is not a delicate form of suppression.

May Hill Arbuthnot, probably the most widely known writer on the subject of children's literature, also sanctioned "limited biographies," for, paradoxically, giving a more accurate view of the whole man. [11] "Adult peccadilloes," she maintained, will distort the essential character. One instance she cited was of "one of our historical heroes" who—as other frontiersmen—took an Indian wife and then deserted her. One might well ask whether a typical practice can be ignored (or even justified) merely for its "normality"; whether on the contrary, if the incident were included in the book, the child might gain better understanding of the plight of the American Indian. If the "hero" were, except for this part of his life, a decent sort, the child might still feel him worthy of reading about. My own feeling is that such heroes need humbling. Elsewhere, May Arbuthnot agreed that

144

while a biography was, by her definition, a story of a hero, that hero should be presented with weaknesses and obstacles. Such a presentation, she felt, would give young people "courage to surmount personal or social difficulties." [12] She did not mention what these weaknesses were.

Some persons are never mentioned, are never subjects, for children's biographies. Those people whose sex lives were "irregular" are not considered appropriate: George Sand, Oscar Wilde, Lillie Langtry, or Casanova. Nor are "love-linked" people given twin billing: Nicholas and Alexandra, The Duke and Duchess of Windsor, Scott and Zelda Fitzgerald. Those who have led violent lives outside the "establishment" are also disqualified—Dillinger, for instance. Most show people who are "entertainers" rather than "legitimate" actors are considered too "trivial" to be models for children. Often their psychological background is considered disturbing: Marilyn Monroe, Lana Turner, Tiny Tim. Prominent political figures are excluded on the grounds that they are uninteresting: Governor Rockefeller. Other people whose lives may be worthy and inspiring are excluded or not examined because their contributions are considered too difficult for young people to grasp: Thorndike, the psychologist; Simone Weil, mystical philosopher; Horace Walpole, writer and art collector; and James Joyce. Among these left-out subjects for children, there seem to be no lives of cooks or critics, farmers or pharmacists, mothers or merchandisers. [13]

Biographers for children not only differ in what material is selected or in what person is regarded as an appropriate subject but in how the chosen material is structurally included. If a work is categorized as biography rather than biographical fiction, it follows a plot closely parallel to the life, usually chronological, of the characters and incorporates valid situations and behavior which can be documented or deduced from sources. (Rarely, however, are these sources listed in biographies for children.) What is distinct in a biography for children is the extensive use of dramatic devices rather than narrative or expository ones— imaginary conversation to convey essentially accurate facts, behavior, or actions. Information or description is also frequently injected to supply a clearer or more vivid account of the people or times. In a life of Pocahontas, the author pauses to describe how herbs are used to make healing drinks and ointments, and to describe how the young squaws look when they perform a dance for Captain John Smith.

A comparison of the way a life is told for an adult and for a child is interestingly clarified in "News Notes from the Feminist Press." Reah Heyn, the writer of Challenge to Become a Doctor: The Story of Elizabeth Blackwell, discovered how she needed to revise her book to appeal to children:


BEFORE        Best of all, Elizabeth now had a partner. Her name was Marie Zakrewska, called by everyone Dr. Zak. Marie had been chief-midwife and professor at a hospital in Germany, but lost her job due to the jealous anger of the men doctors. Dr. Zak than travelled to America, hoping to find more opportunity, but her friends kept telling her to be satisfied with a nursing career.

AFTER         On the morning of May 15th, 1954, a young Polish woman walked into the dispensary. She could hardly speak English, but Elizabeth knew enough German to understand her.

"My name Marie Zakrewska , " the woman said. "I came to America . . . continue medical work . . . from German."

Elizabeth was astonished. "Tell me your background."

Groping for the correct words in English, Marie described her past. "Age 23, I was chief midwife . . . professor at hospital Berlin. Students devoted . . . but much jealousy among doctors . . . they say I should be nurse. Support myself for year by sewing. Someone told me your name . . . I come for guidance."

Elizabeth took a deep interest in this determined woman. "First, I shall give you English lessons, and then you must go to college and get your medical degree. Meanwhile, would you like to assist in the dispensary?"

Obviously overjoyed, Marie replied, "Oh yes, Dr. Blackwell. Been very depressed . . . I date my new life in America from this visit."

Such biographies, though not necessarily less scholarly in research, are necessarily less complex in detail and less comprehensive in coverage. Writing in Commonweal, Elizabeth Minot Graves comments that these very limitations often require more writing skill than biographies for adults, since the writers must write clearly, and with pace, must make the individuals come to life. The biographer must write this way consistently, or he will lose his young readers.

Arnold Adoff's book on Malcolm X (New York, 1970) is essentially a picture book which glosses over the early life of Malcolm and barely suggests his real impact as a Muslim and as the leader of the Organization of Afro-American Unity. The book for adults—The Autobiography of Malcolm X—is so far superior in what it includes that it would seem advisable for the child to wait until he can read this account. A book on Martin Luther King by Margaret Boone-Jones (Chicago, 1968) is also too vague in conveying either the vitality of the individual or the nature and extent of his political and spiritual influence. King simply works, for example, "to have bad laws changed for better ones."

Though Langston Hughes experienced poverty and suffered the usual indignities inflicted on his race, Charlemae Rollins in Black Troubadour (Stokie, Illinois, 1970) sees the poet as having a rather favorable environment. While some facts are included to indicate economic hardship, the suffering is made conducive to artistic success. The idea is that if you work hard, regardless of background, you will succeed. Milton Meltzer's Langston Hughes, A Biography, also written for teenagers, does not gloss over the poet's difficulties, nor does it see the American way of life with such blurry optimism. The physical and psychological brutality suffered by Hughes as a child is gone into, as are the conditions of the Black ghetto in Cleveland during the earlier part of this century. Later, as Meltzer indicates, during the era of McCarthyism, Hughes was cited as a communist (a charge never proved) for his "radical books." As a result of his having appeared before the "Un-American" Committee, he lost lecturing jobs. Not for epitomizing the American Dream is Hughes acclaimed in Meltzer's book, but rather for giving voice to social injustice, to the importance of the Black "soul," to the causes of the migrant workers and other deprived groups. [15]

For older children and adolescents, surely figures of economic or political importance are capable of being humanized, but they tend to disappear as people in the panorama of chronology, geneology, contemporary personalities, politics and statistics. We are often only faintly aware of the physical person, his environment, his family relationships. The aim of the biographer is to present palatable history, but usually the effect is to present an enigmatic figure moving through a muddled sequence of events. Zapata, by Ronald Syme (New York, 1971) is certainly both an over-simplification of character and a mystification of Mexican history. Leader at Large: The Long and Fighting Life of Norman Thomas by Charles Gorham (New York, 1970) is more satisfactory as history as well as in humanization, but the author often loses Thomas to circumstances and political experiences. When Thomas does reappear, the author views him less as a man than as a movement to be pondered on and praised. Harry Fleishman's book, Norman Thomas (New York, 1970), an "adult" source to which Gorham admits some indebtedness, is also enthusiastic in its endorsement of Thomas the man and of the socialism Thomas advocated. But the book is more acceptable as a biography because it provides a fuller perspective of the subject—the child, student, husband, and social reformer.

As an "establishment" figure, Andrew Carnegie provides a startling contrast to Thomas in his complete acceptance of a social code through which he eventually finds personal satisfaction and vast public success. In Andrew Carnegie (New York, 1964), Clara Ingram Judson reveals the reasons for Carnegie's achievement, but also promotes the work ethic. Carnegie may have lived by the Calvinist doctrine, and the writer here makes him into the allegorical American figure of "the go-getter." The repeated implication to the child is, "If you work hard, have strength and resolution, show initiative, are proud of what you are doing, are persistent in your effort, uncomplaining in your unremitting diligence, never refuse the opportunity to better yourself, show honesty and thrift, undertake responsibility, show, above all, ambition to better yourself—you, too, will make your million." Carnegie may have been devoted to such principles, but it is questionable as to whether his devotion was this fanatic. However Carnegie felt, the obvious didacticism here makes the character unbelievable.

Written by Clara Judson's daughters, the foreword to this book explains their mother's aim in writing her numerous biographies—to reveal how these "leaders," "threads in the tapestry of America," helped realize the beliefs that Americans hold: faith in government by the people; devotion to freedom; belief in education; and the conviction that each individual is important. Andrew Carnegie, then, is one of the threads in that glorious American flag, an embodiment of nationalistic goals.

Carnegie's treatment of labor is never critically or fairly examined. However amiably Carnegie exercises a tyranny over his workers, he is still a tyrant. In accepting the idea of a union in writing, yet advising that all mills be non-union to prevent disputes over wages, he reveals some duplicity; and his so-called "interest and concern for workers" (p. 124) is never convincingly demonstrated. The so-called champion of workingmen actually denied the Homestead workers a national union, and gave all workers an inadequate wage, determined by "a sliding scale." In 1892, after the Homestead strike, the leaders lost everything, and rates for the workingmen were cut even further. Workers labored seven days a week on a twelve-hour shift. As a biographer for adults points out, "And Carnegie went on giving libraries and wondering why so few adults made use of his magnificent gifts." [16]

Clara Judson refers to The Gospel of Wealth as a truth. This work affirms Carnegie's notion that wealth in the hands of a few can elevate the race much more effectively than wealth distributed more equitably. Mrs. Judson seems, then, to confirm this notion that the "man of wealth" is "a trustee in the community" and deserves to be since he is obviously much superior to "his poorer brethren." This was a concept particularly common among Calvinists of the period, and one still held by many people, but not all, and it can only be maintained in Carnegie's biography by allowing for certain omissions from the whole story, as I have cited above.

If Carnegie is the American hero, the self-made man and the fulfillment of the American dream, then Karl Marx is the arch-villain, the Satan who throws down all who would ascend the ladder to the golden heaven, where the God of the Dollar reigns supreme. Written for adolescents, Karl Marx, The Father of Modern Socialism, by Albert Alexander, is not really biography but a diatribe against the economic philosophy Marx espoused and a defense of the American system. It is a "loaded" book. Marx is hateful because he represents a hated doctrine. As a child, he was totally unlikeable; as a college student, he was totally irresponsible; as an adult, he is best characterized as an atheist who, unable to bear most people and incapable of understanding life in general, escapes from living through philosophical abstraction.

The author implies that the 10-point program in The Communist Manifesto is somehow invalid because many of the goals in that program have since been accepted. Marx's thinking is criticized as being confined to the era in which he lived, derived from Marx's observance of hopeless conditions of that day—not in any sense a far-reaching explanation which can have relevant application. Das Kapital is disapproved of for revealing how wealth can come to be concentrated in a few hands. Income and inheritance taxes are viewed by the author as effective means of preventing such accumulations. Thus Marx as a philosopher is pictured by Alexander as a self-deluded, selfish individual who simply plays games with abstractions in order to avoid honest work.

Generally, if one is to be an honest-to-goodness hero—either in this country or elsewhere—he must have known some kind of economic deprivation. Riches are not justified if the rags have not been flaunted beforehand. In biographies of Andrew Carnegie for children, either written by Katherine Shippen (New York, 1958) or by Clara Judson (discussed previously), the hero's early life is marked by poverty. Poor from what perspective? one might well ask. How comparatively poor as immigrants in the mid-nineteenth century? And is one really poor with relatives and friends in Pittsburgh, close by, who can lend money, give jobs, provide contracts?

Financial difficulty is also a means to strength of mind and inspiration to effort in Explorer of the Unconscious: Sigmund Freud, by Adrien Stoutenburg and Laura Nelson Baker (New York, 1965). The assumption seems to be that a lack of funds necessarily means poverty. Actually when Freud had "no money available" and was "worried about debts," he was, at the same time, collecting primitive sculpture, taking long summer vacations, and sporting stylish clothes. His contribution to psychology did not depend on either his id, ego, or superego having known "real" want.

Even the poverty of George Washington is stressed. Elsie Ball in George Washington, First President (New York, 1954) sees poor George at eleven inheriting only "a large tract of land which was not very fertile" (p. 14) and Ferry Farm—not really his, but to be used as a family homestead. George, then, has "to make his own way in the world."

This misleading notion that fame and fortune come to those who work hard and long and that, conversely, those that have fame and fortune always deserve it, can well arouse psychological and even physical violence, once the realistic situation is confronted by the child and he recognizes how he has been biographically brainwashed.

Presenting a cultural and chronological perspective can diminish the possibility of distortion. In other words, if the person is poor, why poor, how poor, and, perhaps, how comparatively poor today? Why brave, how brave, and to whom? How brave today?

Sitting Bull by La Vere Anderson (Champaign, Illinois, 1970), for the 8 - 11 age group, is a clear and lively book, sympathetic to an understanding of the values of Sioux life. In the Sioux battle with the Crows, "Slow" (the hero's original name) is regarded as brave after he is the first to strike a Crow Indian from his horse. Killing, in this case, is regarded as respectable, even deserving of reverence, as it probably always has been so long as the death comes to an enemy. To his own people, though, Sitting Bull is always gentle and compassionate. He abolishes slavery in his band. He tells stories, creates pictures, composes songs. He is wise. How comes such a man—or any man—to kill?

Perhaps the biographer needs to regard violence and its particular value to this Indian tribe; perhaps he should suggest how certain types of destruction are worshipped today. Peace-abiding citizens and "family men" may also destroy and yet be acclaimed heroes.

One would need a team of researchers working for some years to cover every facet of the treatment of biography for children. More research needs to be done on how a "life" is viewed for the young as compared with how the same life is viewed for the adult. More studies need to be made of the treatment of evil in children's books. Also, an investigation is desperately needed of the hiatus in the treatment of sex in all children's books, including biographies. The supposedly "brave" children's biographies of the pioneer in birth control, Margaret Sanger, have a curious habit of omitting her rich love life, including her marriages. Certainly these had some bearing on her crusade.

All in all, I see two major needs. The first is to encourage the writing of biographies of great human beings who are not famous, and who may be greater for this very reason, that they did not seek or obtain renown. We all have known such people and could wish for nothing more for our children than that they be like these quiet great ones. The second need is to give the subjects of biographies for children a fuller treatment—not to talk down to the child. The danger in the half truths of so many current biographies for children is that when that child reads the total account of the life in an "adult" book, he is understandably likely to distrust all adult information and instruction, and throw the good out along with the bad.

---

[1] John A. Garraty, The Nature of Biography (New York, 1957), p. 28.

[2] Learned Bulman, "Biographies for Teen-Agers," Readings About Children's Literature, ed. Evelyn R. Robinson (New York, 1966), p. 412. Reprinted from English Journal, 47 (November, 1958), 487-94.

[3] Richard Ellmann, "That's Life," The New York Review of Books, June 17, 1971, p. 3.

[4] Garraty, p. 140.

[5] André Maurois, "The Ethics of Biography," Biography and Truth, ed. Stanley Weintraub (New York, 1967), p. 50.

[6] Richard D. Altick, Lives and Letters: A History of Literary Biography in England and America (New York, 1965), p. 85.

[7] Harold Nicolson, The Development of English Biography (London, 1928), p. 146

[8] Jean Karl, From Childhood to Childhood: Children's Books and Their Creators (New York, 1970), p. 7.

[9] Lillian Hollowell, ed., A Book of Children's Literature (New York, 1966), p. 241.

[10] Hollowell, p. 242.

[11] May Hill Arbuthnot, Children's Reading in the Home (Glenview, Illinois, 1968), p. 261.

[12] Arbuthnot, p. 259.

[13] See for instance, Doris Solomon, compiler, <u>Best Books for Children</u> (New York, 1970).

[14] As discussed in "News Notes," <u>Feminist Press</u>, Baltimore, Maryland. (Spring, 1971), p. 7.

[15] Milton Meltzer, <u>Langston Hughes, A Biography</u> (New York, 1968).

[16] Joseph Frazier Wall, <u>Andrew Carnegie</u> (London, 1970), p. 579.

# ALICE OUR CONTEMPORARY[*]

Jack J. Jorgens

In his discussion of the fairy tale, W. H. Auden nicely sums up the stereotypi-
cal view of children's literature. The world of the fairy tale, he says, is an unam-
biguous, unproblematic place where appearance reflects reality. It is a world of
being, not becoming, where typical, one-dimensional characters (either good or
bad) behave strictly in accordance with their natures, and always receive the
appropriate rewards or punishments. It is a predictable world where events occur
in fixed numerical and geometrical patterns. And above all, it is a world without
intense emotion or awareness where even the most violent acts are viewed by
characters and readers with detachment, as not horrible but somehow fun, playful. [1]
But children's books are written by adults, not children, and one need not be a frequent contributor to American Imago to see that they reflect not only the author's
ideals of what children ought to like and be, but his own fears and fantasies. The
sense of freedom many writers feel when they are addressing an audience that they
consider to be more imaginative and more innocent than any other often leads to
works which are strange distorting-mirror images of social problems and upheavals,
personal compulsions, and philosophical dilemmas. The fanciful is also the uninhibited and the unrepressed.

The limitations of the stereotype of children's fiction become clear when one
applies them to the greatest of such works—Alice's Adventures in Wonderland and
Through the Looking-Glass and What Alice Found There. In them we find not only
the typical characteristics, but negations and parodies of them as well. Alice is
at once simple and complex, predictable and unpredictable, sentimental and tough-
minded, escapist and realistic, humorous and satirical, melodramatic and tragic.
Carroll took the problems children face while growing up—their dreams, their imaginary worlds, and their games—and combined them with the problems of adult life:
the labyrinths of conflicting values, the struggle to meet the demands of society
and self, the coming to terms with mortality. All these he fused in an imagination
heated by intense pressures within him—his sexual longings, his seizures of
"unholy thoughts", and his despair. In Alice (written for the little girls he was so
attracted to) Carroll embodied both the quest of modern man for meaning in what
seems to be a grotesque nightmare and his personal quest for the still, quiet center.

The success the Alice books have had with children grew out of Carroll's pro-
found understanding of children and their problems. On those innumerable after-
noons of tale-telling and games with his young friends, he learned just how to delight them, how to frighten them and then provide release in laughter, and how to
warp or exaggerate life until it became ridiculous or wonderful. To children, who

---

[*] One of a series of lectures on children's literature delivered at the University
of Connecticut in 1970.

have constantly to adjust to the new, Carroll often presents a world of wish-fulfill-
ment where the heroine is skillful enough to adjust to any situation, or powerful
enough to shape it to suit herself. If the spectre of school becomes too much, let
it be transformed (as it all too often is) into reeling, writhing, ambition, distraction,
uglification, derision, mystery, seaography, drawling, stretching, fainting in
coils, laughing, and grief (p. 129).[2] If books with no pictures or dialogue bore us,
or a winter's afternoon makes us lonely, let us chase a rabbit down his hole or walk
through a mirror into another world. Let all those dull poems with morals at the end
be re-written. Let them tell us how crocodiles eat the little fishes rather than how
the industrious bees demonstrate that idle hands are the devil's tools (p. 38). Let
our poems tell us that old people are, among other things, crazy, fat, ugly, slack-
jawed, not just that if you are careful of your health and remember God you will
have a golden old age (p. 68). Let them tell us that the prudent "lobster" speaks
contemptuously of the "sharks" only in their absence, not that sloth is a thing to
be abhorred (p. 139). Let adults recall how it feels to be ruled by people whose
time is always worth a thousand pounds a minute (p. 217). Let them recall the pain,
the disorientation, and the embarrassments of growing up—the difficulty of keeping
up with inconsiderate long-legged adults (p. 208), the shyness and self-conscious-
ness (p. 217), the perplexing fact that our feet do not want to go in the same direction we want to, and the dilemmas resulting from the outgrowing of old selves or of
burying them within new selves so that" . . . it's no use going back to yester-
day, because I was a different person then" (p. 138). Let them remember the ogres
that haunted our dreams—the Jabberwock, the Bander-snatch, and the Snark—and
our fear of the darkness, but also that we take delight in things like Mr. Tenniel's
surrealistic scene with the toves, borogroves, and raths wandering about a sundial (p. 271), his grinning cats, and his strange, horrible beast the Jabberwock
(p. 198). Let them see how ludicrous it is that they justify themselves by crying
"I'm older than you, and must know better" (p. 45), and how inexplicable to a
child an adult's lightning changes in mood are: "the Queen turned crimson with
fury, and, after glaring at her for a moment like a wild beast, began screaming,
'Off with her head!'" (p. 109).

Of course the adult reader's view is more complicated than the child's. We
see Alice from two perspectives—the child's and the adult's—and are therefore
sometimes amused at her naivete and her parroting of her parents. Part of her
charm for adults is the mixture of her stern, sensible, "adult" side (cf. her concern for eating and drinking the right things) with her mischievous, insecure "childish" side (frequently the two selves separate and talk things over between them).
It is amusing to observe (and recall) the smugness of a six- or seven-year-old who
knows that all questions have answers and all answers questions, that the world
is an orderly and logical place and that what she has been taught to be good and
right is good and right. We smile as Alice flaunts her moral superiority on her
journeys just as she flaunts her knowledge and her big words. It is not so amusing,
however, to feel with Alice what it is like to hear, "didn't you know that?" (p. 202)
or "it's my opinion that you never think at all" (p. 203), or, from the White Queen,
described by Carroll as "cold and calm . . . formal and strict . . Pedantic to
the tenth degree, the concentrated essence of all governesses!" (p. 206 n. 5),

"I don't know what you mean by your way . . . all the ways about here belong to me . . ." (p. 206). Least comforting of all is what Alice dreams of doing to adults when she fulfills the wish every child has of being bigger than anybody: she would behead us, as she threatens to do with the flowers—"If you don't hold your tongues, I"ll pick you" (p. 202)—or blow us all away like a pack of cards, or play cat-and-mouse with us: "Nurse!  Do let's pretend that I'm a hungry hyaena, and you're a bone!" (p. 180).

As a number of literary critics have recently pointed out, Carroll's Alice books are much more than skillfully written vehicles for childish revenge and adult complacency.  This new appraisal grows largely from our realization that many of the problems of modern man are really extensions of those of children (hence the growing interest in early development), that myth and the unconscious cut across the lines dividing children from adults.  William Empson pointed out a number of important themes and patterns in the course of his well-known discussion of Alice as Swain.[3]  He reveals that there is in Alice a curiously Darwinian retelling of Genesis where Alice is born out of her own sorrow (her salt tears are the amniotic fluid), and a whole Noah's ark of animals emerge from that "sea" as man, according to evolutionary theory, did long ago.  There are, beside the parodies of snobbishness, politics, progress, and industrialization, recurring death jokes (e.g. pp. 27, 32, 64) and a persistent linking of puberty with death.  There is Alice's growth in her womb-house where she feels cramped and fears that her food and air will be cut off.  In addition, there is the curious zoo of post-Darwinian animals which represent facets of Man (the Cheshire cat = intellectual detachment, abstraction, an inner world), and demonstrate the vicious natural struggle for survival in which man is involved (Alice often squeamishly shies away from some proffered "naked lunch").

Out of the links Empson made between Carroll's life and his books grew Phyllis Greenacre's Freudian biography [4] which establishes that Dodgson, like Verlaine and Joyce, poured his inner life into his works, and in doing so touched the universal.  Far from limiting herself to the listing of suggestive holes and elongated objects, the author makes several penetrating observations including the basic one that the world of Alice, with its disorientations of time and space, mysteries of cause and effect, confusions of animals and humans with the inanimate, its amorality, threats of extinction, and frightening female authority figures, is a reproduction of the stage of child development from about fifteen to thirty months—the stage in which crude sensory awareness and primal demands complicate themselves into memory, anticipation, self-awareness, and self-criticism (p. 210).  She links Carroll's female-dominated upbringing with the powerful females of his books and the singular lack of strong, well-respected adult males (p. 219).  And (to mention only her major points) she demonstrates how Carroll's passion for order and dismay at the aging of his young friends led to his attempts to preserve them for all time in his photographs and books (p. 213).  She shows (p. 245) how his fear of loss of memory, consciousness, and sanity (he kept careful records of his voluminous correspondence and carefully filed all his photographs and negatives) is incorporated in, and lends power to, Alice's journeys.

Building upon Empson and Greenacre, Donald Rackin in "Alice's Journey to the

End of Night,"[5] has skillfully shown how Alice in Wonderland may be viewed as
". . . a comic horror-vision of the chaotic land beneath the man-made groundwork
of Western thought and convention" (p. 313). When Alice goes "below ground,"
she seeks meaning in terms of the rules and conventions of Victorian society and
when they fail her, she is so terrified that she flees back to her comparatively
safe, logical world "above ground." In the course of her journey, "practically all
pattern, save the consistency of chaos, is annihilated" including mathematics,
logic, social convention, language, time and space (p. 313). Alice for Rackin,
is a grim comedy in which our laughter grows not from self-assurance, but from
our fear of meaninglessness. Alice's "curiosity" is madness—it leads her to a
dream world of black humor where, when man seeks to know reality through symbols, he manages only to become lost among them.

To the historian of literature, what is interesting about Carroll as seen in his
books is the tension between his restrained, rational, conservative "Victorian"
self and his wildly imaginative, satirical, "romantic" self. To critics who are
concerned primarily with what meaning literature has for us today, what seems important about works such as Alice and Shakespeare's A Midsummer Night's Dream[6]
is not their undeniably forgiving qualities—their gentle humor, wonder, and playfulness. Rather it is their absurdist traits, their dark ironies, their grotesque-
ness. Carroll's works have been extremely influential among avant-garde writers
since the turn of the century. Their "warping, stretching, compressing, inverting,
reversing, distorting" (p. 182 n. 4) of the world, reflected in Tenniel's illuatra-
tions of the Jabberwock and the Toves around the sundial placed them solidly in
the tradition of Surrealism. As Gardner points out (p. 193), Lear and Carroll, the
leading nonsense poets of their time, were precursors of the Dadaists, Italian
Futurists, Gertrude Stein, and Ogden Nash. Journeys underground, journeys to
the end of night or into mirror-worlds proliferate as writers like Celine and Genet
despair of finding meaning in the world. The fall of Humpty Dumpty achieves
mythological status in Joyce's Finnegan's Wake, and one could easily mistake
Alice's train ride or the trial of the knave of hearts for Kafka's work. Vladimir
Nabokov's first book was a translation of Alice into Russian, and his nymphet-lov-
ing hero Humbert Humbert resembles Carroll not a little. Echoing T. S. Eliot,
Jorge Luis Borges has noted in his essay "Kafka and His Precursors" that "every
writer creates his own precursors. His work modifies our conception of the past,
as it will modify the future." If this is so, then Borges, the author of so many
"fictions" about dreams within dreams, doubles, mythological creatures, and voy-
ages to strange worlds, "created" Alice as part of his own tradition.[7] From the
first, Alice was recognized as a forerunner of the theatre of the absurd with its
syntactic dead ends, philosophical mazes, and grotesque, cartoon-like characters.
Alice even has its own "Catch-22"—"We're all mad here. I'm mad. You're mad."
"How do you know I'm mad?" said Alice. "You must be," said the Cat, "or you
wouldn't have come here" (p. 89).

As important as these critics and creative artists have been in discovering the
contemporary Alice, I believe it has been most skillfully brought into focus by a
group of actors who humorously called themselves The Manhattan Project, under
the direction of Andre Gregory.[8] Because the production so graphically illustrates,

in their original context, the aspects of _Alice_ that have attracted modern artists and critics, it is an important bridge between the critical world that describes _Alice_ and the artistic world that draws upon it.

There have, of course, been numerous stage versions of Carroll's works (the earliest having as collaborator Carroll himself), and films have been made by Paramount (1933) and Walt Disney (1951), but only in this production was the importance of _Alice_ to our time made clear. The mode Gregory has chosen for his _Alice_ is the strenuous one evolved by groups such as the Open Theater and the Performance Group. From Artaud's Theatre of Cruelty he borrowed moments of savage eroticism, violent physicality, anarchic humor, and a burning focus on the actor. For a decor he chose the rags and junk of Grotowski's Poor Theatre which stripped the production of all gaudy, slick, showmanship. When we entered the tiny, crowded lobby of the small converted church, we were swept like Alice through a rabbit hole and a long corridor and bunched up on risers with old chair seats nailed to them (at random so nobody _fit_ very well). From there we looked down on a small square stage which looked like somebody's old attic or a seedy pawn shop. This playing area, "half circus—half nursery,"[9] had a torn canvas floor, an old parachute spread out over it for a roof, a stack of chairs, a bench, and table, a ladder, an old gramophone, and a curtain at the back made of old newspapers.

As in Weiss's _Marat Sade_, the play was acted out by a mad chorus. All save Alice were insane, hopelessly wrenched out of "normality", swept into forgetfulness and euphoria, or smashed against each other by fits of rage. Their chaotic costumes reflected their minds: a tattered, soiled petticoated dress with an apron (like the one shown by Tenniel) for Alice, a coat and tails grubby overalls for the White Rabbit/March Hare, a stack of hats and old suit coat for the Mad Hatter. The White Queen and the Narrator/"Balloon Prince" wore quilted shirts and pants which through dream-transfer mirrored the padding from a bed or (to us) invisible walls of an insane asylum (Gregory, quoted by Lahr, p. 61). The sound effects, which like the setting and costumes provided little sensual pleasure, were raucous and harsh. Marches and tunes from the twenties were shouted by the chorus or blared out over the old gramophone. The air was full of groans, whistles, ticking clocks, long agonizing silences, cuckoo birds, foghorns, bells, and screams (of pain? delight? terror?). Through this world travelled Alice, "homeless, forgetful, nostalgic, fragmented, emotionally and physically warped" (Lahr).

There was no break in the production and the acting was exhausting to watch— as exhausting as trying to read _Alice_ with close attention to everything in it. Hewes, like many spectators, admired the "totally engaged life-and-death ensemble playing of the actors that gave their confrontations the desperate urgency of a nightmare." The atmosphere was hyperactive, frenetic, compulsive, and the silences and pauses seemed to grow out of exhaustion. It was an atmosphere which provided a perfect dramatic representation of Carroll's intense Wonderland/Looking-Glass world which constantly assaults Alice and pressures her into readjusting to it Through questions, insults, and dream-like changes of scene. Within these cycles of feverish energy and fatigue Gregory captured the book's rich and varied humor, whimsical, grim, farcical by turns. Barnes underscored this variety, yet accurately listed that "humor is not the play's purpose. The purpose is fear. Mr. Gregory

156

noticed a very, very obvious fact. We laugh when we are afraid."

When working on <u>Marat Sade</u>, Adrian Mitchell and Peter Brook were struck by the play's ability to force the audience to repeatedly shift their focus, opinions, and emotions, to make them reformulate their ideas about what is happening and what it means. As in Shakespeare, the impressions come too fast to permit relaxation. "A good play sends many such messages, often several at a time, often crowding, jostling, overlapping one another. The intelligence, the feelings, the memory, the imagination are all stirred."[10] The <u>Alice</u> books have that quality, and it is a measure of the success of Gregory's adaptation that playgoers were stirred by "states of dread, of sexuality, of absurdity, of bewilderment, of wonder, of fear, of giddiness, of giggliness, of madness, of contraction, of elevation, of 'growing pains,' of terror, of playfulness, of ecstacy" (Kalem).

Both of Carroll's books have idyllic openings. The feeling in <u>Looking-Glass</u> is one of comfort and security, as Alice sits by the fire in a snug, warm chair and watches the snow kissing the windows and covering the trees and fields beyond. <u>Wonderland</u> begins with a leisurely, dreamy journey down the Thames as Dodgson spins tales of fantasy to three little girls on a golden afternoon. Yet I have always felt these openings are deceptive ones—as deceptive as the pictures of Dodgson with his boyish face, or accounts of his quiet, professorial life at Oxford. One cannot deduce the nature of <u>Alice</u> from its beginning any more than one can deduce what kind of book a stammering, shy bachelor who preferred the company of little girls could write. The production made both these points economically and powerfully.

The virtue of Gregory's production was its ability to string together great theatrical moments which skillfully elucidated the book. An anarchy of hair and padded bodies and junk would suddenly clarify itself into beautifully honed sequences from Carroll. In the opening scene, we hear back in the darkness the slow, excruciating tearing of a hole in the newspaper screen, and a clump of characters mumbling "Jabberwocky" enter. Alice in her tattered "little girl" dress comically struggles to escape this sticky blanket of nonsensical sounds, this group-grope, when suddenly the scene disintegrates and, after a silence accompanied by the ticking of a clock, it re-forms itself into the river scene at the start of her first journey. In a deep, confident voice, the narrator begins the prefatory poem "All in the Golden Afternoon" as a kneeling actor mimes paddling the boat down the Thames, imitating vocally the leisurely sh-h-h, sh-h-h, sh-h-h of the paddle. But slowly the compulsions and repressed drives most readers sense beneath idyllic narrative come to the surface. Carroll stumbles over his part, collects himself, begins again, stumbles again until he becomes totally confused and forgets everything. As he sweats and strains his memory, the paddling becomes more vehement, goes faster and faster until in a crescendo of violent exertions of mind and muscle, the scene explodes and suddenly we are confronted with Alice's tortuous journey down the rabbit hole. She is tossed, twisted, flung, rolled, assaulted by members of the chorus; the descent is a blend of sexual initiation, dizzying nightmare, madness, and death. Our journey into Carroll's mind has begun.

The Alice of Gregory's distinctly adult version was a modern kind of innocent, not the priggish little Victorian Miss of the original. In order to involve us in

Alice's journeys (who can identify with a snobbish little prude?) Gregory gave us a much more earthy, sympathetic heroine, naive and curious but able to look out for herself, a tomboy—unrestrained, "assertive, ornery, and often rude" (Brukenfeld). There was much less distance between this likeable tomboy and the audience than there is between the reader and the Alice of the original; when we are taken to the edge of madness with a tough, sensible girl who is in touch with her own feelings as much as any of us were when we were young, we cannot shrug it off so easily.

Through Alice, much of the playfulness and humor of the books is preserved. As long as she remains untouched by her "adventures" or at least is able to spring back from them, we can enjoy Gregory's elaborations on Carroll's fantasy world. Two good examples are the mirror-double of Alice, who mimics all her motions and perversely gives her the wrong answers to mathematical problems, and the "dirigible prince" who eludes her shrinkings and growings, who when punctured "skitters to the floor like a deflating balloon, twisting every which way" (Kerr). Often however the fun becomes uncomfortable. We chuckle at the hilarious caucus race, with the whole cast running in place until they collapse in exhaustion, but the scene ends with a cruel little turn: out of revenge, the birds who "choked and had to be patted on the back" (p. 50) gleefully make Alice eat her thimble. While we are amused by the mouse's body, which curves and sways as he narrates the mouse's "tale" of Fury's arbitrary hatefulness pursued out of boredom, the sense of claustrophobia becomes overwhelming as the "house" (made of actors) closes in on Alice.

The caterpillar scene was also both funny and unsettling. Atop several actors forming a mushroom, the thoroughly stoned caterpillar (in the book he speaks in a "languid, sleepy voice" and is "quietly smoking a long hookah and taking not the smallest notice of her or of anything else") inhales on the arm of one of the actors with long ecstatic breaths and eventually gets Alice silly/high. But his persistent questions about metamorphosis and identity shake her deeply, and like Carroll we are not so secure about who we are as to remain untouched.

Alice survives the duchess' crazy kitchen, the (boy, naturally) baby's transformation into a pig, and the grinning Cheshire Cat, but in the marvelously conceived mad tea-party Gregory makes it clear that Alice moves near the abyss, and does not recover as easily as she does earlier. The sinister, threatening Mad Hatter with three hats stacked on his head, rules the scene with barely preserved calm. Violence erupts when he is ridiculed by Alice and as he fixes her in a ferocious stare, he murderously squeezes a stick of butter in his fist. The Dormouse, wearing a World War I helmet, takes crushing farcical blows on it from the Mad Hatter. He stuffs his mouth with bread until he cannot speak, and turns the stomach of every one on and off stage by cramming a whole stick of butter into his mouth and eating it. The jittery, panicked March Hare nibbles his bread frantically. His actions are totally disjointed: he suddenly juggles three pieces of bread, plays footsie with Alice, waltzes her around the room, and then tries to rape her.

After some Marx brothers antics (actors scrawl "LEWIS LIKES LITTLE GIRLS" on a wall, the paranoid Queen of Hearts pops front-row spectators on the head with a huge plastic hammer, and a croquet game is played with human mallets and balls), we enter a weird, quiet land where trees (actors with ragged umbrellas folded down over their heads) sway in the dark, the wind whistles, and the gently, lyrically mad White Queen dances and spins verbal mazes about us. A tattered umbrella throws a swirling speckled light over the whole errie scene. Here Alice is lured toward the beauty, the quiet still place of madness — the misty place where distinctions between past, present, and future are obliterated, where memory becomes the future, where crime follows the punishment and trial, and where one cries out in pain before the wound is inflicted.

Alice confronts in Humpty Dumpty the chaos of words breaking loose from their agreed upon meanings. And all the while Humpty Dumpty, like Jerry in Albee's Zoo Story, is secretly thinking not about his "opponent's" dilemma, but about how to time his suicide correctly, how to play the game. This cynical philosopher-gamesman constantly catches Alice in word traps, treats the world as a riddle (which, Alice is learning, is true), insults her, and argues that even if communication were possible, it is irrelevant. He, like the Red King, "means what he says," but chooses any word he likes and makes it mean exactly what he wants it to. Humpty Dumpty dismisses Alice's (and our) questions about whether he can do such a thing with the definitive statement on the matter: "The question is which is to be master—that's all" (p. 269). Alice is staggered. When he suggests a suicide pact to her (p. 266), she is upset enough to consider it seriously, but things are not allowed to go any further. Tottering on a pile of chairs, held up by four imaginary guy ropes which are held with great difficulty by straining actors, Humpty Dumpty falls to the ground crushing an egg against his forehead as he strikes the floor. We feel Alice is free, but we are wrong. She stares in horror, and it dawns on us that she thinks it was she who was responsible for his death (again like Zoo Story). The trap has snapped shut.

In the following (final) scene, the White Knight brings Alice to a crisis. He is a summing up and intensification of all that has come before—a kaleidoscope of hate, fear, love, desire, disgust, wild imagination, and fearsome literalness. He violently assaults Alice and then becomes a child whose head must be cradled in her lap. The frank, friendly, flirtatious, good humored, little hoyden—conventional but curious, naively vulnerable—is destroyed by this Thomas Edison gone berserk. The humor is gone, and with it the release of laughter, watch a man conscious of his madness and pathetically struggling to escape it, but being sucked back into chaos by his weakness, his fear of the "sane" world, and his fatal attraction to the flashing jewel, madness. Alone in his maze of inventions and visions, he needs desperately to draw Alice in with him. The agony and attraction becomes unbearable for her, so she flees and awakens, taking back to the world above ground the dreamer's incredible knowledge—knowledge like Leda's knowledge of the Swan, or Cassandra's knowledge of the future to which we all are doomed.

As the more perceptive critics, writers, and theatre artists of our time have shown, far from being isolated from the world, Carroll's "children's books" lead us to its heart; they are a microcosm of it. We too are caught up in that intense nonsense played according to arbitrary rules which is unfortunately not confined to games. (Alice, like most of us, is a pawn until the end of the dream. The paradoxes of "Underground" and the "Looking-Glass World" are painfully contemporary. In the midst of a print explosion and cursed with the shifting sands of memory, which of us does not run as fast as we can to stay in the same place? In our world too, walking directly toward something only carries you further away from it—progress breeds regress, punishments become worse than crimes, inhumanity is proposed as our only humane course, and the last thing we can do to alleviate poverty (we are told) is to give money to the poor. What thoughtful observer of governments today can doubt that in deciding what words are going to mean, the only question is who is master? All too many "world leaders" respond in a crisis as the White King does: "You alarm me! I feel faint—Give me a ham sandwich!" (p. 281). Carroll's alarm and sense of loss at the aging and coarsening of the little girls he adored serves as a metaphor for all the effects of time: weakness, forgetfulness, inconstancy, disease, death. And the ironic twist is there too. Just when is despair we learn the melancholy lesson that time washes away loyalty, friendship, love, that the rushes we pick up will, like Alice's, fade and lose all their scent and beauty, we are confronted by the Red Queen who screams "When you've once said a thing, that fixes it, and you must take the consequences" (p. 323).

---

1 "Interlude: The Wish Game," The Dyer's Hand (New York, 1962).

2 The Annotated Alice, ed. Martin Gardner (New York, 1960). All quotations from Alice are from this edition.

3 English Pastoral Poetry (New York, 1938).

4 Swift and Carroll: A Psychoanalytical View of Two Lives (New York, 1955).

5 PMLA, 81 (October, 1966), 313-326.

6 See Jan Kott, Shakespeare Our Contemporary (Garden City, New York, 1966); Michael Taylor, "The Darker Purpose of A Midsummer Night's Dream," SEL, 9 (1969), 259-273; Alan Lewis, "A Midsummer Night's Dream—Fairy Fantasy or Erotic Nightmare," ETJ, 21 (1969), 251-258.

7 Labyrinths (London, 1970), p. 236.

8 Their adaptation of both Alice books under the title Alice in Wonderland opened at the Extension Theatre in New York September 31, 1970, but had been originated the previous year at NYU, and played at The Loft (New York City), where it won an Obie award before officially "opening," New Brunswick, Syracuse University, the Loeb Experimental Theatre at Harvard, and the Berkshire Theatre Festival in Stockbridge, Massachusetts. It was also shown recently on educational television (a medium not at all suited to productions like Gregory's Alice) and is going on world tour this Spring.

[9] Henry Hewes, <u>Saturday Review</u> (October 31, 1970), p. 12. The major reviewers, hereafter identified only by last name, were: Clive Barnes, <u>New York Times</u> (October 9, 1970); Dick Brukenfeld, <u>Village Voice</u> (May 14, 1970); Mel Gussow, <u>New York Times</u> (September 7, 1970); T. E. Kalem, <u>Time</u> (October 26, 1970), p. p. 93; Walter Kerr, <u>New York Times</u> (October 18, 1970); John Lahr, <u>Evergreen</u> (September 21, 1970), pp. 59-64, (this last is the best). Minor notices included: <u>Variety</u> (October 21, 1970); <u>Christian Science Monitor</u> (October 26, 1970); <u>Village Voice</u> (October 22, 1970); <u>Cue</u> (October 17, 1970); <u>Newsweek</u> (October 19, 1970); <u>National Review</u> (February 9, 1970). Also useful are Elenore Lester's interview with the director, <u>New York Times</u> (November 1, 1970), and the photographs in <u>T D R</u> (T48), 14 (September, 1970), pp. 94-104.

[10] Peter Brook, Introduction to <u>Marat/Sade</u> (New York, 1966), p. 5.

John Tenniel's illustration for <u>Alice in Wonderland</u>

Courtesy, Bodleian Library, Oxford

# CHILD READING AND MAN READING: OZ, BABAR, AND POOH*

Roger Sale

This essay began some years ago when I reread the Oz books in order to begin writing an appreciation of them. I had read them fairly often since childhood, but found that the prospect of trying to say something paralyzed me; I was, I discovered, being haunted by my own experience as a child reading these books. I could, it seemed, live with that experience only as long as I was silent and asked few questions, and it became haunting when I imagined writing for an audience that of course had not had my experience. As long as I tried to speak simply as a man, as a literary critic, I could perhaps say a great deal, but I would be running from the ghost that haunted me, and I did not want to do that and was not sure I could. The present essay is an effort to turn my difficulty into my subject: child reading as a fact in man reading, the differences it makes in the way the man reads that the child was reading those books before him. Inevitably I was thrown back on my own experience, though I can hope that the kind of thing that happened to me happened to others, with the same or different books from those I am going to discuss. Oz, Babar, and Pooh are my subjects because I read them all and loved them as a child, because they are quite different from each other, because they fall into the category of children's books and so avoid the problems and difficulties raised by fairy tales, folk stories, or adult classics adapted for children, where the original or natural audience is not children exclusively. Each of those reasons will, I hope, begin to seem relevant as I go along. I want to start by taking up the books in the order listed, working first with passages and episodes and working up my generalizations from them

At the opening of Ozma of Oz, the third of L. Frank Baum's series, Dorothy Gale and her Uncle Henry are on a ship bound for Australia, and a storm comes up. The captain is not alarmed but advises everyone to stay below, but Dorothy has been dozing while this message is being delivered, and so, when she wakes and does not find her uncle, she goes on deck. She sees there, clinging to a mast, a man that might be Uncle Henry, and she rushes toward him but gets no closer than a chicken coop lying on the deck when the storm doubles its force and she is hurled from the boat, holding on to the coop:

> Dorothy had a good ducking, you may be sure, but she didn't lose her presence of mind even for a second. She kept tight hold of the stout slats and as soon as she could get the water out of her eyes she saw that the wind had ripped the cover from the coop, and the poor chickens were fluttering away in every direction, being blown by the wind until they looked like

---

* Address at the Thirtieth Annual Session, The English Institute, Columbia University, September 9, 1971.

feather dusters without handles.  L. Frank Baum, <u>Ozma of Oz</u>
(Chicago, 1907), p. 19.

The storm is not so much a storm as it is an event that creates situations and problems.  A moment later, Dorothy climbs into the coop:

"Well, I declare," she exclaimed with a laugh.  "You're in
a pretty fix, Dorothy Gale, I can tell you!  and I haven't the
least idea how you're going to get out of it."  (p. 20)

Both Baum and Dorothy are surprised, but unexcited.  If you go off for Australia you
can get caught in a storm, and if you get caught in a storm you are liable to be
blown overboard and be in a pretty fix.

When the wind dies Dorothy sleeps on the floor of the coop, and in the morning
she discovers one remaining hen at the far end.  The hen has just laid an egg, and
she and Dorothy start a conversation.  Dorothy said to herself after a minute or
two:

"If we were in the Land of Oz, I wouldn't think it so queer,
because many of the animals can talk in that fairy country.
But out here in the ocean must be a good long way from Oz."
(p. 26)

Indeed, the ocean is a long way from Oz, and a long way from Kansas, too.  Just
as one expects animals to talk in Oz and not to talk in Kansas, so one isn't sure
what to expect on the ocean.  So the two find themselves discussing the hen's
grammar, which turns out to be rather like Dorothy's.

After a while the coop lands on a sandy beach.  They find a key, and an admoni-
tory inscription in the sand.  Both are hungry, and this leads to a long conversation
about whether it is better to eat live things, like bugs, or cooked dead things, like
chickens who have eaten bugs.  The hen gets her bugs, and Dorothy finds a grove
of trees on which grow lunch pails, filled with food.  Later Dorothy discovers a
door with a keyhole, so she tries the key she found on the beach, that being the
only one she has, and it works.  Inside is a mechanical man named Tik-Tok, and
though he turns out to be "magic," his makers, nonetheless, are Smith and Tinker,
American mechanical geniuses.  Baum's instinctive rightness about tone and detail allows us to move from a real world to an improbable world to a magic world
without any fanfare.  The sentences come easily, and imply they were no harder to
write than it would be to take the journey they describe.  His way is to fix himself
in the present, and to have Dorothy respond to each new detail with the same un-
shakable acceptance and curiosity with which she faced the one before it.  Our
problem is not to classify each detail according to how realistic or likely it
seems, but to do as Dorothy does and take each one as it comes, because that,
as we have always known, is the way to get out of pretty fixes.

At night people go to sleep, in the dark they look for light, in the morning they
search for food, in the face of a disused mechanical man you look for a key to
to wind him up.  It is precisely the atmosphere of Baum's writing not to be atmos-
pheric, or faerie, or invoking, mysterious, gripping.  The one false note in all
the early chapters is the sentence about Dorothy's not losing her presence of mind
when thrown overboard by the storm; for the rest, Baum does nothing to separate
himself as a narrator from his heroine.  It is her story, her acceptance, her

curiosity and inventiveness, and he implies he could do no better than she does at taking a journey to a magic country. In the next passage it is quite striking the way everything is unselfconsciously merged into the dramatic present, with no sense of Baum considering or calculating the past, the future, or the possibilities of magic. Princess Langwidere of the land of Ev, who has a collection of thirty heads she can put on and take off as she pleases, is assessing Dorothy's head:

"You are rather attractive," said the lady presently. "Not at all beautiful, you understand, but you have a certain style of prettiness that is different from any of my thirty heads. So I believe I'll take your head and give you No. 26 for it."

"Well, I believe you won't!" exclaimed Dorothy.

"It will do you no good to refuse," continued the Princess, "for I need your head for my collection, and in the land of Ev my will is law. I have never cared much for No. 26, and you will find that it is very little worn. Besides, it will do you just as well as the one you're wearing, for all practical purposes."

"I don't know anything about your No. 26, and I don't want to," said Dorothy firmly. "I'm not used to taking cast-off things, so I'll just keep my own head." (pp. 97-98)

What Dorothy is so grandly accepting here is much more important than Langwidere's No. 26 head, which she is not accepting, and that is the fact that she has such a head. Dorothy is totally inside the situation, the moment, and not the least bit interested in how heads might get off and on, or even in how best to deal with this imperious princess. She wants only to make clear her indignity, and what she is or isn't used to—in Kansas, or in Ev.

All this seems to me marvelous; I reread these pages with undiminished admiration for Baum's assurance with Dorothy and Dorothy's acceptance of herself and her present tense. I say "undiminished" admiration because it has always been one of my favorite sequences in the Oz books. This, and others similar to it where Dorothy or Tip or Trot or Betsy Bobbin takes a journey to a magic country, filled me, when young, as I remember it, with a powerful if undefined sense that it is morning and the world is fresh and possible. To be able to go, unintentionally, into a strange world and to accept each moment there—somehow, for me, that was and is morningtime; and I am sure that the value I placed on this possibility, and the value I thereby placed on the Oz books, is something that other children reading these books, to say nothing of adults coming to them for the first time, simply do not feel. When, for instance, the six-year-old son of a friend of mine says he doesn't much care for the Oz books because they are too cinchy, I know what he means, and in many ways I agree with him. But the child I was who read those beginning magical journeys to magic countries insists to the man who reads them now that he never be caught saying the Oz books are too cinchy, because that, for child and man, is not the point. When I was six it did not matter to me that the journey I liked best, in The Road to Oz, ended up at Ozma's long and boring birthday party; I said the book was my favorite anyway. Nor did the insipid satire and wit that mar so much of the middle sections of The Land of Oz keep me from loving the book because of its wonderful opening, with Tip, Mombi, Jack Pumpkinhead, and the trip to the Emerald City with the Sawhorse. Whenever I go back to these I feel their enchantment all over again, feel the delighted and exhilarated sense of its being morning and on a road that is magical not because its end is the Emerald City but because the heroine or hero at each step along the way is totally and unselfconsciously inside the situations that are taking them farther and farther from home. If I once read these sequences and did not feel this, then I would have lost part of myself.

But it is not the vividness of any particular memory concerning the Oz books that keeps me tied to the child that read them; I don't think that distinctness of memory is all that important. I have no single memory of Oz as clear as that of being frightened by a picture of a cat in a book called <u>Little Sally Mandy</u>, but the vividness of the memory and the fear does not make the book an important one for me. The experience was of the sort that every child knows, and could have been provoked by any one of hundreds of pictures or stories where an animal looms up in a frightening way. Neither the book nor the fear nor the memory of either is particularly interesting, whereas the opening sequences of a number of the Oz books, though my memory of them is less distinct, gave me something that nothing else could give.

I want to return to this point later, after looking at Babar and Pooh, and try to see it again in the context created by all three groups of books. The sequence from Jean De Brunhoff I have chosen, from the second Babar book, <u>The Travels</u>, is not, like that from <u>Ozma of Oz</u>, distinctively good, but instead characteristic of all of De Brunhoff's books. Near the middle of <u>The Travels</u>, Babar and Celeste are rescued from a tiny reef by a huge ocean liner, but their relief soon gives way to frustration and anger when they discover the captain of the ship will not let them go ashore and instead puts them in the stables:

> "They have given us straw to sleep on," cried Babar in a rage. "And hay to eat as if we were donkeys! We are locked in! I won't have it; I'll smash everything to bits! Jean De Brunhoff, <u>The Travels of Babar</u> (London, 1935), p. 23.

Celeste then offers the advice we usually associate with the name of Uncle Tom: "It is the captain. Let us be good, and he may set us free." Babar acquiesces, and on the next page we see only their large and seemingly defiant posteriors facing the captain who is selling the elephants to an animal tamer who wants them for his circus. Even though Babar and Celeste have gotten for her advice what others called Uncle Tom have often gotten, on the next page she is still counseling patience: "We won't stay in the circus long; we will get back to our own country and see Cornelius and little Arthur again." We then switch back to the elephant country where little Arthur is exploding a firecracker on the tail of an old rhinoceros named Rataxes, and Cornelius is unable to calm down the old rhino who is now threatening war.

It is a sequence different from anything in Baum, destructive and apparently cynical. The false sense of security raised by the original rescue, the avarice of the ship's captain, the arrogance of the animal tamer who imagines it is he who trains animals already highly civilized, the folly of Celeste for trusting the captain and then for imagining that seeing Arthur and Cornelius will set everything to rights—every move that does not seem to instruct us in cynicism is rudely undercut. And throughout the Babar books we see that De Brunhoff does despair that life is ever more than momentarily free of trouble, or that hoping does much good, or that we can make rules for whom to trust or what to expect. He shows us misfortunes and disasters of a kind not usually found in children's books: betrayal, desertion, cruelty, adventurousness and curiosity rewarded with danger and punishment, poisonous snakes and mushrooms, house fires, nightmares, capricious weather, homesickness. But this list falsifies. De Brunhoff does relentlessly deal with these facts of life, but his total effect is nowhere near as Gothic or as gloomy as my descriptions imply.

The major reason for this is that there is no register inside the story to carry the burden of the pains and sorrow, and we are thus not asked to imagine ourselves inside these terrible situations. When the savages attack Celeste while she is taking a nap, we are given no sense of surprise or danger, no sense that the savages are doing anything extraordinary; when, shortly thereafter, the whale who has befriended Babar and Celeste leaves them on a reef while she goes in search of food and then never returns, we are not allowed to think the elephants have been sorely betrayed. De Brunhoff exhibits great assurance in all this, and offers therefore great reassurance. Instead of dwelling on the disasters, De Brunhoff is always moving on, thereby mitigating the possibilities for both hope and despair. The rhinoceroses do go to war with the elephants, but Babar and Celeste escape from the circus, too, and return home in time for Babar to devise a ruse that routs the enemy. De Brunhoff then says, "King Babar was a great general," and in exactly the same tone with which he says "It was a great misfortune" when, in The Story of Babar, the original king of the elephants dies from eating a bad mushroom. Nothing is allowed to be taken at its highest or most emotional pitch; in De Brunhoff's hands words like "cruel," "happy," "great," "fled," "choke," "poison," "play," and "help" are all defused, robbed of their capacity to excite or alarm. For him equilibrium is the great goal and achievement, and it is gained not so much by finding a single tone or an implied state of rest as by constantly juxtaposing and thereby reconciling disparate attitudes and possibilities.

If I ask myself how much of this did I see as a child, my answer is, Enough. I saw it, of course, in the pictures, which I loved, stared at, and returned to as I did to no others. De Brunhoff puts two Vs in the brow of an elephant chef to show anger, and I would stare, but not in fear; he takes the tusks off the nurse of Babar's children to show how frightened she is that Alexander might be killed, and I would stare, but without anxiety for Alexander; he makes whole murals of elephants at work or play, and I would stare, though not with any sense of their exertion or pleasure. It may seem that the pictures are at odds with the text, that the child is absorbed mostly with what is piquant or odd in the illustrations while the adult is mostly aware of De Brunhoff's superbly French acceptance of misfortune and disaster. Yet they do not work at cross purposes, nor does De Brunhoff bring them together by turning the dreadful into the piquant. When I stared at the Vs in the brows of the elephant chef I could afford to be fascinated because I knew, without knowing how I knew, that there was no reason to be scared. The chef is angry because Zephir has fallen into his vanilla cream, but in the picture no one is frightened or alarmed—Zephir himself is just forlorn—and the text assures us the moment will pass. The last sentence of the episode is "Celeste took Zephir away to wash him," and on the next page we are at a garden party on the grounds of the Palace of Pleasure (<u>Babar the King</u>, pp. 19ff). The absence of any strong or consistent register, plus the way the story loosely juxta-poses events rather than push deeply into one set of complications, plus the im-passive tone of the narrator—these are De Brunhoff's techniques, and I had absor-bed enough of their effects to know even as a very small child that I could stare at any one picture as long as I liked. De Brunhoff himself is similarly released into playing in his pictures, to delight in showing elephants using their trunks to hold glasses and pencils and chalk and to take baths and eat cakes and swing tennis racquets. The reassurance offered by the sequences is strong enough to withstand De Brunhoff's insistence on showing us a great many of the natural shocks to which flesh is heir, and the child can even be fascinated by the pictures showing disasters—the king of the elephants turning green with poison, the gar-goyles and goblins of Babar's nightmare—because everything is working to con-vince him that this moment, though real, is transitory, something to be accepted as a part of life.

The child cannot say anywhere near as well as the man how all this is done, but he can receive the essential message of the text without being much interested in it; if for him the message is, "Look at the pictures," that is not the wrong message at all. It is not an accident that my happiest memories of reading aloud to my children are all of the Babar books. The effect of the relation De Brunhoff creates between his text and his pictures is to make a kind of alliance between child and man reading that allows each to do what he does in his own way without there being any necessity of either interfering or overlapping much with the other. If I cannot now stare at the pictures as my children could, as I could as a child, I can receive their witty truths my own way.

This point about Jean De Brunhoff's allying child and man so they can arrive at the same place by different routes, can help us see what is good and bad about the Pooh books of A. A. Milne. In reading the Babar books the child and the man operate independently, and the child need never feel that the man doing the read-ing is trying to guide or instruct him. Milne, on the other hand, openly and self-consciously tries to make an alliance between child and man. Not only do Milne and his son appear in the story as "you" and "I," but everything else is arranged so the child reader will agree to pursue those goals of good manners, good spelling, and obedience Milne is nudging him towards. There are many reasons why children do not read the Pooh books, as a rule, after they are old enough to read to them-selves, but one reason is that the books depend on being read aloud in the spirit of a cozy relation between reader and read to.

Let me start with a passage that shows Milne pretty much at his worst:

"We are all going on an expedition," said Christopher Robin, as he got up and brushed himself. "Thank you, Pooh."

"Going on an Expotition?" said Pooh eagerly. "I don't think I've ever been on one of these. Where are we going on this

Expotition?"

"Expedition, silly old bear. It's got an 'x' in it."
"Oh," said Pooh. "I know." But he didn't really.
"We're going to discover the North Pole."
"Oh," said Pooh again. "What is the North Pole?" he asked.
"It's just a thing you discover," said Christopher Robin, not
being quite sure himself. A. A. Milne, Winnie-the-Pooh
(New York, 1926), pp.112-113.

People and things are always being put in ranks; you calculate your superiority to
someone and then worry about who is superior to you. Milne makes Christopher
Robin feel superior to Pooh because Pooh can't say or spell "expedition"; then
he wants Christopher Robin, or any child being read to, to feel inferior because
they don't know how to get to the North Pole. Milne assumes it is important to
know how to spell as well as he and I can, which it isn't, and that we would know
how to get to the North Pole, which we don't. Milne is constantly vulnerable to
the charge that the fun of his stories is based on a very shallow snobbery.

But Milne is more interesting than that, and we can perhaps get at it by noting
the popularity of the Pooh books among adolescents. So many people in high
school and college have told me they liked Pooh that I started asking what they
liked, and invariably they would name something from this list: Pooh's hums,
especially "The more it snows, tiddely pom" and "I could spend a happy morning
Seeing Roo"; the spotted and herbaceous backson, Trespassers William, Piglet,
Eeyore's gloominess, Poohsticks. All are part of that aspect of the book that is
relaxed, lazy, cozy, nonsensical, and therefore, so the argument seems to go,
really right about life. This is the Forest seen as Utopia.

What the adolescent sees is really there, but the Forest is no Utopia. The two
books are essentially about the fact that Christopher Robin is now too old to play
with toy bears. First he is given a world over which he has complete power, and
if he is not very attractive as a deus ex machina in story after story, if he seldom
is as interesting as the Pooh and Piglet to whom he condescends, the pleasures
of his power are perfectly clear. But, secondly, he is now going to school, doing
sums, spelling words, worrying about not getting things right, about being ridiculed, and all he can do, in effect, is to take his fear of embarrassment and his need
to rank and his schoolboy facts, and impose them on the animals in the Forest.
Pooh in fact is not a bear of very little brain, but Christopher Robin puts Pooh in
situations where he will think he is because that is just what others are doing to
Christopher Robin in his hours away from the Forest. Seen this way, Milne is a
good deal shrewder and harder-headed than the adolescents' view of him. If he
has none of Lewis Carroll's power and wisdom and resembles him only in his
social prejudices, nonetheless most children do not like the Alice books because
they are about the fear of growing up, and many children do like the Pooh books
because they alter the focus slightly and are about how it is sad, but all right,
that we grow beyond our early childhood.

I speak here as an adult, but suspect I was aware of a good deal of this when I
was young. I can remember the strong effect that the most explicit statement of
Milne's theme, in the closing sentences of The House at Pooh Corner, had on me:

168

So they went off together. But wherever they go, and whatever happens to them on the way, in that enchanted place on
the top of the Forest, a little boy and his bear will always be
playing. <u>The House at Pooh Corner</u> (New York, 1928), pp. 177–178.
I find it hard to read that without something like tears beginning to move toward
the surface of my eyes. Nor do I think this is sentimental of me, though I am quite
aware that my tears are not so much for what is in the book as for my having read
these sentences and wept over them as a boy. The lies they tell are known to be
lies, which saves everything. Pooh and Christopher Robin do not go away together,
and we know it. The Forest is now forever closed except in memory, and that is not
a sentimental fact.

But Milne does not work this way most of the time. What I never saw as a child
but see everywhere now is the way the Forest is becoming tainted long before the
end by the alien values of Christopher Robin's and Milne's world. The primary
activity of the animals is deferring, often bordering on syncophancy. As Pooh and
Piglet in their clumsy ways, and as Rabbit and Owl in their more knowing but stu-
pider ways, attempt to manage and control things, they constantly imitate Christopher Robin, or wish they could. Christopher Robin always wins because he can be
lazy and mindless with Pooh and Piglet, or knowing and organizing with Owl and
Rabbit, and his presence is felt everywhere, except by Kanga, herself a mother,
and Tigger, the outsider. What is worse, Milne's view of schoolboy and adult life
is limited, empty, formalistic. It can be seen at its worst in Rabbit's efforts to
unbounce Tigger, at its most pathetic in Eeyore's triumphant making of the letter A,
its best in Christopher Robin's announcement that the stick in Pooh's hands is the
North Pole. Even there, though, where Christopher Robin is finding a neat way out
of his problem and is also making Pooh feel splendid, the idea is still that you
keep control over others by hiding your ignorance from them. Candor is seldom
found in the Forest, and a man reading the Pooh books to a child is bound to worry
that the child who really seems to like them is or will become a little monster.

But, interestingly, that seldom happens, because the alliance Milne seeks between adult and beginning schoolboy is just not that interesting. Most children do
not object to Pooh, and find them good for some laughter, but still, they seldom
read them to themselves. <u>Winnie-the-Pooh</u> and <u>The House at Pooh Corner</u> are about
the loss of early childhood, and I suspect that is a much more interesting fact to a
boy of sixteen than to a boy of six. The wit is surface wit, verbal playing, fun
to hear but forgettable. The child reading wants the adult reading in some relation
other than the one Milne offers, and a child who really knew what he liked might
well turn from the Pooh books and seek as antidote something like the Norse legends of the grimmer of the Grimm tales or something else he will be able to read
with pleasure for the rest of his life.

If at this point I were going to try to draw some single conclusion about the
effects of child reading on man reading, then I should either have chosen different
examples or argued them differently. In the case of Oz the child guides the adult,
in the case of Babar the child and the man seem to get to the same place by different routes, in the case of Pooh the child and man see different things and only part
of what the man sees is the result of the child's having seen it before him. And

other books give me quite different relationships with myself as child reader. For instance, I find Dr. Seuss' <u>And to Think that I Saw It on Mulberry Street</u> very pleasant, but barely read it as a man at all and lapse into remembered childhood reading with it, while, at the opposite extreme, my experience as a man with the stories of Beatrix Potter has been so enthralling that it has blotted out the much fainter experiences I had with them as a child. And so it goes. There seems to be no way to calculate or predict the relation of child to man with any given book.

But more can be said. The obvious fact to an adult is that all three of my examples are very different from each other and one way to express that difference is to label them American, French, and English. Baum's belief in the bouyancy and practicality and simple dignity of his heroines and heroes, his fascination with machines, some of which, like Ozma's magic picture and Glinda's book of records, he thought of as magical but which we call television and computer, his insistence that evil is only grown-up people acting like naughty children—all these are characteristics we think of as American. Jean De Brunhoff is distinctively French, much more knowing than Baum, more impassive, more civilized; in my more extravagant moments I have wanted to contend that those qualities for which Flaubert and Proust are best known they share with De Brunhoff and if they are better they are not any purer than he. All this is not only different from Baum, but from Milne, too. De Brunhoff is witty but never funny, and with Milne it is just the other way around; De Brunhoff is very much a grown man and Milne is an arrested child; De Brunhoff seems able to take in almost anything for his subjects while Milne's world is excluding, enclosed, snug, and whimsical.

Each author gives so purely that the child by reading them must learn a great deal about what it is to be American, French, and English: Baum with his faith in the American child left on his own to cope with things; De Brunhoff with his faith only in his intelligence; Milne with his faith that if one learns how things are named and done then everything turns out for the best. Put that way we have almost parodies of national types, but the authors don't really put themselves that way, though when we start contrasting them it is the purity and completeness of each that is striking. I know that one of my pleasures with the Oz books was that each one started off with a different situation and often a different set of characers, such that it seemed a totally distinct book, and then each became an Oz book, and shared with the others Baum's essential tone and manner. In other words, at the beginning of each book it was still and always morning. So too with Babar and Pooh, because their authors need only a page or two to evoke their worlds in their completeness. It is like learning the difference between the taste of milk, water, and orange juice, and the tastes, once learned, are not forgotten or felt to be unimportant, and as long as one goes on reading these books and tasting those tastes, there will be a distinctiveness to each every time he returns, and one which also can become a way to know or recognize other things not obviously similar. The opening sentence of <u>The Road to Oz</u> is "Please, miss," said the shaggy man, "can you tell me the road to Butterfield?" Within fifteen pages the road to Butterfield leads out of Kansas into no place, then into a country recognizably magical, then into the city of the foxes, then to the discovery that we have somehow been on the road to Oz all along. It seems to me the most enchanting thing in all the

Oz books, and whenever I hear or am reminded of any one detail in the sequence the whole thing comes back to me, so completely and purely does Baum make his details adhere one to another. Almost inevitably the relation of roads to Butterfield to roads to Oz has become my way of knowing all sorts of roads. Baum's magic journeys to magic countries came into my life when it was relatively unpopulated, nowhere near as varied or shifting in its values as it was to become, so the roots planted by these stories went deep and are always potentially in my experience, able to become consciously a part of it at a moment's notice.

But this fact about the purity of the experiences offered the child reading can also lead us to a converse fact, not about the distinctness of Oz, Babar, and Pooh, but about their commonality. For the effects of this early reading not only need not be but probably cannot be single. One word I used in writing about each author is "acceptance," because each in his different way is offering a kind of imaginative dogma about accepting. Baum, De Brunhoff, and Milne all are assurers, consolers, celebrating the actual and the possible in the midst of magic, confusion, loss, and lostness. Though I did not know this as a child, the more I think about it now the more it seems that I was ready to hear the different versions of the imaginative dogma each offered. Reduced to a single statement, the dogmas would be: for Baum, accept the present as being crucial, for the ability to deal well with each immediate circumstance is a kind of magic; for De Brunhoff, accept misfortune and the indifference and even the cruelty of others, not only because they are part of our condition but because their pains and sorrows are as transitory as the joys and peace that will follow; for Milne, accept the play of early childhood, for it is precious, accept that it is lost, accept the schoolboy and adult worlds that replace it. That which makes each writer pure, distinct, complete, is thus only part of the story; that which binds them together is at least as important.

What these writers taught me was not, I presume, to accept. The desire and the beginnings of the capacity to do that must have been present in me even before I knew them. But they could give me the terms of acceptance, the tone, manner and importance of so doing. I envied Dorothy Gale greatly, not so much because she could go to Oz as because she did so beautifully every step of the way, not by being strong or brave but by accepting and living inside each new situation. By comparison legendary figures like Arthur, or the boy David or Prometheus touched me less because they seemed fantastic. They were strong or brave enough to fight through or even to ignore their situations, and the appeal of that kind of figure had been pre-empted for me by the earlier and more appealing truths told me by Baum, De Brunhoff, and Milne; the more exceptional some feat was the less important it seemed. I read Superman desultorily. I created fantasies myself—as a rubber-armed pitcher, a winner of the World Series, a king of the sky—but I never invested much energy in them because in fantasies you do not have to accept.

I was, thus, a daylight reader, living in a daylight world. Those qualities about the Oz, Babar, and Pooh books which make them seem thin or tinny to others did not make them seem that way to me, and conversely, though I was fascinated by many fairy tales, I read them as something of a stranger, and their mysterious routes down to our deepest wishes and fears have never been as open and unclogged for me as they have been for many. All this I began to realize and put together only

171

comparatively recently when I understood who were, for me, the irreplaceable authors: Spenser, Fielding, George Eliot, William Empson, all large and wise writers, all seeking our possibilities in consideration and acceptance of our condition. These are for me the writers who count most. Others, more daring and exciting, like Shakespeare and Lawrence, taught me how to speak, but Spenser, Fielding, George Eliot, and Empson seem to have had a deeper effect even than that, and on parts of me that are silent and would be, but for them, dumb. When I realized that fact, it was not difficult to see that they began to become irreplaceable for me long before I had heard of any of them, when I first read Baum, De Brunhoff, and Milne. My knowing and caring for them as a child made them capable of coloring everything that followed, and those who did not read about Oz, Babar, and Pooh as children or, even more, those who did but did not like them, those people are in some important respects very different from me.

The child reader defines not only the man reader, but the man, and on this score I doubt that I am alone. In going back to the books of our childhood and to the experiences we had with them, we discover a great deal; not that it was bliss in that dawn to be alive, but what most matters to us, even why. This truth is in itself similar to those told us by my particular authors, Baum, De Brunhoff, and Milne, and can lead us back with renewed awareness of one of the really permanent truths, that we are fathers, but not masters, of ourselves.

# CONTRIBUTORS

Richard Arnoldi is in the doctoral program of the English Department, University of Connecticut

Robert J. Bator, Ph.D., Loyola University, is an Associate Professor at Olive-Harvey College of the City Colleges of Chicago

Lee Burns teaches children's literature in the English Department, University of Connecticut

Francelia Butler, Ph.D., University of Virginia, is associate professor of English, University of Connecticut

Laurence Gagnon is a Woodrow Wilson Fellow and candidate in the doctoral program of the Philosophy Department, University of Connecticut

Harriet Korim Hornstein is teacher and coordinator of a children's program in the Inner College, University of Connecticut

Jack Jorgens, Ph.D., New York University, is an assistant professor of English at the University of Massachusetts

Marilyn Jurich is an assistant professor in the English Department, Suffolk University, Boston

Hugh T. Keenan, Ph.D., University of Tennessee, is an associate professor of English at Georgia State University, Atlanta

R. Gordon Kelly is an assistant professor of American Civilization, The Graduate School of Arts and Sciences, University of Pennsylvania, Philadelphia

Mrs. Julie Carlson McAlpine, Ph.D., University of Connecticut, is an assistant professor who teaches children's literature there

Mrs. Meradith Tilbury McMunn is the first candidate in the doctoral program in Medieval Studies at the University of Connecticut

William Robert McMunn, Ph.D., Indiana University, is an assistant professor of English, University of Connecticut

Robert G. Miner, Jr., who is writing a doctoral dissertation on <u>Aesop's Fables</u>, teaches children's Literature at the University of Connecticut

Taimi M. Ranta is Professor of English Literature for Children and Young People in the English Department, Illinois State University, Normal

John Rodenbeck, Ph.D., University of Virginia, is an assistant professor of English, University of Michigan, Ann Arbor

Roger Sale is Professor of English at the University of Washington, Seattle

Dominique Tailleux, a doctoral candidate at the Sorbonne, Paris, teaches in the French Department at the University of Connecticut

R. Loring Taylor, Ph.D., University of California, is an assistant professor of English at the University of Connecticut

Alison White is Associate Professor of English at the University of Alberta, Canada

SUGGESTED TEXTS TO BE USED IN CONJUNCTION WITH THESE ESSAYS

For Fables     (the essays on "Aesop as Litmus" and "The Sage of LaFontaine")
Sir Roger L'Estrange, <u>Aesop's Fables</u>. Dover.
Leo Tolstoy, <u>Fables and Fairy Tales</u>. Signet.
<u>Fables of LaFontaine</u>, tr. Marianne Moore. Viking Paperback.

For Rhymes     (the essay, "The Child as Rebel in Song and Rhyme")
William S. Baring-Gould and Ceil Baring-Gould, <u>The Annotated Mother Goose</u>. Clarkson N. Potter or Meriden.
<u>The Nonsense Books of Edward Lear</u>. With a Foreword by Howard Moss. Signet.
Rudyard Kipling, <u>The Jungle Books</u>. With an Afterward by Marcus Cunliffe. Signet. (for the chants)
Iona and Peter Opie, <u>The Lore and Language of Schoolchildren</u>. Oxford.

For Folktales   (the essays, "Children's Literature in Old English," "Children's Literature in the Middle Ages," "Red Riding Hood," "Out of the Ordinary Road: John Locke and English Juvenile Fiction in the Eighteenth Century")
<u>The Story-Telling Stone</u>. <u>Myths and Tales of the American Indians</u>, ed., Susan Feldmann. Dell.
<u>The Blue Fairy Book</u>, ed. Andrew Lang. Dover.
<u>The Violet Fairy Book</u>, ed. Andrew Lang. Dover.

For Fantasy     (the essays, "Pilgrim's Progress as Fairy Tale," "From Fantasy to Reality: Ruskin's <u>King of the Golden River</u>, St. George's Guild, and Ruskin, Tennessee," "Parallels between <u>Our Mutual Friend </u>and the <u>Alice</u> Books," "Tap Roots into a Rose Garden," "Philosophy and Fantasy," "<u>Alice</u> Our Contemporary," "Death in Children's Literature")
<u>The Annotated Alice</u>. Introduction and Notes by Martin Gardner. Clarkson N. Potter or Forum.
Lewis Carroll, <u>Alice in Wonderland</u>, ed., Donald J. Gray. Norton Critical Edition.
Kenneth Grahame, <u>The Wind in the Willows</u>. Avon.
John Ruskin, <u>The King of the Golden River</u>. University Microfilms. Ann Arbor. (paper)
George MacDonald, <u>The Golden Key</u>. Farrar, Straus and Giroux.
L. Frank Baum, <u>The Wizard of Oz</u>. Avon.
Beatrix Potter, <u>Peter Rabbit</u>. Warne.
A. A. Milne, <u>Winnie-the-Pooh</u>. Methuen paperback.
Antoine de St. Exupéry, <u>The Little Prince</u>. Harbrace paperback.

C. S. Lewis, <u>The Last Battle</u>. Puffin paperback.
J. R. R. Tolkien, <u>The Hobbit</u>. Ballantine books.

For the Contemporary (the essays, "The Ambiguous Legacy of Wilhelm Busch,"
"The Tin-Tin Series" Children's Literature and Popular Appeal,"
"What Finnish Children Read," "Sendak Confronts the 'Now' Gener-
ation," "What's Left Out of Biography for Children," "Child Reading
and Man Reading: Oz, Babar, and Pooh")
Contemporary fiction, biography, or comics of the reader's choice

## FURTHER BACKGROUND READING

Aries, Philip.      <u>Centuries of Childhood</u>. Tr. Robert Baldick. Vintage Giant,
1962. First published, 1960.

Brophy, Brigid, Michael Levey, and Charles Osborne. "Peter Pan" in <u>Fifty Works
of English and American Literature We Could Do Without</u>.
Stein and Day. New York, 1968, pp. 109-112.

Chesterton, G(ilbert) K(eith). "The Ethics of Elfland" in <u>Orthodoxy</u>. Garden City,
New York, 1908, pp. 81-118.

Greene, Grahame.      "Beatrix Potter" in <u>The Lost Childhood and Other Essays</u>.
Viking Press. New York, 1962, pp. 106-111.

Green, Peter.      "The Wind in the Willows," In <u>Kenneth Grahame A Biography.</u> John Murray. London, 1959, pp. 239-263.

Hürlimann, Bettina.      <u>Three Centuries of Children's Books in Europe</u>. Tr. and
Ed., Brian W. Alderson. Oxford University Press, 1967.

Jung, Karl.      "The Phenomenology of the Spirit in Fairytales," in <u>Four
Archetypes</u>. Bollingen Series. Princeton University Press.
Princeton, 1969, pp. 85-132.

Lane, Margaret.      <u>The Tale of Beatrix Potter</u>. Frederick Warne & Co. London,
1964. First published, 1946.

Lewis, C. S.      "On Three Ways of Writing for Children." <u>Only Connect</u>.
Oxford, pp. 207-220.

Littlefield, Henry.      "The Wizard of Oz: Parable on Populism," <u>American
Quarterly</u>, XVI No. 1 (Spring, 1964), pp. 47-58.

Muir, Percy.      <u>English Children's Books, 1600-1900</u>. B. T. Batsford.
London, 1969.

Rackin, Donald.      "Alice's Adventures to the End of Night," <u>PMLA</u>, LXXXI,
No. 5 (October, 1969), pp. 313-326.

Rosenback, Donald.      <u>Early American Children's Books</u>. Dover. New York, 1971.

Speaight, George.      <u>The History of the English Toy Theatre</u>. Studio Vista.
London, 1969.

Speaight, George.      <u>Punch and Judy</u>. Studio Vista. London, 1970.

Thompson, Stith.      <u>The Motif-Index of Folk Literature</u>. Bloomington, Indiana,
1956.

Tolkien, J. R. R.      "Tree and Leaf On Fairy Stories," in <u>The Tolkien Reader</u>.
Ballantine, 1966, pp. 3-73.

# CLASSROOM METAPHYSICS

Most literature for children assumes a quality of perception in its audience that literature for adults must create: what T. S. Eliot, in speaking of the metaphysical poets, called "the direct sensuous apprehension of thought." Most non-children have lost this capacity, in part at least as a result of the enforced segregation of responses that modern education has deemed basic to its process. Perhaps, though, this is changing. In the theatre these days the audience is being asked to become part of the play. In the classroom a similar process is taking place: students are demanding a more complete experience from their subjects—the real meaning of that unfortunate word "relevance"—that is, they want classes to become part of their lives.

With this in mind, the following activities are designed to provoke a more unified and immediate response to literature. Unorthodox as they may seem, all have been tried on classes of varying size and make-up and found to be surprisingly successful. After all, the study of this literature, especially, need not be such a deadly earnest thing. A sense of fun adds new dimensions of understanding. Readers can participate in a way that could not be done—or could it?—with the works of say, Henry James or Norman Mailer. And, just as the fusion of the Man and the Intellect suggests the metaphysicals, so also does the relationship between humor and high seriousness in learning. Yet another poet on the metaphysicals, Robert Brooke, in his essay on Donne, speaks of the way in which Donne's "lack of solemnity" serves to "heighten the sharpness of the seriousness."

Fables

1) Try writing your own, based on your own experiences.
2) Have the class do spontaneous doodles expressing what they take to be the essence of particular fables—to help develop awareness of the levels on which fables work.
3) Develop and build luminous paper mobiles of the fable creatures. During lecture on the subject have them set in motion, illuminated with black light, in darkened classroom. The effect is disturbing and comic at the same time (like good fables)—a fluid series of chance encounters among characters, which helps release imaginations crimped by rigid abstractions and, like animated prehistoric cave paintings, offers a sort of hallucinatory "trip" into the primitive regions of the imagination. The student is helped to do the kind of active visual imagining that younger children (and great visionary adults) do and therefore enjoys a more complete response to the magic of fable.
4) Do charades of the fables.
5) Write some fables to indicate changes in moral values since Aesop or to "up-date" the morals.

Rhymes

1) Athletes and exercisers skip. To feel the rhythms of poetry and prose as one feels music or dance, try skipping the Mother Goose rhymes, Lear's limericks, your own rhymes, skip-rope rhymes.

2) Write your own rhymes.

3) Write a limerick.

4) Search out the bits of Mother Goose rhyme in current popular music.

5) Track the themes of protest, loneliness, and love from Mother Goose rhymes into current music.

6) Do a choral reading of Lear's "Akond of Swat," with the leader reading the stanzas and the group shouting the two-word question in each stanza.

7) Do an extemporaneous pantomime of Thomas Campbell's "Lord Ullin's Daughter." (Almost every word of this poem lends itself to pantomime, and should be played in an exaggerated way, with nineteenth-century Delsartean gestures.) Choose a "Chieftain," a "bonnie bride," a "lover," "horsemen," and a "boatman." For props use blankets as costumes for the men, an old curtain for the bride, a piece of heavy tinfoil to make thunder, a tin tub as a boat, a broom as an oar. Two volunteers can create the thunder and also swing a sheet to represent waves.

8) Chant Kipling's "Road-Song of the Bandar-Log," "The Law of the Jungle," and "Hunting-Song of the Seeonee Pack." The group should beat out the rhythms by tapping their fingers on table tops or desks and should shout the choruses.

9) Play the traditional play-party games which "sprang from pagan ceremonies of our European and British ancestors" (Richard Chase, Singing Games and Play-Party Games, Dover Publications, 1967). They can be studied in Traditional Games of England, Scotland, and Ireland, ed. Lady Alice Gomme, London, 1894 (Dover reprint, 1964), or in Games and Songs of American Children, William W. Newell, ed., New York, Harper and Brothers, 1903 (Dover reprint, 1963).

10) Trace the archetypal figure of the Lady on the Hilltop through myth, ballad, rhymes, and poetry. (It is also the subject of an old singing game, "The Lady on the Mountain.")

Folktales

1) Someone dressed in Russian costume can give a dramatic recitation of a sharply cut version of Alexander Pushkin's Ruslan and Ludmilla. Parts of this long dramatic poem can be summarized and narrated, parts read from a translation of Pushkin. (Ruslan and Ludmilla is an old Russian folktale. It is commemorated by statues of the characters in a large children's park in the Crimaea.) Music from Glinka's "Ruslan and Ludmilla" can be used in conjunction with the reading.

2) The folk story of "Prince Ivan, the Firebird, and the Gray Wolf"

can be narrated. Then, a large puppet Firebird, with gold plumes for wings and a red velvet body can be made to do a ballet to Stravinsky's "Firebird."

3) Volunteers can tell a very well known folktale, such as "Red Riding Hood," in various ways:
   a) The story can be narrated with each narrator in succession saying only one word and doing the story from memory.
   b) The story can be acted silently with one narrator speaking from memory.
   c) Next, it can be acted, with the actors using the A B C's instead of words.
   d) Now, it can be acted with words.
   e) Finally, the actors can pretend the characters are apes.

4) From Embassies, (the Japanese Embassy, for instance) it is often possible to obtain movies or recordings of folktales set to music and enjoyed by children in their dances and games. One can view these or make a study of how folktales unify some cultures by entering their religion, politics, drama, dance, music, early schooling, novels.

5) Find folktale plots in modern novels.

6) Produce a Punch and Judy Show, or a Mummers' play. A good text is Diana John's St. George and the Dragon and Punch and Judy. Penguin Books, 1966.

7) Write plays for the West based on Japanese kyogen. A good text is The Ink-Smeared Lady and Other Kyogen, tra. Shio Sakanishi. Charles Tuttle, Rutland, Vermont, 1967.

8) Adapt folktales for dramatic presentation.

9) Study archetypes, masks and shadows (in Jung's terms) in folktales.

10) Consider underlying meanings and attitudes toward life in folktales.

11) Become familiar with the folktales of your own ethnic group. If not familiar with them, explore the subject not only through written literature but through the oral tradition. What variations occurred in the tales when immigrants re-told them in America?

12) Study tales of folk heroes for qualities which constitute an American hero—John Henry, Casey Jones, Molly Pitcher, Paul Bunyan, Davey Crockett, Daniel Boone, Johnny Appleseed, Tatuba, Squanto.

Fantasy
1) Tolkien's The Road Goes Ever On. Music by Donald Swan. Ballantine Books. Have someone sing these songs in conjunction with study of Tolkien's Hobbit.

2) Play the record of Tolkien's "Songs of Middle Earth" (Caedmon).

3) Create a fantasy by group selection of characters, place, and conflict. Volunteers might act it out as the group develops the

story, or it can be recorded on tape.

4) Society enclosing human beings. Do a production based on the various containers in which Lear put so many of his characters in the limericks, possibly using a scene from Beckett's _Endgame_ as a model.

5) Write your own fantasy.

6) Produce the essay, "Philosophy and Fantasy" in _The Great Excluded_ as a dialogue between puppets.

7) Have a colloquium on the logic of fantasy, using G.K. Chesterton's essay on the Ethics of Elfland in _Orthodoxy_ for background reading.

8) Discuss the various kinds of journeys or "trips" in fantasy.

9) Discuss Locke's attitude toward fairy stories: justified? in connection with Robert Bator's essay on "Out of the Ordinary Road: John Locke and English Juvenile Fiction in the Eighteenth Century."

10) Discuss economic propaganda in fantasy, particularly Ruskin's _King of the Golden River_, Grahame's _Wind in the Willows_, and Baum's _Wizard of Oz_. For background, see a biography of Ruskin, Peter Green's biography of Grahame, and Henry Littlefield's article on _The Wizard of Oz_ in _American Quarterly_, XVI No. 1 (Spring, 1964), pp. 47-58. Also, the essay, "From Fantasy to Reality, Ruskin's _King of the Golden River_, St. George's Guild, and Ruskin, Tennesse."

11) Baum tried to write a great American fantasy and only partially succeeded. What elements might go into producing such a fantasy? Could folk heroes, economic exploiters, racists, the good and evil, be taken out of time and fused to give an identity to the varied facets in American society?

General     Arrange addresses or colloquia on:
Sex and violence in children's literature
Superstitions in children's literature
Comics
American Indian folklore (an Indian, if possible)
African folklore (an African, if possible)
Illustration of children's books
Music and children's literature (songs, for instance, from George L. Spaulding, Simpson-Fraser, Liza Lehmann, Victor Hely-Hutchinson, Bainbridge Crist, Robert Schumann, Hugo Wolf, Aaron Copeland, and Benjamin Britten)
Dance and children's literature (ballets including "The Firebird," "The Sleeping Beauty," "Petrouchka," "Bluebeard," "The Nutcracker")
Blake's poetry: Its Roots in Children's Songs
Huckleberry Finn
Current Fiction for Children
Children's Plays

AREAS FOR RESEARCH

Since so little research has been made by humanists into children's literature, almost any serious study is likely to turn up fresh material which will enrich knowledge of the field. Such material can be considered in discussion sessions or developed in papers.

Possible topics:
Children's Books by Famous Writers for Adults (Joyce, Eliot, Faulkner, Ionesco)
Puerilia by Famous Writers (Brontes, Ruskin, Tennyson, Louisa M. Alcott, Daisy Ashford)
Standards of Criticism for Children's Literature
Literature for the Disadvantaged Child: Should the Classics Be Restated?
Foreign Folktales (Italian, Polish, Serbian, German, Spanish, Colombian, Eskimo, Swedish, Chinese, Hungarian, etc.) Told in America: Variants Occurring When the Tales Are Told by Immigrants in a New Environment
The Father Image in Folktales or Other Stories for Children
Antoine de St.Exupéry's The Little Prince as a Literary Expression of Existential Philosophy
Local Folklore
Revenge in Children's Stories
Changes in Social Attitudes as Reflected in Old Magazines for Children
The Novalis Fairy Tale Formula and Its Relationship to Drug-Induced Hallucinations
Christopher Smart's Writing for Children
The Poetry of Randall Jarrell for Children
The Image of the Black in Thornton Burgess' Stories for Children
Emotional Disturbances Reflected in the Tales of Hans Christian Andersen
Changes in the Hero Image
The Tom Thumb Archetype in Various Cultures (or in England)
How Great Writers Have Been Influenced by Their Reading as Children
Oxford Professors and Children's Literature: Carroll, Ruskin, Lewis, Tolkien, Auden
"The Sleeping Beauty" and Freud
"Snow White" and Grimm, Freud, Barthelme
Fighting Evil in Children's Stories
Political Cartoonists Who Illustrated Children's Books
The Seven Champions of Christendom: Its Literary Impact on Children
Biblical Parables as Children's Stories
Why There Are Few Great Children's Plays
Poetry for Children in the Victorian Period

Children's Books and Athletic Christianity: Thomas Y. Hughes (or Charles
          Kingsley)
Symbols in Children's Literature (werewolf, apple, flower, egg, river, etc. ad
          infinitum)
The Student as Hobbit
Economics in E. Nesbit's Books for Children
Zen for Children
Religious Propaganda in Children's Literature
Andersen-Nexö, Astrid Lingren, Selma Lagerlof:  Scandinavian Writing for Children
Commercial Propaganda and Children's Literature
Comics as Literature
African Folktales and Uncle Remus
Sholem Aleichem's Writings as Literature for Children
Rousseau's Emile and Pinocchio
Psychoanalyses of Selected Folktales
Special Qualities of Fairy Tales from Indonesia
Politics and the Development of Variants in Folktales:  Taiwan
The Death of the Family in Children's Stories
God on a Lazy Susan:  Attempts to Unify Religious Faiths through Children's
          Literature
The "Hang-Ups" of Famous Writers of Fantasy:  How Reflected in Their Work?
War in Children's Literature
A Linguistic Study of Winnie-the-Pooh
Current"Adult" Books Which Could Also Be Enjoyed by Children
The Quiet Moment:  Meditation in Children's Literature
The Hidden Preaching in Modern Children's Books
The Child as Victim in Children's Literature
Science Fiction as Children's Literature
Thingism:  Giving Human Qualities to Machines in Children's Literature
Haiku for Children
Social and Moral Values in American Folklore
Women in the Oz Books
Economic Propaganda in Children's Books in Russia, Bulgaria, and China
Does the Teenager Need His Special Literature?
Similarities in the Folklore of Various Ethnic Groups:  A Bridge Across Prejudice
Humor and Fatalism in Jewish Folktales
Is Mother Goose a Bad Influence on Her Children?
Series of Books for Children:  Good and Bad
Children's Plays from the Child's Point of View
German Romanticism and Children's Books
Horatio Alger and the Protestant Ethic
Trends in Children's Literature
Children in Shakespeare's Plays
Shakespeare's Plays as Literature for Children

Christian Theology in C. S. Lewis' Narnia Series
The Continuity of Life as a Concept in Children's Literature
The Grimms and Their Folktales
<u>Pericles</u> as a Children's Play
The Theater of the Absurd:  Beckett and Children
Mary Lavin's Writings for Children
Rex Warner's Writings for Children
Children's Autograph Books as Literature
Louisa M. Alcott's Books for Children as a Reflection of Social Attitudes
Similarity of Ethical Teachings in Western and African Folktales
Poetry of Children in Agony:  <u>I Never Saw Another Butterfly</u> and <u>The Me Nobody</u>
                <u>Knows</u>
The Dream as a Device in Children's Stories
Life as a Myth in Contemporary Stories for Children
Children's Literature and the Counter-Culture
Children's Films as Literature
Literary Style in Children's Stories
Edward Lear and Ionesco
Social Criticism in Children's Literature:  Saturday Morning with the Cartoons
Fantasy Fulfillment in Children's Literature
"Little" in Literature for Children
Satire in Children's Literature
Rebellion Against Authority in Children's Literature
Realism Versus Fantasy for Children
Tolkien to the Reader
The "Uncle Toms" in Children's Literature
Wittgenstein and Fantasy for Children
Arthur Clarke's <u>Childhood's End</u>
Kurt Vonnegut's <u>Children's Crusade</u>
Middle Class Ideals:  The Hardy Boys and Nancy Drew
Robin Hood:  Man and Myth
Publishers of Children's Books:  Their Literary Standards
Are All the Newbery Prize Books "Literature"?
The Treatment of Theft in Children's Literature
Robbe-Grillet and the Problem of Formalism in Children's Literature
Sports in Children's Literature
Peter Pan, the First Hippie
Supernatural Beings in Children's Stories
Relations between Anansi, Navajo, and Japanese Folktales
Alienation in Children's Stories
The Anansi Stories of West India and West Africa
Aesop's Fables:  Are the Moral Values Always Valid Now?
Pennsylvania Dutch Tales for Children
Kate Seredy and Hungarian Legend

Children and "X" Rated Adult Books
Tarot Card Symbols in Children's Literature
Fantasy and Religion in Children's Stories
Regional Poetry for Children: James Whitcomb Riley
Karma in Jaime de Angulo's Indian Tales
Quarreling in Children's Stories
The Mask in Children's Stories
Expendable Animals in Children's Stories
Witchcraft in Children's Literature
Blake's Songs: Their Roots in Children's Songs
Women in Andersen's Tales
Puppetry for Children
Rapunzel and Rampion
Literature for Deaf, Blind, or Other Physically Handicapped Children
Television's Role in Children's Literature
The Deterioration of the Folktale
Children's Literature and Rock Music
East European Jewish Literature for Children
Literature for the Child of the Future
Are There Sex Differences in Reading Interests?
Sesame Street
"Goldilocks" as a Children's Story
Stream-of-Consciousness in Children's Stories
Andersen and Auto-Eroticism
Homosexuality in Peter Pan
An Analysis of MacDonald's At the Back of the North Wind (or The Golden Key)
The Santa Claus Image in Children's Stories
Children's Literature and Cultural Deprivation
The Tales of Seuss: Are They Literature?
The Wind in the Willows and the Bible
The Microcosm of Winnie-the-Pooh
Dragons in Children's Stories: the Trend toward the Sad, Happy, or Otherwise
                     Harmless Dragon
Women in Tolkien's Tales
The Raggedy Ann Stories and James Whitcomb Riley
The Hobbit: Its Relation to Beowulf
An Analysis of Tolstoy's "Ivan the Fool"
An Analysis of Sozhenitsyn's "Matryona's House"
Old Age in Children's Stories: The Folktale of "The Blanket," etc.
I. B. Singer's Fiction for Children
Relationships between Children and Nature: Kipling's Jungle Books
Metamorphoses of Animals to People: The Frog Prince, etc.
Robert Raikes, the Sunday School Movement, and Commercialism
Negative Criticism of Tolkien's Hobbit

Criticism of One's Own Stories
Hamlet for Children
Huckleberry Finn as Fantasy
Swift's Gulliver and Children
Indian Myths as Science
The Power of Love in Children's Stories
St. Francis, "The Wolf of Gubbio" and Love as Toleration
A Marxist Interpretation of The Wind in the Willows
"The American Way" in Uncle Wiggily
Classics for Pre-School Children
Humor in Children's Literature
Fear in Children's Stories
Codes of Values in Grimm's Fairy Tales
Portuguese Rhymes and Mother Goose
Attitudes Toward Children as Revealed in Children's Literature
The Fool in Children's Stories
Folktales Wherein the Sense of Justice, Order, and Cause and Effect Does Not
        Exist
The Cat in Children's Literature (historical or contemporary)
Thornton W. Burgess' Stories and Ecology
Sir Thomas Elyot and Aesop
The How and Why of Talking Animals
The Character of Mary Poppins
Themes in American Folktales
Comparison of Greek Myths and American Indian Folktales
Br'er Rabbit and the American Slave
Sex Role Implications in The Blue Fairy Book
The Concept of Truth in Children's Stories
Jung's Collective Unconscious as Evidenced in Certain Folktales
Women in Newbery Award Books
Poetry for Emotionally Disturbed Children
Oscar Wilde's "The Happy Prince": An Analysis
The Role of Business in the Publication of Children's Books
International Academic Trends in Children's Literature
Chesterton's Essay on "The Ethics of Elfland" and Antoine de St. Exupéry's
        Little Prince
Landscape and Mood in Children's Stories
Poverty in Children's Stories
The Folklore of New England
Magic: Primitive and Literary—A Commentary on the Relation Between the Two
Greed in Irish Folktales
Reward and Punishment in Children's Stories (folktales or contemporary)
Realistic versus Stereotyped Animals
Toys and Children's Literature
Musical Mother Goose That Talks Down to Children

Sometimes, the best research projects are interdisciplinary, in which scholars relate their interest in children's literature to their own special fields. For instance:

Stimulating creativity in young children by programing classics into a computer in such a way that children are induced to develop their own variations in the stories

Photographic illustrations which tie classics, such as <u>Alice in Wonderland</u>, to contemporary life

Developing machinery to test the reception of classics by retarded children

Studying what literature for children is most appreciated by the deaf or the blind